CREST OF A WAVE
Some good old days in Africa

This is a description of a joyful but often harrowing safari through Africa by two young people in a Landrover in 1965. Everywhere, hopes for a grand future were riding on the crest of a wave.

This travel book, roughly drafted in 1966 and completed in 1993, is published for the first time in print. It is both historical and nostalgic. Historical because the journey was taking place through countries which had just recently obtained freedom from colonial rule, from Algeria to Zambia, and nostalgic because the conditions and the ambience are of an era which is now long past and will not be seen again.

The journeying began in Durban, South Africa, where the author left his wife and children, and started with a four-week voyage by tramp-ship to Barcelona. The fitting out of the new Landrover and finding a companion took a month or more, and then the big adventure commenced with the crossing to France.

Camping roughly off the road and occasionally putting up in simple hotels, eating food bought in local markets or in rough local restaurants in towns, they traversed the Mediterranean coast of North Africa. Surprised by the sudden closing of the border at Aswan, they had to take ship from Port Said to Mombasa. Three months were spent exploring East Africa and living in a lonely beach shack before taking the long dusty road to South Africa. Denis Montgomery was home with his family, but 'Barbie' had then to return to her own life in London. Unsettled, Montgomery went on to Cape Agulhas at the end of Africa before facing the necessary adjustments in returning to a normal life.

Dear James
With love,
Dad.

CREST OF A WAVE

Some good old days in Africa

"Only those who know can tell how sweet it was under the ancien regime."
- attributed to Talleyrand, (1754-1838)

Denis Montgomery 12/1/2007

DENIS MONTGOMERY

By the same author:
The Reflected Face of Africa, 1988
  - Second edition, 2006
Two Shores of the Ocean, 1992]
On the Internet : www.sondela.co.uk
Seashore Man & African Eve
Golden Rhino
Da Gama Septet
and short stories.

© Denis Montgomery, 2006

Produced with WordPerfect v. 13. Cover photograph by Denis Montgomery

African Insight

CONTENTS

'Landie' on the edge of the Great Ruaha River flood-plain, in the Great Rift Valley in Tanzania. October 1965

'Barbie' and the author, celebrating the end of the grand safari in Durban, November 1965.

INTRODUCTION

I made two north-south trans-continental journeys of personal exploration in Africa. The first was in 1965 and the second in 1985-86. The first was in my own Landrover with one companion and the second in a 12 ton 'overland' truck with an average of eighteen companions. On both occasions more than 25,000 kilometres were travelled on the ground. I have made numerous shorter journeys, including several east-west traverses, but none had the grand soul-stretching of 1965 and 1985/86.

In 1965, Africa was riding on the crest of a wave and in the prevailing optimism few people could believe that the wave was going to crash onto such jagged rocks of social, political and environmental degradation.

I intended to write a book about my travels and observations in immediate post-colonial Africa and a start was made in 1966, and then abandoned. I knew that I did not know enough. A year later in Lucerne, Switzerland, I discussed my dilemma with a senior editor from McMillan and Co. of New York, whom I met casually in the Hotel Flora. She told me quite seriously: "Of course, you will have to *live* a little more..." I never forgot her friendly injunction.

I wrote much of this story in rough draft in 1966 and then abandoned it. When I had seen *The Reflected Face of Africa* published twenty two years later, it seemed a good idea to complete the book about the earlier journey, and here is the result. It was written in sporadic jumps in between other activities and was based on diaries of the journey, the manuscript from 1966 and my fading memories supported by photographs. I had to 'think' myself into how I felt and thought in 1965, and that in itself was an adventure. Africa seems to have been so *innocent* then; I have no better word to use. We were innocent too.

Because this account was written as a story and not as a kind of serious historical record, there must be inevitable errors of detail. Of course, conversations did not occur exactly as I have narrated them.

The philosopher, Baroness Warnock, in a TV programme on the British Channel 4 on the 21st November 1993, said that she believed that memory and imagination are part of the same mental process. When remembering the past it is like creating a story out of a series of important and significant separate events. I understand exactly what she means: we all like to tell stories about things that we have done or been part of, and they don't follow a simple flow of accurate facts. And every time you tell a story, either to others or internally to yourself while 'remembering', the story gets subtly changed and re-imprinted as a refined memory. The way this problem of accurate recording of folklore in illiterate societies was solved was by designating particular people to remember history or prayers by rote and in endless chanting, instilled by rigorous discipline. Songs and epic poems were the history books of pre-literate people. This book is not reinforced by epic chants and nor is it history; it is reminiscence.

In the sub-title I refer to the "good old days" and this may be seen to be frivolous, patronising, biased towards European colonialism or traditional tribalism. I am sure there is a measure of those things. But it is also an honest statement. Nostalgia for my own youth apart, I believe that they *were* better days in Africa and I would be delighted to debate the argument with my African contemporaries, sitting around a fire under a tree, passing the beer around. If there are some who think that it is a 'racist' remark, there is nothing I can usefully say in response.

I salute my family for understanding my obsession to travel across Africa at a principal watershed of history. After nearly thirty years, my feelings of affection and gratitude towards 'Barbie' for her staunch companionship, honest friendship and for sharing the trials and excitements of that experience with me, are undimmed.

Denis Montgomery
Belmont, Lancashire. December 1993

Although there has been temptation to change the text or refine opinions in this book here and there, I have resisted it. Editing was carried out to remove as many typographical errors as could be found and improve the style. The events, my thoughts and emotions and the conditions we experienced are portrayed as faithfully as possible after the elapse of more than forty years.

Denis Montgomery
Chedburgh, Suffolk. December 2006

PART ONE : DURBAN-ALGIERS

CHAPTER ONE : *M.V. KLOSTERTOR*

Seen from the heights of Kloof, Durban was sharp and clear. A cold weather-front had passed over the previous evening and swept away the smog and dust. Driving into the city with my wife, Sue, and our two children, I was proud of my home town. The sun was bright and the colours rich. A hint of cool autumn breeze kept it from being too hot and the people in the streets were going about their business with smiling faces. It was April 1965. It has become a long time ago.

The ship that I had been waiting a week to catch lay at the coal wharf where it was loading nine thousand tons of fine-quality South African anthracite to help with the smog of Barcelona. The accommodation on the ship was sealed tight against the anthracite dust, so I left my bags in my cabin and walked with my friend, Tony, across the rails of the marshalling yard to a wood-and-iron hotel.

The hotel was an old sailors' pub nestling against the thick green bush wall of the Bluff that shelters Durban harbour and its bay from southerly winds. Our feet thumped on the wooden floor and the gravel and coal dust that they carried in scrunched loudly. From the outside came the wailing of steam locomotive whistles, the clatter of shunted trucks and the steady roar of the coal conveyors. Inside, the Indian barman played a radio and an off-duty railwayman threw darts endlessly at a battered old board. His boots went clump-clump every so often as he went to retrieve his darts. Sometimes he exclaimed in Afrikaans at a good or bad shot.

"How does it feel?" my friend asked.

"I don't know," I said. "Empty, I suppose."

"I supposed it would seem that way," he said.

"Yes. I know that."

We drank the iced beer and looked at the old advertisements preserved behind the bar. There was one for Plymouth Dry Gin which looked a hundred years old.

"How old is this place?" I asked the barman.

His brown face split in a grin. "Older than me, that's all I can tell you."

"About 1900, I'd guess," Tony said.

"Must have seen some wild sights," I said, sipping.

"Yes, can you imagine those men coming in here after a voyage round the Horn or from India and Australia."

We ordered more beer which did not seem to be affecting me much. The colours were brighter and the noises sharper, but my stomach was still terribly empty.

"You'll be changed when you get back," he said after a while.

"Probably," I said, not really thinking about it.

"You can't do what you are doing without being changed."

"It's not really unique," I said, uncomfortably.

"There're not many doing what you're doing, and they are all different."

"Sure I'm different," I said, grinning.

"You know, you are. You silly bugger!" He punched me lightly on the arm.

"Have another beer," I said.

He got up off the stool. "No. I must be going."

"You only see me off on a thirty thousand mile round-trip once in a while," I protested.

He grabbed me by the shoulder and shook it gently. "Look after yourself," he said softly. His feet clumped to the door. There was warmth in my eyes. It wasn't only Tony going, it was the departure from my family and all those familiar things which were suddenly fading into a different reality. Structures were changing: I was sitting there in the old wood-and-iron pub, a ship was waiting with my bags on it, the familiar world was departing. Which was real? I suddenly did not know and I wanted to rush after Tony and go back with him. I had the too-close images of Sue and my children being so-cheerful and jolly as they wished me luck. Somehow I knew that those images would be with me for ever: not just during the months of strange parting that lay immediately ahead, but forever. Thirty years later, all those images are still sharp.

I had another beer by myself and played with the condensation rings on the scarred counter, making shapes. It was suddenly very lonely by myself and the barman was intruding, carrying clinking boxes of empties to the yard at the back, so I went out into the glaring sun.

At the end of the wharf was a whale slip and I went there to have a look. Three rusty whale-catchers were tied up to the pier and big winches at the head of the slip were pulling the whales out of the water onto low railway trucks. A dirty little diesel engine was waiting to haul them around to the whaling factory on the other side of the Bluff where its stench was somewhat confined away from the city. There were many neatly sliced holes in the blue-black sides of the whales where sharks had come in for a mouthful of white blubber and I reckoned that the holes were about the size of a man's abdomen. Looking at the giant corpses with the white scars and the rich wine-coloured blood staining the water and the general stink of dead whale worried me and I walked back towards my ship.

A gang of stevedores came towards me and one of them stopped as I passed to gesture with his hand which had an unlit cigarette between the fingers. He was a tall black man, his face fatigued and shining with sweat. I lit his cigarette and he blew out a gust of smoke, raising his hand in a gesture of thanks. He was the last South African I met for nearly a year.

The ship, my home for four weeks, had finished loading, the hatches were closed and the crew were busy hosing the upperworks. Some were hosing each other and laughing and joking in German. There was a little crowd seeing off the other three passengers and the saloon was filled with forced-hearty people. A dark, attractive girl was looking at me. "You're a writer?" she asked with an English accent. Somebody had been talking about me.

"I'm trying," I said. "Are you coming with us?"

"No, I'm seeing my friend off."

"I'm sorry about that," I said smiling and quite sincere but the clichéd remark irritated her because she looked away.

I was feeling a little drunk from the beers and smoky heat in the saloon, so I went to my cabin where the German steward lad with a Beatles haircut was opening the port to let in the evening breeze. Water from the hoses on the deck above sprayed and dripped past and the air smelled salty.

Beyond the blue of the Bay with some yachts and busy launches, I could see the clean buildings of the city and the tree-clad suburban hills behind against the sunset. I lay on the bunk, listening to the drum of a diesel generator and the occasional clunk of metal on metal from the deck above where the crew were working. After a while, I slept.

When I woke, it was dark and the ship was at sea. I had missed the leaving of Durban and for a while I felt a return of that sharp and empty sadness, much worse than ordinary homesickness. There was some fear too: not physical fear of course, it was the fear of the huge step I had taken and that it may have been a serious act of folly. I was completely alone, too, and that is always fearful.

The *Klostertor* was a motor ship and my cabin was next to the funnel casing so that the bulkhead shook all the way to Barcelona. Some trick of the ventilation made the air drum with the piston strokes of the big engine down below which sounded: "whuppa-whuppa-whuppa-whuppa". I smoked a cigarette at the open porthole, feeling the cool breeze on my face. It was black outside and I could not see anything. I had not said good-bye to Durban, my home town that had made me feel proud, all clean and bustling and strong at noon. I felt more waves of sadness about all of the business of leaving. If I thought of my family too much it would have been thorough misery, so I steered my thoughts away towards the future. After another cigarette at the porthole, I took off my clothes and lay on the woollen blanket of the bunk, feeling it press against my naked skin as the ship heaved over the swells. I often lay naked in that hot cabin in the days that passed.

*   *

We stood far out to sea when rounding Cape Agulhas, the southernmost point of Africa, because the Captain took advantage of the strong west-flowing current, so I only saw a grey-brown rounded mass in the mist of sea-haze. But it was the end of Africa and I watched it from the bridge and was thrilled at an important moment of my long journey. All that night I stood on the bridge end and picked out the great lighthouses of Danger Point, Cape Hangklip and Cape Point that marked the turning point as we rounded the Cape of Good Hope. I knew them from several transits when I was in the Navy. I went to bed in the early hours when the lights of Cape Town city appeared. We had left the Indian Ocean and entered the Atlantic and were going north. There was enough phosphorescence in the sea where our bow wave crashed through the swells to light up the side of the ship as we passed from warm to cold water at the meeting of the oceans.

The Captain was a good man with a great deal of understanding of people and life, but he was a pessimist and cynic. He had precious little respect for the world and that made him drink a lot. He was glad to have me on board because he was lonely, like all captains, and I was prepared to go to his cabin after dinner on some nights and sit talking while he lowered the level of the brandy bottle on the table. He did not respect the other passengers who were a wash-out for late talking and drinking and his position prohibited him from being close to his officers. The younger members of his crew exasperated him with their lack of discipline, the new fashion of long girlish hair and the Beatles-type music which they listened to on the short-wave radio or their gramophones.

He told me that between 1942 and 1945 he had commanded small aviation-gasoline tankers running from Kiel up the Norwegian coast. In all those years he had never returned to his home in Hamburg and he had been frightened all the time. At first he had been terrified but after some time, months or a year or so, the terror became a slow smouldering fear. It was because of the many thousands of gallons of 100 octane petrol that he carried and the British Beaufighters and torpedo boats that were always searching for him. Later, it became a children's game of cops and robbers and the fear seemed like a child's fear in the breast when hiding from a playmate. They used to drink a lot all the time, and laugh a lot, trying not to be serious, to keep it to a game. After the war, there was no work and he did not know how a man could be treated so badly by so-called civilised authorities that he could never hope to influence.

When the bottle got low in the middle of the night he would get very angry and bitter about these things, and there was too great an age gap for me to offer true sympathy. He was about fifty and I was thirty. But I understood and could feel his frustrated anger. He revealed the strangeness of Germans at that time which I had not thought about much until then. Although he was intelligent and had seen the world and spoke several languages, he did not believe the Holocaust of the Jews.

"American propaganda!" he would shout, banging his glass. "They got to the punishment camps and sealed them off and made it all up. Germans cannot behave like that." He would stare at me, his face glistening with sweat. "How could Germans ever do those things? I don't know any German after fifty years of my life who could do those things... It has to be fake. It has to be American propaganda! We Germans cannot be that way!" Then his face would change and his voice would be pleading: "What else can it be? What do you think?"

I felt sad for all Germans of his generation who felt the agony that he showed me. When the second bottle of brandy has been opened at two in the morning there is nothing to say. When I went down and lay on my bunk, still stirred by the alcohol and the poignant conversation, I would think about our differences. There was the difference of our ages, of course, but there was the huge gulf of our nationality. I had been old enough to understand what was going on during World War II, after all I had relatives who fought, and I still had the arrogance of certainty that I was part of a British Empire which had been on the moral high ground. I had never questioned that. And yet, I had met a mature man whom I respected and for whom I felt a kind of privately shameful sympathy, who had been an 'enemy'. My own Naval service was still quite close. During training we had been indoctrinated with films such as Noël Coward's *In Which We Serve* and our instructors took us through war games which always used Germans as the enemy. Soviets, when I was in the Navy in the early 1950s, had not become the model antagonist.

On another night the Captain said that as a South African I had to be a good brandy drinker; white South Africans drank more brandy per capita than any other people, he told me. He kept trying different brandies on me as the nights rolled by. He said that you could not appreciate any brandy until you had drunk a bottle of it and could decide your reaction when you woke up next morning. Brandy should be served ice-cold like schnapps, he said. He had a small refrigerator in his cabin where he kept several kinds of German, Austrian, French, Spanish, Portuguese and South African brandies; Hamburger schnapps (for his officers) and lager beer for when he was thirsty from drinking brandy. There was a case of Scotch whisky beside it for customs officers which he never opened for himself. He could buy brandy from ship's stores for the equivalent of six shillings (30p) a bottle.

It was his custom to have two shots of ice-cold schnapps with the first officer and chief engineer at noon each day, just as the second officer sounded the siren to mark the hour. I was invited to join this ceremony which was conducted with serious dignity: a careful raising of the small, brimming glass, a gruff "prosit", then a quick sinking of the perfumed biting liquor. Meals were formal and the

14

food, which was common to all on board, invariably excellent, superior to any passenger liner's fare. The Captain always supervised the cook's menu himself because he believed that the crew were entitled to better food than that they would have if they were living ashore in soft jobs. He was an old-fashioned martinet who hated Beatles hair styles, but he also had an old-fashioned respect for German professionalism and the honour of the seamen under his command.

There were three other passengers on the ship. A middle-aged Belgian couple who had spent their lives in Africa, in the Katanga Province of the Congo, and had retired because they could no longer stand the terror of civil war and massacres. He was a mining engineer and was neurotic and had a complete mental breakdown because of his experiences. His hands shook and he spoke nervously. She was quite a 'grand' lady and it was a disgrace to be travelling on a German tramp-ship. She told me many times about going first-class on fine Belgian liners to the Congo. On several days they never emerged from their large cabin with portholes opening onto the foredeck which was the best on the ship, the 'owner's suite'. My noisy, hot little box was designated for the Third Engineering Officer and one was not being carried on that voyage, but we all paid the same fare.

The fourth passenger was an English girl from Sussex who had emigrated to South Africa and was returning home after an unfortunate love affair. She was pregnant and I thought she was very brave about it all, pretending that her motherhood did not exist. Although she usually sat quietly by herself, her conversation was always happy and gay and I admired her for that because she was only nineteen and was estranged from her parents. They did not know her circumstances or that she was returning to Britain and she was not going to contact them. The Captain thought that it was my duty to comfort her in my bunk in the night hours, but I did not believe she would be interested. The young steward boy with the Beatles haircut definitely thought that it was his duty and he told me that he was sure that a pregnant girl would be good experience for him. He could learn a lot for the future, he explained seriously. But she disagreed with him and told me that she thought he was a funny little boy and his sexual suggestions were a real joke.

The Belgian couple were distraught. They had lived all their adult lives in the colonial world of the Congo and had enjoyed it so much before independence five years before. On retirement, they had returned to Belgium but they could not tolerate the new urbanisation, the greyness, the hard impersonal world of post-war Europe, the decline of morals, TV and all that. So they had tried South Africa, but the South African cities were almost as bad. Nothing was like the Congo when they were younger. She said that if they had to live with super-highways and skyscrapers they would prefer America and they were leaving South Africa because they could not stand black faces any longer. Black faces made her sick in her stomach and her husband got very nervous so that he stayed indoors all the time.

They could not forget the things they had seen in their last year in the Congo. A black face reminded her of blood and intestines of young African men in the dust and a white women friend dead in her bed, lying naked on disgustingly sodden sheets with her ankles tied out to the bedposts. When she told me these stories I was also sick in my stomach. Otherwise, her conversation was about the cost of living in Las Palmas, the climate of Crete or the price of land in Florida or the Virgin Islands.

I had been in Ibadan in Nigeria in 1960, just five years before, when the first horrors of the Congo mutiny had been exposed to the world. I remembered Kano airport and seeing a crowd of exhausted women sitting desolated or lying on the floor. I heard that they were Belgian Catholic nuns from Stanleyville who had been raped several times and some had been beaten. Their pale, blank faces with hollow eyes haunt me now. I wondered what they were thinking, if they were thinking, and could not imagine what it could be. I remembered my Nigerian sales supervisor, Azike, coming to me one morning in our office and standing before me with pained embarrassment. When I asked him what was the matter, fearing some personal disaster, he told me how shamed he was at the terrible news from the Congo where white women were being abused. I could never forget my friend, Azike, and the little ivory head he gave me later, and it all came back when I listened to the introverted horror-stories of the fat little Belgian woman on the *Klostertor*. It had all happened close in time.

The Captain despised the Belgians but he used to shake his head and mutter about the uncivilised *schwartzers* in the Congo.

"You see what happens in Africa," he pontificated. "They have no discipline and so when there is no more proper government, they become savages. Wait and you will see what is happening in the Congo will start all over. Now, we Europeans have many centuries to learn discipline, especially we Germans."

16

He paused in thought and sipped at his brandy. "But, I will tell you something. Look to China, they have also learned strong discipline. There is the danger for the future. We were in Shanghai last year to load cereals. For ten days they made us wait in the river tied to buoys. I was going mad, but they just said to wait because they were getting ready for my ship. One day, a tug came and we were taken to a wharf. About two or three hundred men were brought in old army trucks, very old but all washed and clean. Doors of a warehouse were opened and these men carried the sacks of maize and wheat on their backs onto the ship and down into the holds on wooden ramps. I offered my derricks, but they were refused. Men with guns watched and little brass gongs were beaten to make the rhythm for the running men. After some hours when the men began to fall and drop their loads, they were taken away and another ten truck-loads were brought. And again, when those were exhausted. And so on. In sixteen hours, seven thousand tons of cereal in jute bags were loaded by hand. I have never seen such a thing." He looked at me over the rim of his glass. "Now, you understand what I mean?"

I used to walk with the pregnant girl up to the stemhead to watch the flying fish skittering away from the bow wave, their wings flashing green and silver, irridescent like transparent mother-of-pearl. She would clap her hands with pleasure and wore an ecstatic smile. On the big Union-Castle liner going out to Durban she had never seen these things as there was no freedom to go everywhere on the ship. One day we were followed by huge schools of dolphins which churned the sea as far as the horizon. They surfed in the bow wave below us, twisting away at the last moment, racing and curving. One day we passed a small herd of whales, so close that the spray of their blowing wet the deck.

Towards the end of the voyage, the pregnant girl brought a pile of winter-weight skirts to the saloon or the deck to painstakingly let out the waists, sitting quietly for hours with her needle and cotton.

*   *

I celebrated my thirty-first birthday in mid-Atlantic on the 26th April and went down to the liquor store to spend one pound, ten shillings on whisky, brandy, beers, Cinzano and Dutch cigars for my guests. I invited the Captain, First Officer, the Radio Officer and the other passengers and we had a jolly time after dinner. Horoscopes were fashionable and we worked out who were supposed to be compatible.

I should be linked to the Captain, the Belgian man and the girl. The Captain thought I was older than I was and the girl younger, which was interesting for I thought it would have been the other way around. The Belgian couple were in quite good form, but they left after two glasses of Cinzano each and we settled down for a good party until after midnight. I wanted the girl to have a swim with me in the canvas pool that had been built on the after deck, but she refused, saying she had grown too big and did not have a costume to fit her. She laughed off swimming without one.

There was a grand party on the day that we crossed the Equator. It was a holiday for the crew who normally spent their time chipping rust and painting in a never-ending battle against the salt air. The First Officer told me this was because the ship had been built shortly after the war when steel was terrible quality, mostly scrap from the battlefields of northern Europe.

It was the ship's custom to celebrate the holiday with a shooting match on the poop-deck. The sea was calm but the poop rattled and shook to the beat of the screw below. I was told that as I had been in the Navy I would have to join in. I was an excellent shot but did not know the .22 rifle they had and I was not used to the shuddering of the poop and the paper target fluttering in the wind. However, I got the highest score which embarrassed me, but they all seemed pleased. Maybe the result removed the tension of old rivalries on other voyages.

That night there was the traditional party and it became an unforgettable event. Each crew member contributed ten marks, which was the equivalent of twenty bottles of beer, or a bottle and a half of schnapps. There was also a contribution from the ship and the profits from the shooting competition in case of need. My prize had been a case of Becks beers and I threw them into the kitty. The ship's company was forty three officers and men. There were two officers and four men left on watch and the rest congregated in the machinist's mess, a space thirty feet by ten and a quarter of the floor area was completely covered by cases of Becks beer which had been in the cold room all day.

By midnight twenty dozen beer bottles had been tossed out of the portholes. We were so happy in that hot steel box together, all those men with their shirts ringing wet from the sweat running from their bodies. The box heaved gently over the sea, shaking to the rhythm of the engine and outside the port holes the black sea stretched to the blue-silver sky in which floated a full moon. Outside,

18

no land for a thousand miles, inside thirty seven happy men beginning to sing songs to echo in the shaking steel box. They sang German drinking songs, dirty sailors' songs, Bavarian mountain songs, Afrika-Korps marching songs and Rhine folk songs.

At one point, they had to sing in English with respect for me, their shooting champion, and there was long involved argument. They tried to sing 'Tipperary' but only the war veterans knew the words and it petered away. The Captain called on the Bootsman to sing and there was a roar of agreement. He stood, swaying, sweat pouring, waving a bottle and sang an old sailing ship shanty. He had a good voice and everybody knew the chorus. It was a slow shanty for raising the anchor and was sung all the way through.

I sat in a corner feeling the slow swoop over the empty, moonlit tropical sea and listened to those sentimental male voices singing that nostalgic old sailors' song. The faces of the hard men were solemn, eyes downcast, their lungs filling and emptying, calloused hands gripping the bottles, slowly beating time. The wooden tables trembled to the huge volume of deep bell-sounding choruses. It was the most beautiful singing I had heard. I could raise a lump in my throat easily thereafter by remembering: "Blow, boys, blow - for Californ-I-o..." There was a danger of drunken sadness setting in after that, but the Captain knew that and started a competition for the best Bavarian clapping dance.

Later, the First Officer and I fell fully clothed into the canvas swimming pool and watched the sun rise with arms clasped around each other in fraternal bonhomie, swearing eternal friendship. I learned about ordinary German men during that voyage in a way that I could not have done through any amount of reading. I re-read Eric Maria Remarch's *All Quiet on the Western Front* soon afterwards with new understanding.

*   *

The weather changed as we closed with Dakar and neared the westernmost point of Africa. The ocean currents were cooler and the air was foggy. The colour tones were a deeper blue and it was difficult to pick out the line of the horizon. The land slowly crept up on us after many days at sea: yellow-white land, the edge of the Sahara Desert. We entered the spacious harbour guarded by the fortified slave-trade island of Goreé and within there was a flotilla of French, Brazilian, Polish and Nigerian warships, whose purpose I did

19

not learn. A vast Japanese tunny-fishing fleet swamped the inner harbour. The facade of the city was neat and modern with a distinct French style and I imagined the French colonial officers, and their famous Senegalese soldiers in Zouave jackets watching the tricolour rising only a year or two before.

The Captain was unhappy about entering Dakar but he had to refuel. The newly-promoted black officials wanted bribes, but his company managers had decided that bribes were not permitted, so the captains had to donate whisky from their personal supplies and hope that would be sufficient. He was closeted with a group of men in his cabin for some time and we waited several hours tied up to an empty quay before the fuel lines were eventually brought to us and pumping began.

I stepped on shore to walk along the quay to be able to say that I had been to Senegal, but had no inclination to try to get permission to go into town. A taxi driver cruised by and stopped to tell me that Dakar had the best girls in West Africa. They were in all colours from White with real blonde hair all over to virgins just down from up-country. I told him I had no money, which was true.

"Before, it used to be a good 'run-ashore'," the Bootsman told me, standing at the rail and watching the sun go down, a huge red ball falling through the dusty sky towards yellow rock cliffs. "Now, p-f-f-f-t. Not good. If you get drunk, and of course you will get drunk, you get beat-up and robbed of everything. The police don't care."

Africa! I thought, what is happening to Africa?

The pilot was a giant of a black man and he took us out to sea in the dusk with practised ease, without the help of tugs. It was a fine piece of seamanship which the Captain grudgingly acknowledged.

*   *

We were three weeks out from Durban when a flashing light showed up in the dull dusk and I went up to the bridge to find out. It was Cape Trafalgar; Nelson was there a hundred and sixty years before. On the other side there was another light which was Cape Spartel. We were entering Odysseus' Pillars of Hercules and passing the northernmost parts of Africa. I stayed on the bridge all evening.

The Captain and the First Officer were together conning us through the straits because there were many fishing boats and the currents were strong. I was shown the small radar screen with a mist of orange light around the centre and the Captain told me how he had complained about his inefficient radar. "The owners said that I am ninety percent of my time on the ocean when I do not need radar, so this old model is enough. I told them that one day maybe the ship will hit an invisible vessel in fog in the North Sea and that will be the end of me and the ship. They said at the beginning of the war there was no radar anyway, but I said that before the war there were many fewer ships." He and the First Officer kept rushing from the radar to both bridge-ends and occasionally calling alterations of course to the helmsman.

By midnight we were through. Gibraltar was astern to port and the lights of Ceuta off our starboard beam. I went to bed with the now-familiar "whuppa-whuppa-whuppa" of the engine in my ears and my thoughts confused. I had learned to love this German tramp ship and its people. We had entered the Mediterranean Sea and the voyage was coming to its end. But there was excitement in my belly at being there in the ancient sea, corrupt with history, overripe with civilisation. My family and South Africa seemed very far away now both in time and space. I thought about them, of course, in flickering moments of every day; but they were in another dimension however precious.

I don't remember much about Barcelona because it seemed a mad rush and I was mentally stretched out. After four weeks of isolation at sea, the transition to decision-making, another foreign language, thinking in foreign currencies, finding out about trains to Paris and Calais and all the bustle of a big city caused a sort of mental paralysis with everything happening automatically. A machine inside my skull took over, steering me about. At two o'clock in the morning I had been talking about Kafka and Dostoevski with the studious Radio-Officer and at eight o' clock in the evening I was on the train north. (The second-class fare from Barcelona to Calais was £12.) The between hours were dim with a blur of faces saying good-bye and a dull, grey cityscapes behind them. We had been carried ashore by a tired motor boat from where the ship had to anchor awaiting a berth and the dockside streets were dirty and flanked by old buildings needing repair.

The rails in Spain were uneven and the train crawled, bucking and jumping, with luggage falling from the overhead racks. Three hours from Barcelona we changed at Port Bou and the luggage had to be carried a quarter of a mile and be checked by customs in between. The pregnant girl was with me, of course, and I had to

21

manage our things while she stood guard. The border officials were tired and irritable and they gave me a hard time over my cameras, threatening documentation and putting them in bond. Luckily, I could show them a through-ticket to Calais. The French train was packed with eight to a compartment and we rolled slowly north. In the early hours, I squeezed out of the stuffy compartment and stood in the corridor for hours. I watched the cool misty dawn spread over the bare green of northern France at the end of winter.

I had forgotten how crowded Europe was, how everything was pushed to the limits of capacity, how busy and unfriendly the cities were with dirt and frenzy. Where were all these singularly madly-moving people trying to go? The taxi-driver in Paris abused us with genuine bad temper because we had so much luggage and the girl could not instantly lift her own heavy case.

I waited twenty minutes to buy a postage stamp and then we had a few moments for coffee and large cognacs outside the Gare du Nord in spring sunshine with the Belgian couple, saying good-bye. They had travelled first-class of course and had slept well in a couchette. They were suddenly strangers but he seemed to be at ease at last in a French-speaking country. We did not eat until we were upon the cross-channel ferry where the sandwiches were stale.

There was a big crowd of returning British tourists wearing tweed jackets, check shirts, yellow sweaters and pork-pie hats, buying half-bottles of Dimple Haig and cartons of Players for the 'duty-free' allowance. I listened to superior public-school voices, penetrating and cool, and felt lonely and far away from South Africa and my German ship. There were few working-class tourists, and they seemed to ape the style of their so-called 'betters'.

I was exhausted and floaty after no food for thirty-six hours and little sleep for forty-eight and I worried about the girl who was wincing in obvious discomfort from her swollen belly. But she was cheerful and chirpy as always: an independent and staunch girl, refusing attention. We said an embarrassed good-bye when we docked; we both faced unknown events and an England which was suddenly unfamiliar.

At Folkestone, there was a queue for taxis and some kind of official managing it. I said I wanted to go to Hastings and asked the price. He said if I would share it would be quite reasonable, which it was, so I was put in with an immaculately dressed teenage French girl who was returning to boarding school at Rhodean. 'My' girl from the ship was squeezed out of the customs shed as our taxi started his engine and I called out to her to get in as far as the station. Her face lit up and she was struggling towards me with her suitcases when the taxi queue manager stopped her.

"Here! You can't do that. You'll have to wait your turn, miss," he said, barring her way and my driver let out his clutch and we pulled away. I felt sudden desolation and a pang of resentment at the crude ways of civilisation.

That evening I had dinner by myself in a so-called posh restaurant in Hastings where I was to stay for a month in digs arranged by a friend. It was going to be a private celebration and I wanted to cheer myself up. A pseudo-French maitre d'hotel made me a 'Bearnaise' sauce to go with my indifferent steak on a spirit lamp beside me, using American tomato ketchup, Worcestershire and HP sauce! I watched this performance with jaundiced disappointment and made some good-humoured remark about its obvious spuriousness. But he gave me a look which I suppose he thought might freeze me. What a bloody joke, I thought. I could eat far better at half the price, without snobby pretensions, in my 'colonial' hometown in South Africa.

I drank a bottle of acidic red table-wine and thought of my family saying good-bye with forced cheerfulness and the beers with my friend in the wood-and-iron dockside pub; I thought of the tall black stevedore giving me a wave as thanks for the light; I thought of the Bootsman singing the shanty on the Equator. I thought of the fixed smile on the face of the pregnant girl while she waved to me as my taxi drew away from her at Folkestone a few hours before. I could feel her grey eyes boring into mine as she cried after me: "Thanks for everything!" Years later, I couldn't remember her name. I think it may have been Yvonne.

23

CHAPTER TWO : *SO MANY THINGS TO DO*

They had begun talking about 'swinging Britain' and I found that I liked it. Britain was breaking out, somehow, becoming more international superficially and accepting foreign ideas. People seemed more relaxed and I could sense some real chinks in the class barriers with everyone beginning to look at each other and not only at their clothes or judge instantly by the accent of their voices.

I suppose it was the informality that I noticed most strongly. There were men in restaurants who did not wear ties. Not all the girls had changed to mini-skirts, but many had, especially those pseudo-leather plastic ones. I was aware of the different pop-music. In South Africa at the time, the imported music was mostly American and much of it still in the old ballad style, although Bill Haley and Elvis were being played on the radio. In England there were the Beatles, Sandy Shaw, Cilla Black and the Seekers. The off-shore pirate radio stations had new virility. TV had become universal and everyone seemed to discuss the popular programmes and personalities. It was all fresh and new and cheerful, optimistic and brash. Colours seemed brighter and the cities cleaner. It was six years since I had been in England.

I stayed in digs that an old pal from my years with The United Africa Company in Nigeria had arranged for me. He had written that it was owned by a woman who was eccentric and preferred foreign guests. I was happy there for the weeks of preparation. She had students studying at the local polytechnic at the time. There was a girl from Thailand learning English, a technician from Kuwait, an older fellow from Ghana and a bright young man from Libya. With the daughter of the house who came at week-ends from Guy's in London where she nursed and myself, the South African traveller, we were a cosmopolitan mixture.

Only once did politics come up and the topic did not last. The Ghanaian had been reading a letter from home: "It cannot be as bad in your country as it is in mine," he said to me moodily. His father was a political exile and he had not been back home for five years.

"Could I earn good money in South Africa?" the Kuwaiti asked. He was bored with Britain and people did not like his dark colour. "There are no opportunities at home for me."

"Are the black girls pretty?" the Libyan wanted to know. "Could I be allowed to sleep with them if I am an Arab? Are your police as strict as ours?"

"Do you have many Americans there?" the Thai girl asked sympathetically.

"Politicians are shit!" said the Kuwaiti. He was proud of his colloquial English. "They have the money and their kids get all the best jobs."

"UNO is no good," said the Ghanaian. "They listen to all the worst of our corrupt politicians and never believe the truth about life for ordinary people. They have done nothing for us in Africa...."

"That's life today," I said emptily, not sure what I should contribute. To discuss *apartheid* with these diverse young people from other nations ruled by harsh demagogues seemed pointless.

The pretty Thai girl was always a little sad. She sighed and shook her head. "Politicians not good," she said quietly to herself.

My friend from Nigerian days came around on two weekends and we had a couple of nights out in local pubs. Bruce had been the manager of UAC Motors in Freetown, Sierra Leone, with several prestigious agencies including Land Rover and General Motors and was now working as a salesman with Bristol Motors, in their commercial vehicle department. So although he was enjoying a somewhat devil-may-care life he was depressed about the let-down and lack of prospects. He drove a two-year old 2.6 litre Jag on which he had lavished much attention and it was fun to speed about the country roads together. He talked of buying a boat and sailing round the world and said he greatly envied me my adventure.

He understood what I was doing maybe better than anyone at the time because he had driven back from Sierra Leone the previous year around the bulge of Africa through Senegal, Mauritania and Morocco. I told him I envied him that, because it was more adventurous than what I was doing; who ever heard of driving that route? I think we supported each other at a time when we were both feeling insecure and worried about the future, for different reasons.

Bruce's wife, was trying to find herself with painting and sculpture and between them they had literary friends. We picnicked with some of them one sunny Sunday. They knew Osborn well and the other 'angry young men', which made me feel somewhat inferior and exaggeratedly colonial. When I mentioned the South African, Roy Campbell, in a snobbish literary discussion of contemporary poetry, my remarks were given that exquisitely subtle, cool reception that the English manage so well. I kept quiet after that.

Afterwards, Bruce said: "You floored them with your talk of Roy somebody-or-other. They'd heard of him but not read anything of his, so they thought you must be seriously literary and a real dark horse!" We both thought this very funny.

*   *

I had put an advertisement in the *Sunday Times* personal columns asking for a companion to travel rough with me through Africa. I had 272 replies which was startling, and significant about the new Britain of 1965. I wished I could publish all the letters because they were magnificent. I had letters from retired Indian Army colonels, from a schoolboy wishing to collect butterflies, a girl with a pilot's license, many students wanting to write papers or theses on every conceivable subject, typists in Geneva, a teacher in Athens, a South African desperately down on her luck in Spain, a fashion photographer, two colleens from Dublin (one to cook and one to sing to me when we were lost in the desert). There was a doctor in Edinburgh, budding journalists, actresses who were resting, au pair girls from Sweden, a sensible engineer from Holland, jaded TV staffers, so many tired-of-cities young people. It was painful to read those letters over in my room at night: so wistful, so earnest and sincere, so wanting it badly. I wonder if one would get any replies at all these days; what I was doing uniquely then is commonplace in the 1990s.

I sat up until two and three in the morning reading and sorting; each one different, each one with a particular wrench at my heart or bringing out laughter. I would put the pile of letters aside and smoke a cigarette and think of society which was so lacking in adventure, so painful, that its youth was desperate to get away. If I had some national publicity and been on TV I might have expected that response, but only a little one inch advertisement in the personal columns. I supposed that people read every line every week, hoping for something exciting. One writer said that she had been watching for two years for an opportunity like mine to come up. With a few exceptions I would have taken any one of them, sight unseen. Their letters were enough.

One of the many problems to solve in a few weeks was to find the one out of 272 that I should take. First, I eliminated all those who were too far away to meet easily, then all those that were under 21 and over 35, and those that could not come because of their own time constraints. Most of the students were included in that group. I was left with about 100 candidates.

Some I could telephone and chat with, but most I had to write to because few had access to phones in those days. I piled on the problems and difficulties to put them off. I told of the heat, the loneliness, breaking down, camping in the wild African bush, insects, all that sort of thing. That reduced a lot of the enthusiasm. Out of twenty letters of that sort, seven replied with unabated enthusiasm.

Two were not easy to meet so they were kept in reserve. One was a young man that I liked, but he had to drop out to take up a cherished university place. A serious writer agreed to come and then was offered a challenging job with one of the new independent TV production companies. An interesting girl who had lived in West Africa was desperate to join me. She had a boyfriend who was experimenting with abstract nude photography. She was his model. Avant-garde photography was serious then.

Her parents were adamant that she should not cross Africa with a stranger but she said she was ready to do it anyway, but I refused to take the responsibility. A delightful young Scot hitch-hiked down to see me but I feared that he was too immature.

An Australian girl wrote on one page in reply to my dire warnings: "If that's all you can do to scare me, you'll have to try harder."

We met at Victoria station under the clock and went for a cup of coffee. She told me that she only had fifteen minutes before a date and I thought that I had come all that way from Hastings and she only had fifteen minutes to spare to decide on such an important matter! Anyway, I pulled out my map and started talking about the possible route and what the gear and vehicle would be. She stopped me after five minutes and put out her hand.

"Yes, I've got the picture," she said, impatiently. "If you want me, I'll come."

Bemused, I shook her hand, and that is how it was decided that Barbie would be my companion.

*   *

Now, I had so much to do. I picked up my brand-new long-wheelbase Landrover with pick-up body and plain metal panel-van top from the works near Birmingham, travelling up by trains and then a bus. There were no side windows, because I expected to sleep in the back most of the time, and there was a sturdy factory-fitted roof rack. It smelled so clean and driving back to London and the south coast I loved its firm clutch and tight gearbox and the crisp note of its exhaust. It had no rattles. I told myself to savour it while it was new, before it became loosened-up on African roads.

I had a new British passport to get to see me through the mire of newly independent African politics and then visas for all the countries of North Africa. At the Automobile Association headquarters in Leicester Square I got my all-important Carnet de Passage that would take the Landrover through a myriad of customs posts. The AA also provided introductions to their associates in East and South Africa and the Rhodesias. I asked for whatever guides they had for trans-Africa motoring and I was sold a marvellous publication of the AA of South Africa in Johannesburg called *Trans-African Highways*, revised to 1963, which became a Bible. All the through routes north and south and east and west across the continent were described in detail of road surfaces, weather systems, fuel and repair facilities, tourist attractions and accommodation. It was also filled with useful practical tips that made sense to me. I used it to add to my own lists of important spares and medical gear. It must be a classic collectors' book to-day.

I hunted about the south coast looking for equipment. I needed all sorts of spares and complete sets of tools. There were two spare wheels, inner tubes and tyre repair kits. For reserves, I bought metal cans for sixteen gallons of petrol and plastic drums for fifteen gallons of water. I put together a medical kit for burns, fungus and eye infections, malaria, pain, stomach bugs and infected cuts or grazes. I was determined to eat off the land everywhere and only had a reserve of canned food for a few days. Gradually I accumulated two campbeds, foam mattresses, cotton sleeping bags and blankets. (I did not want proper sleeping bags because the temperature would vary so much.) There were Primus stoves, cutlery, cooking utensils and pots, plastic plates and enamel mugs, washing bowls and a bucket, folding chairs and table, lamps and torches, transistor radio and batteries. I kept making lists and crossing things off. I had brought my clothes from South Africa, a simple outfit including one presentable set with a white shirt and tie in case we had to stay in a hotel in East Africa.

I drove along to Rye one lovely day to order a special lean-to tent or awning that could be fixed to the side of the Landrover and to two sets of poles with guys. I did not expect much rain, because I had studied the weather systems well, but shade is very important in the tropics. I went to Rye to get it made at an old-fashioned sailmaker's loft where the people enjoyed the challenge of making something different and romantic.

When I thought that I had most things we would need, I asked my Australian companion if she could take a week-end off to do a trial camping expedition. We arranged by correspondence that she would come down to Hastings on a Saturday morning and we would set off for Hayling Island where I was told there was a big, open camp-site without any parked caravans. It was late May, so I did not think we would be embarrassed by crowds of regular holiday campers.

I was terrified that we would not recognise each other or that there may have been a mix-up over arrangements. We had only met for a quarter of an hour two weeks before and Barbie did not have access to a telephone so we had only exchanged a couple of brief letters. I did not want to start choosing a companion all over again from all those applications so I was very anxious that we would be all right together. Despite her surface calm, Barbie had to be nervous too.

From Hastings we took the main A259 road through Eastbourne to Brighton and then the A27 in bright cheerful sunshine. Being a Saturday and the weather good the traffic was busy and I began to wonder if we would find a quiet camp-site for what I was sure would be a clumsy experiment. I was also worried because our lean-to awning was open along the outer length and I explained all of this to Barbie, but she did not seem concerned. As I wrestled with the traffic on the first long journey in the Landrover with a fair load in the back we talked about ourselves in the usual way of strangers getting to know each other.

I talked a lot, telling about the Navy and my experiences in Nigeria, boasting about the bad roads and how I had to ford swollen rivers with loads of cash and armed policemen in the back. She told me about a camping-trek she had done on an old bus into the

Outback of Australia and climbed Ayres Rock. She told me about another camping-trek she enjoyed in the previous year into the Sahara in Morocco and had lived for a while with an officer in the Moroccan Army who had wanted to marry her.

I was not sure, in my mind, whether she was exaggerating her stories, because I knew that I was exaggerating mine a little. I knew that we were both out to impress the other. I had the feeling that we were both quite experienced in unusual travelling but that we each had a different style. She spoke of a number of different boys and men she had, in a quiet sort of way and I realised that she had more experience in that direction than I. But there was no flirting, she was not inviting anything from me and I began to understand that she was a very straight person. She was intolerant of subterfuge and hypocrisy and I appreciated that. We were both from third generation colonial families and I think that straightness was still a characteristic then. We told each other something of our backgrounds. Her father's family were originally Welsh miners recruited for the coal and iron mines of New South Wales and she had been brought up in a small mining town near Newcastle, NSW.

I told her my great-grandfather had gone to Natal with five pounds in his pocket by sailing ship and that my father came from farming stock in Northern Ireland. He had emigrated to Australia to join a relative on a rough smallholding in Victoria on the Murray River and fought with the ANZACS at Gallipoli.

She had some bad things to say about Aussie in the early 1960s; how she had found it provincial and narrow-minded after she left school, which is why she had left to spend some years in England. She did not know when she would go back. It would depend on the right man in her life, but she was in no hurry to get married. She did not want kids for a long while, there were too many things to do first and her childhood had not been that good. I began to relax and to like her.

I was sure that I had chosen well and that she would be a good tough Aussie girl to have by my side: a good 'mate' in the old colonial way. She had tinted black hair, quite long at the sides and cut in a fringe across the front and very big grey eyes that sometimes had a veiled look. Her skin was smooth and sallow. She looked Welsh. She was dressed for the week-end in blue jeans and a violet blouse and was wearing lots of eye make-up. From her stories of going out a lot in 'swinging' London, especially around Earls Court, I supposed that she was quite a fashion-conscious girl. She was attractive and looked

30

rather sexy and I wondered if that would be a problem for me. I bluntly asked if she wouldn't miss having a good time and going with all these different guys and she gave me quite a hard look.

"If I was looking for that, I wouldn't want to go with you in Africa, would I?" I found her accent difficult to follow sometimes, but I understood that alright.

We checked over 'business' things, about inoculations and visas, money and how to arrange our mail and so on. She asked about our domestic equipment and I told her all the things that I had bought so far and she suggested buying a good supply of powdered detergents, soap, toothpaste, shampoo, sugar, salt, and other easy bulk necessities because she had not seen a lot of them in Morocco, especially manufactured goods. The markets had all sorts of fresh foods but there were no Boots' chemists, Woolworths' or Home and Colonial Stores. She said she would have sewing needles and that kind of thing and would have a supply of all her own private toiletries. That was useful advice because my experience was limited to West and South Africa where you could usually get all simple essentials, even if the towns are often far apart. I said that I was sure that the big towns in East Africa like Nairobi would be alright for things like face cream, quality hair shampoo, tampons and so on, that she worried about.

Hayling Island was mostly farmland. I knew Portsmouth from visiting friends in the Navy and was pleased that suburbs had not spread there. We found the camp-site easily enough towards the end of the road near the small village of West Town, and it was as I hoped it would be. There were a couple of tents, but most of the open meadow was deserted. We chose a spot away at one end and spent the afternoon getting all the gear out, looking it over and sorting, and then put up the awning for the first time. It was made of stiff new green canvas and more-or-less fitted. It was too big along the side of the Landrover so there were some little sags but the sailmakers said that it would shrink, so they had allowed for that. Anyway, by pulling the guys very taught it seemed to stand quite securely. We learned how to put up the campbeds and arranged the cooking and eating equipment how we thought we would do it regularly, and everything fitted in under cover. We sat on the bright new folding chairs and had a cup of tea made on one of the Primus stoves which burned with a clean bright blue flame and a fine roar.

"We'd better take good English paraffin so that it burns well," Barbie observed and I made a mental note. It felt good sitting there in the misty sunshine drinking tea and smoking well-deserved cigarettes. My plans were working out.

After a meal of warmed-up tins, we walked to the nearest pub along the road leading to the seaside. There were only a few quiet locals there who took no notice of us so we had a couple of pints sitting in a corner before going back in the dark. The inspection lamp on a long lead that I had labouriously wired up to a plug on the dashboard worked well.

Silently, with some awkwardness, we got undressed and into our beds. It was very still and quiet after I put the light out. I could see trees silhouetted against the loom of distant Chichester in the sky to the eastward. In a way it seemed strange to be sleeping in England looking out of our open-sided awning-tent into the open air; stranger than in Africa. There was a naked feeling, but it was a pleasant nakedness, an adventurousness. I thought of the many nights across Africa and how different they would be.

"All right?" I asked Barbie in the dark.

"Fine," she answered sleepily from three feet away. "It's a lot more civilised than I expected."

*   *

Everything seemed in order after the trial week-end. I gave Barbie a time and date three weeks off and she told me that she would be waiting at her digs in Earls Court, packed and ready.

"You won't let me down," she said with the direct look that I was getting used to. "I'm going to give notice at work and to my landlady. It isn't easy to get another good job like I have."

"There's no reason for anything to go wrong, except illness or something serious, in which case I'll send you an urgent rate telegram," I said. But I knew she meant something more than that. "No," I added. "I'm not going to let you down, I'll be there in Earls Court just as I say I will."

"Alright. I'll see you," she said as she got on the train.

I packed and left Hastings which was sad because I had enjoyed the landlady and the others. It was like leaving the *Klostertor* in Barcelona, but different, and I knew that I had to become conditioned to a nomadic life. For the next two weeks I would be with my family in Devon and Staffordshire and in all that time Africa and camping seemed remote, but always there was the loaded Landrover parked outside to remind me, and there was a continual little turmoil

32

of excitement in my stomach. The days flashed by as I was torn between parting from family and security and starting the incredible adventure.

*   *

Three weeks later, the Landrover found a parking place a few doors from Barbie's digs in Earls Court and I deliberately waited until the very exact hour before knocking on her door. She opened it immediately and her bags were all packed up and waiting. She had a cold lunch for us and her flat-mates would clear everything away. A new girl was coming in to take her place.

I was excited and in a mental turmoil, my stomach churning. We were starting!

CHAPTER THREE : *FAREWELL TO EUROPE*

We left Earls Court at 4 o'clock on the 14th June, 1965, after rearranging the load to fit Barbie's luggage; one suitcase and a squashy bag.

It felt quite warm and muggy driving down to Newhaven from London. The sky had that yellow look it so often has around the metropolis and the people had that dishevelled look that goes with being used to dressing for cool weather and then being caught by a hot and humid day. The air smelled of diesel smoke and dust as we struggled to pass the labouring Albion and Bedford lorries, crawling up the hill to Streatham.

When I lived in London in the mid 1950s, the building where I worked stood at the junction between Old Kent Road and New Kent Road in Southwark, on the A2 outlet to Dover and Folkestone. In summer, I could look down on the traffic immediately below and watch the lucky people going off for a continental holiday, their cars full of luggage, new GB plates on the back. The cars that really had me groaning in envy were the smart Triumph TR2s and Austin-Healeys which always seemed to be driven by a suave man in tweeds with a Tyrolean hat and a luscious girl with blonde hair tied with a paisley scarf, reading a road map. Tweeds and patterned waistcoats were 'in' then and skirts were long and nobody had dreamed of the Beatles.

Here, we were setting off in the days of blue jeans and Cilla Black and I would never have believed it ten years before, looking longingly out of my window in Southwark. I told Barbie about those dreams of Interlaken or Nice with a growling, red sports-car and Grace Kelly by my side.

"We're going a lot further than those smart Poms you used to envy so much," she said with satisfaction.

"You don't like the English?" I asked. She had made several disparaging remarks about them.

"Well, it's not that exactly. But those sort of people you describe give me a real pain. They are so bloody superior. When they hear your Aussie accent, or colonial, or whatever, they look down very long noses."

I laughed. "I'd always heard that Aussies were hostile."

"You should hear some of your 'Yippee' friends around Earls Court."

"'Yippee'?" I queried.

"That's what South Africans are called around Earls Court."

"Oh yes. You mean, *Jaapie*. It's an abusive nickname for Afrikaners from World War II. It means a sort of stupid farm-boy."

"That's right: 'Yippee'. They are very hostile about your race problems and all those Black slave camps you have down there. All that."

She was serious and we were verging on our first argument. "Do you believe the slave camps?" I asked.

"It's what we read in the papers," she said belligerently. "And I know how bad our Abos get treated at home in Australia, so I'm sure that 'Yippies' are probably worse. There's a lot more Blacks in South Africa to keep under the jackboots."

"So why are you coming all the way to terrible, awful South Africa with me?" I asked, feeling a sudden sensation of anxiety.

She smiled a slow smile and put her hand on my arm. "When I saw you, I thought you might be different. I'd already met lots of other Yippies," she said. But we had a long way to go.

*   *

We stayed overnight in a bed-and-breakfast pub near the docks in Newhaven and had dinner in a restaurant on the waterfront. We had two bottles of Burgundy and talked and laughed a lot, reminding ourselves that it would be many weeks before we were in an English-speaking land again. We learned more about each other. She was twenty-five and had lived on her own for the past seven years. She was plain spoken, without politeness, and had a passion for the truth, having been hurt a lot as a teenager. She was easy around men and had lost her virginity early.

"What I hate about Poms is that they never seem to say what they mean," she told me, going on from our conversation driving through south London. "If Aussies think a thing is crap, they say it's crap. In England they say it a hundred different ways and in the end you don't really know what they mean."

"What about your English boy-friends?" I asked, pouring more wine.

"They think they're God's gift to little girls. The Irish are fine, I like them, and the other colonials, except most Yanks. But I only went out with Continentals over here. If you let an English boy take you out to dinner, they reckon you have to repay them smartly in bed and I can't stand that shit. Going to bed is when you know each other well, you have some special feeling and respect each other."

After dinner, we walked slowly back to the pub, buoyed up by the steak and wine, savouring the beginning of the great adventure. We undressed and climbed into our twin beds, feeling strange.

Sharing a room for the first time was another psychic border line to cross. I knew that we were going to live more intimately and on top of each other than most married couples for the next months, but that was the first time we had actually undressed and climbed into bed in the same room. This was real and it was an event that became commonplace and ordinary, something that was automatic.

There was no relevance to the usual conventions of personal space and privacy in what we were doing.

*   *

Up early, we stood on the deck of the ferry *Falaise* for Dieppe as the sun rose, both of us subdued. I watched the shore moving slowly away, thinking of all the things I had arranged and wondering if I had forgotten anything. I thought of the months of planning and preparing that were behind me, and the adventures I had already had since leaving Durban.

I sighed and pulled myself up. "Let's go for some coffee," I said.

She did not answer and had her hand to her face, turned away from me. I realised that she was crying, shaking with heavy silent sobs. It made me feel warm to her and I put my hand on her shoulder and she stood with it there for a moment before moving away and pulling out her cigarettes. I walked away across the deck, my own eyes filling in sudden sympathy, thinking my own sad thoughts. It was suddenly so sharply emotional, watching the white cliffs drawing away behind us and I thought that I seemed to be passing through one great divide after another, as if I was going down a long corridor with one great door thudding shut behind me after another. After a while, we went down to the saloon and had coffee.

She told me that she broke down because she felt sad at leaving England after all and had been worried whether she could stand the trip and if she would let me down, because she knew how important it was to me, even if I did not talk about it that way. I had passed some kind of a test as far as she was concerned, she did not know if she would pass a test with me.

*   *

Driving through Le Mans in the sunny afternoon, I went around the Twenty-four Hour Race circuit and got the Landrover up to 71 miles an hour for a few seconds on the long straight through the trees before slowing to let the new engine cool. We stopped to fill up with petrol and bought Union Jack and Tricolour plastic stickers that had become popular, to plaster on the back and front.

We had dinner that evening at the *Hotel du Commerce* in the village of Ecommoy in the Touraine. We were taken into the warm kitchen filled with steamy aromas to choose what we would like to eat by the fat jolly lady proprietor. It was exactly the kind of rural French restaurant I had read about and never experienced. The tastiness of the food amazed me and we sat on the terrace in the late sunshine with a jug of local red wine and savoured every minute. It was the best meal for a long time.

The night became cold and misty when we pulled off the road onto a farm track near Chatellerault and slept in the back after unpacking the blankets and spreading the thick foam mattresses over the top of our gear. It was the first overnight sleep of so many like that.

It drizzled with rain in the night, but the next day was sunny and warm. The meadows were scattered with wild flowers and red poppies dominated. We ate lunch of French bread by the side of a river and the grapes were heavy on the vines. At Barbezine I had the Landrover's oil changed and the suspension greased while we drank coffee in a square.

We entered the Pyrenees from Pau, which I had always wanted to visit after reading Dornford Yates' *The House that Berry Built* when I was at school. Going up the Col de Pourtelet in the late afternoon the sharp mountain sunlight was grand. Thunderstorms were playing about the peaks, their great purple masses hung above, hiding the mountains with veils of dark rain. Lightning flashed and rainbows formed and reformed. I stopped and we watched the scene over a cigarette. We decided it was symbolic, we were leaving the green land of France for the arid countries of the Mediterranean and Africa and at the Pyrenean gateway the gods were playing, bellowing with their immortal power, deluging the high pine forests with their tears.

We asked the Spanish customs men at the top of the pass where we could camp for the night and they directed us to a meadow between the road and a swift mountain stream below the village of Salient. The sky became clear again on that side of the range and stars came out in the deep blue, the peaks and pines silhouetted crisply black. As we washed up and water from the stream bubbled on the Primus, four young men came walking down the road and pitched a tent. They came over to drink coffee with us and said they were students from Madrid University hitch-hiking around Europe in their vacation. Their English was halting but they enjoyed our coffee, watching us with liquid eyes and asking what we were going to do in Africa. One said he had been born in Spanish Morocco, so he was an African, which they thought was a huge joke.

*   *

Heading south through Huesca and Zaragoza the heat of the Mediterranean summer struck us. Propped up in her corner to catch a breeze from the open window, Barbie dozed; a sight I was to get used to in the months ahead. Dismayed by the stark depression of Zaragoza with unpainted buildings, rough cobbled streets with rattling old trams and ill-dressed people, I got lost and the heat and the seedy old city with its mouldy dirt and battered atmosphere of poverty made me irrationally angry. I thought of the Civil War as I drove on in the heat of noon, of how the Spanish people had been ravaged by the conflict of ideologies. I thought that it was always the gentle, ordinary folk who suffer between the crushing of intransigent regimes in any civil war.

South Africa had been terribly damaged by the Anglo-Boer War, which had also been a civil war. More English-speaking white South Africans had fought on the British side than the whole of the Boer armies at their peak and many thousands of coloured people had been interned with Boer families in British concentration camps.

In the 1960s, the echoes of the Boer War were still sounding and I was sure that much of the dreadful Apartheid system which was being rigorously applied then, which disgusted and worried many of us, was a direct result of that turmoil. The Afrikaners were so deadly serious about never being dominated by another people again. Driving through Spain and seeing the cities that seemed locked in a 1930s time warp made me think sombre thoughts. That fine South African poet, Roy Campbell, had lived in and written about Spain in the late 1930s.

It was a relief to leave the dreadful city of Zaragoza behind and we reached the sea at Vinaroz as the sun lowered. The road was guarded by battered old castles and we glimpsed a magnificent Roman aqueduct. We paddled in the Mediterranean for symbolism and gazed at 'El Cid's' castle looming on a promontory. As the sun set we raced to Peniscola and sat at a beach café and had a beer in the warm air of dusk.

"I feel as if our real adventure has at last begun," I said. "It's the warmth and feeling of lightness. We're getting close to Africa."

"Yes, it's great isn't it? Just look at that old castle, you can feel the history. I loved that movie about El Cid with Charlton Heston."

As the lights came on, the noise of the scooters seemed louder, buzzing like giant angry insects and townspeople and German and French tourists began to fill the pavements. We drove back to Benicarlo and found a place in a crowded camping park. The tourist shop sold us some very expensive fillet steak and a bottle of Spanish wine to celebrate our arrival on the shores of the ancient sea. As we showered the sweat and dust of the day away, a dog stole our meat. So we had fried eggs with bread and cheese and drank the wine. That night we organised ourselves properly for sleeping in the heat, getting out of our clothes and using only the cotton sleeping bags with blankets in reserve. But we had not arranged the load to best advantage, however, and I decided that we should stop further south for a few days to really acclimatise and sort ourselves out.

This we did in a new camping terrain, still under construction at Los Alcazares near Cartagena. Most tourists still concentrated on the Costa Brava around Barcelona then, but we were told that southern Spain would see them in the years to come. We observed Benidorm starting up where some new skyscraper hotels were under construction. Barbie told me that she had heard that old fishing villages, such as Torremolinos near Malaga, were becoming popular with young people following the new 'swinging' pop-music culture. Michener had not yet written *The Drifters* then.

It was going to be a huge camp-site, about ten acres I guessed, and the offices, ablutions, a small restaurant and a swimming pool had already been built, but the rest of the area was still being cleared. Not a blade of grass grew and dust swirled endlessly in the daytime when the sea-breeze blew. Foundations for a small hotel were being dug by a noisy group of young workmen using a home-made pile-driver on wooden tripod legs whose petrol engine racketed away from dawn to dusk. Apart from a French family group the first night, we were the only campers so we could empty the Landrover, scatter everything about without interference, set up our awning in its free-standing mode with extra poles, and take stock in a leisurely way. The first evening, the sun set in a great red ball over desolate mountains.

The proprietor, a small middle-aged Spaniard with a huge suntanned potbelly spoke to us cheerfully about his plans. He reckoned it would be a few years before his grand camping resort began to pay, but he was certain that tourists would come to southern Spain.

"I am the first in this area and I am doing it properly. I have studied the campings on the French Riviera and I will be a millionaire in English pounds before I am too old to enjoy it." He laughed and hugged his sexy young wife. They spent their day in brief swim suits and dark glasses, and she served in the shop or office like that, which seemed strange for Spain in those days. I liked him and hoped his dream would succeed. I'm sure it did.

Having spread ourselves chaotically and set up the campbeds we slept well. I awoke to an already warm morning with the sun bright and hard in its power. I lay smoking, watching tufts of sun-dried weeds nodding in the rising sea breeze thinking of the day and what was to be done. It became a regular routine for me; that fifteen minutes of collection of thoughts each morning before getting up.

Workmen's voices began calling in their unfamiliar Spanish, there were guffaws of laughter and their pile-driving machine started popping, grinding and crashing. I looked over at the other bed and saw only a mop of black hair peeping out of the blankets. I was to learn that I usually awoke first when the birds began to call. "Time to get up," I said. I climbed out, pulled a towel around my waist and went to the ablution block smelling of cement and new paint, knowing that it was a luxury that would soon be a memory. I filled

40

my lungs with the clean air from the sea not far away and savoured the dry heat of the sun on my naked skin. It was freedom I was feeling, freedom from cities and rain and cold. My bare feet kicked up puffs of white dust as I returned to our disordered camp where Barbie was making coffee. I was supremely happy.

That day we sorted our personal possessions and repacked so that 'nice' clothes and reserve toiletries lived in the strongest case out of sight and day-to-day things and dirty clothes lived in other accessible bags. Passports, documents and money were checked and packed away in the built-in lock-up under the passenger seat. We unpacked every box and tin, laid out the food packets, tools and spares, making sure that we both knew what we had and where we would find it. Everything would have its place and would always be put back exactly in an automatic way. Some things ended up having special places, like a particular red-handled screwdriver that lived in a little pocket of space on the ledge under the dashboard and no matter how many times it was used, it was still there six months later.

Quite naturally, various bits of gear or plastic boxes, or tools, began to be animated and were christened with special little names, some rather childish and silly, but all important. Principally, the Landrover became 'Landie'. Most things became companions and acquired characters: our two identical Primus stoves, bought off the same shelf, were definitely different and had to be handled and started up differently. This process began that day near Cartagena without serious intention, sometimes as a joke, but obviously as a reaction to our loneliness and the need to make our little moving world of vehicle and equipment friendly and humanised. It had its effect though, and I will never forget these lessons, because nothing let us down on the long miles ahead, we did not have one puncture and we never lost as much as a teaspoon. I have always believed, since then, that 'things' behave differently if they are treated with the same respect that one should attach to living beings. But that's jumping away ahead in the story.

There were a few minor needs, like an extra spare tin-opener and more spare prickers for the Primus stoves, which we bought in Cartagena.

Late one afternoon I lay on my back on the campbed while Barbie showered, swatting the flies ("Almost as bad as Aussie flies," she complained), letting the sweat dry and listening to the endless 'flap-flap' of the tent canvas in the strong sea breeze and the repetitive grinding and crashing of the pile-driver. The last pieces of the jigsaw of preparation were coming together and we thought the same way about small things which was important.

The next morning we washed everything that needed it and I hosed every corner of the vehicle. It was a symbolic washing away of Europe and also to be sure we were not taking bugs and bacteria from the crowded cities of England with us. In the hot wind, the temperature reached 110°F that noon, everything was dry and purified within hours. I changed the oil in the new engine again, we had come several hundred miles since it was done in France, and spent a couple of hours tightening every body bolt I could get at. We swam in the pool and joked with the proprietor and his girl-wife. If it was my huge investment with only one party camping I would not be so relaxed as they, and I envied them. They encouraged us to try their restaurant for the evening meal because it had not had a client for several days.

We went to eat at eight o'clock as ordered, but were told that it would not be ready until nine. A bottle of sharp cold rosé was brought 'on the house'. We had not eaten much for two days and the wine went to our heads quickly, so we laughed a lot. A big Grundig tape-recorder played interminable Spanish pop-music and a fan rotated over our heads with a sharp squeak-squeak at every revolution. The young manager appeared in a chef's hat and white apron to announce that he was ready, then reappeared in a black waiter's jacket without the hat to serve us. He caught my eye and we all collapsed with laughter, the plates nearly cascading over the table.

We ate delicious grilled fish and stuffed tomatoes, followed by boot-leather steak, green salad doused with vinegar and a carafe of red wine. "We wouldn't give this steak to a dog in Aussie," Barbie said. "Our steaks are the best in the world."

"Better than Texas?" I asked.

"Like a jelly, they're so tender."

"Yuck!"

"Bet your Yippee steaks are like these Spanish shoe soles."

"You'll have to wait and see," I said.

The young manager would not let us go and came and sat with us bringing coffee and Fundador brandy, again 'on the house'. He was lonely, he told us, and we were the first English people he had entertained, and he asked us all sorts of questions. He kept filling our glasses with brandy, especially mine, and I suddenly realised in my fuzzy mind that he was after Barbie by getting me paralytic and her amenable. When he went for more coffee I told her what I thought.

"Don't worry," she said. "I worked that out an hour ago. Stupid creep, who does he think he is? Time to go anyway, I'm ready to fall over."

I tried to pay for the brandy and the wine, but the manager was adamant, although he watched us go with big sad eyes. We walked down a track and found the shore with a moon painting its silver path across the still sea. There was an ancient stone wall by the beach and we leant against it, feeling quiet, breathing the fresh cool air and listening to the soft hissing of water on the sand.

In the dawn I was woken from a dead sleep by an insistent hand. "My stomach's real crook," Barbie moaned. We were both ill that day, running to the ablution block, and I dosed ourselves with chlorodyne and Thalazol. It was the green salad of course, prepared by the incompetent manager.

We left the next day, driving through dismal Cartagena, a city that was covered in red dust from mountainous dumps of iron ore. There were ruined buildings, presumably left from the Civil War, and old warships in the harbour, rusting and neglected.

*   *

Two days later, we breasted a low hill and out of the afternoon haze a huge grey-brown shape loomed, resting on the invisible horizon between sea and sky. It was Gibraltar and we had come to the end of Europe. The Anglo-Spanish dispute over the Rock had begun and the borders were closed so we headed towards Algeciras to catch our ferry the next morning, which was cheaper anyway.

There was a curious camp-site on the edge of town where we stopped. An old farm had been converted and the long lean-to cow sheds were cleared to serve as shelters for tents and caravanners. The strange rule was that the sheds had to be used and camping was not allowed in the open yard, so it was like a weird public dormitory. The shed was full of French, Germans, Belgians and Spaniards. There was only one other English car, a Hillman, with a family crammed into a small tent. The talk and laughter of the international community echoed off the underneath of the corrugated iron roof like a recording of Babel. On one side of our Landie were two young French women school teachers and on the other a wild group of Belgians with super-equipped caravans and complicated gear. The

43

French girls kept going into their tiny pup-tent and shifting about with curses and coming out in different clothes or hair in curlers. I could not understand why they had to keep changing. The Belgian women seemed to cook endlessly while their men kept re-filling their paraffin refrigerator with beer and drinking it before it had a chance to cool.

We drove into town to get our tickets and check the times of the ferry before eating a simple meal at a café, being careful to ignore anything uncooked for Barbie's stomach was still sensitive. We returned after the sun had set to find miraculous peace in the shed. Only a couple of German boys were still about, playing chess by the light of a paraffin lamp. We walked about the spare grass of the old farmyard in the middle of which stood a well and hand-pump strangely decorated with plaster images of sheaves of corn and laden grape vines, all grey and blotched by mildew. Across the bay, the lights of Gibraltar twinkled in rows and far to the south a powerful lighthouse winked.

"Africa!" I said, pointing.

She took my hand. "I haven't told you before how glad I am that I came," she said quietly.

"No, you haven't," I replied. "But, I'm grateful for you saying it."

"I wasn't absolutely, definitely sure until now. I would have gone on, of course, because I believe that I would have been sure sooner or later. I thought you were an awful nut for stopping at that dreadful dust bowl near Cartagena until I understood why you were doing it; to switch over from civilisation to rough travelling and get used to each other. So, I'm sure now." She peered at me in the dim light and squeezed my hand. "Do you understand?"

I nodded.

CHAPTER FOUR : *THE BARBARY COAST*

In the morning, we were early into Algeciras and had coffees and bread rolls sitting on the pavement beside the quay. It seemed a leisurely business compared to the cool efficiency of catching a cross-Channel ferry to Dieppe from Newhaven.

People in holiday mood hung around, some from the campsite, setting off on some kind of African adventure, but none as important as ours I was sure. There were others in Arab dress with battered old Citroëns loaded with family and goods. Were they refugees from the Algerian War returning, or had they prosaically been doing nothing more than visiting family somewhere? The hot morning sun, the flies, the stink of the badly polluted harbour and the sewers under our feet made Africa loom on our psychic horizon. But it was not any Africa I knew, this was the Mediterranean and I was beginning to learn that the lands around that ancient sea belonged to their own particular human and physical geography no matter how many different nations were scattered around it, how many languages or religions were practised.

The ferry, *Virgen de Africa*, took an hour and a half to cross over the pale blue water to Ceuta but it seemed like ten minutes in my state of excitement. In contrast, it seemed like a lifetime since I had sailed the same sea in the middle of the night, standing on the bridge of the *Klostertor*, watching the lights of the fishing fleets. One moment we were nosing out of Algeciras, gazing at the sphinx-head of Gibraltar and a flotilla of lean British frigates manoeuvring at speed, and the next we were tying up to the concrete quay in Ceuta with the brown hills of Africa behind and Monte Hacho off to the left. Suddenly there were men in grey robes everywhere and women with veils across their faces.

"Are you excited?" I asked. She was writing farewell postcards to her friends.

45

She shook her head. "Not yet. I feel stunned. And not like them." She pointed to a group of Swiss boys, loaded with cameras and long lenses, wearing berets and safari hats, laughing and punching each other, sipping at bottles of warm beer. I had noticed them earlier with their battered old jeep loaded with jerrycans and roughly packed boxes. On the side had been painted: 'Zurich-Paris-Timbuktu'. Maybe we were taking it all too seriously, but I did not think so. I doubt if they ever made it.

The echoing announcements were in three languages, none of which were English, and we had to guess what we had to do about clearing the ship. "No English until the Sudan," I said with a sigh. "I suppose we'll get used to it fast enough." I could also see that the signboards on shore had Arabic script alongside faded Spanish.

"We've hardly seen English tourists since Dieppe," she observed. "Remember the campsite last night: Belgians, Germans, Dutch, French, even Danes, but only one other British. Where do they go on holiday; obviously not Spain?"

"Switzerland or the French Riviera," I said. "I suppose Spain is too dirty and raw for them."

"It's certainly dirty enough, and very poor."

At the end of the quay every conceivable brand of petrol was for sale with notices in six languages, (including English), which said 'Cheapest petrol in Europe'.

"So we're still in Europe?" I muttered, then remembered that Ceuta was Spanish territory. It was all somewhat puzzling. Slim Arab boys leapt and gyrated, pimping us to buy. The BP pumps had no cars waiting so I drove to them, feeling patriotic, and filled all our containers for the first time. While I was paying for the incredibly cheap duty-free petrol at less then two shillings a gallon, an older Arab came to the window. He wore a thick, winter-weight grey suit in that heat and a stained tie around the dirty neck of his shirt.

"You want money, best exchange rates in North Africa?" He did not wait for a reply. "Follow me from that taxi."

I looked at Barbie. "Do you think we should, Den?" she asked anxiously.

"Can you remember the official rates of exchange?" I asked.

"Roughly. I've got a list somewhere."

The taxi revved its engine and a brown hand waved frantically. Mesmerised, I followed. Books and movies about drugs and white slaving in Tangier and Casablanca ran in my head, but I remembered that Ceuta was still Spain, still 'Europe'. Barbie was thinking the same: "I met a Scandinavian girl last year and made friends with her. She was gang-raped on the beach in Tangier by three Arab boys while on a conducted tour."

I shrugged, feeling committed.

The battered Mercedes taxi drew up in a quiet cobbled street with sparse eucalyptus trees in the centre where I parked Landie in the shade. The Arab rushed over: "Lock up, lock up!" he cried, hands waving. "Many evil thieves here; you in Africa now." I looked at Barbie and we both grinned uneasily. I looked about the silent street, windows shuttered against the heat, then followed him into a dingy café.

In the dimness our arrival started scurrying movements. An old man asleep in a corner jerked upright, blinking. The proprietress dropped the spoon that she had been using to taste a rich stew at the counter and screamed a greeting or question at our man. A girl was bathing a baby in a plastic bowl and it started crying. A teen-age boy was reading a picture comic-book and a radio exhorted: "*Beve Coca-Cola Grande*". Hardly a hashish den of white-slavers, I thought. The old man was pushed away from his table in the corner and we sat down.

"What you want, vino, Coca-Cola, American whisky, coffee? I pay."

We had thick, strong coffee while rates of exchange were explained which varied considerably according to quantity, the size of bills and cheques. I tried to do mental arithmetic frantically in my head while Barbie repeated the official rates from the pamphlet she had picked up. This little currency black-market we had stumbled into had certainly got excellent rates. Algerian money was being offered at double the official exchange, but I had a premonition about that and in the end we only changed Moroccan which disappointed our friend. He went into a back room to get his cash together while we drank the coffee, feeling more relaxed. I pulled out a cigarette and the teenage boy rushed over and flicked a lighter very carefully and brought the flame to me. The girl with the baby smiled shyly. Two men returned with a brief case bulging with currency notes in neat packages. I noticed Egyptian pounds, Libyan and Tunisian money, sheaves of US dollars and French francs. Our exchange was completed with care and hands were shaken all round. We bought a bottle of wine and groceries from the woman at the counter.

Outside in the baking heat, Landie was waiting unravaged. The contents of the café came out to see us off. "*Hasta la vista!*" They called. The teenage boy's eyes followed mine as we drove away.

"They were really nice," Barbie said.

"Robbed; raped by gangs," I snorted, and we laughed with relief.

*   *

The week spent traversing Spain had got us used to dry heat and different culture, but we knew we were still cushioned by Europe. The next week got us used to the alienness of Africa in the new post-Independence world of 1965; especially the Arab countries. In Morocco and Algeria we sensed antagonism to Whites, but whenever it became clear that we were British, scowling reserve usually changed to smiles. I was glad that I had stuck plastic Union Jacks on the Landie.

In North Africa we were constantly reminded of ancient history; reminded that in the days of Carthaginian, Greek and Roman Civilisations, the countries that we were travelling through had been more developed than Britain. Everywhere there was a sense of ancient days which could not be shadowed by the evident poverty we observed. I began to learn, maybe for the first time from real things about me, that culture and civilisation does not depend alone on wealth and prosperity. The shabbiness and poverty were not dissimilar to that which I had observed in the cities of Spain, but the difference seemed to be that whereas Spain had been a fine modern country by the standards of the time before the Civil War, it had regressed badly since then, twenty seven years ago. North Africa, despite considerable war damage, was different. The wars there seemed to have delayed progress rather than to have created regression. I think I understood the difference, and the different effect on people. The people had not been degraded by the experience in North Africa, maybe they had been psychically strengthened: the Algerian war had strengthened the people, the Spanish war had broken them apart.

I certainly did feel a clear change to a brighter mood after crossing the Straits of Gibraltar which was not just our own excitement of the adventure. I reflected that politically Spain was governed by the hard dictatorship of Franco whereas the North African countries had recently all achieved independence, and I knew that must have had some powerful effect. There was Islam, too, which I knew little about. But there was something else in the air; a quiet, ancient dignity and stoicism of stability that tempered natural striving for progress and personal gain.

Although I had no personal experience to compare with, it seemed to me that if there was obvious change in North Africa it was in the youth which was most vulnerable to the sirens of technology from Europe. Italian motor-scooters gave new personal mobility. Cheaply produced books, transistor radios receiving European 'pop' culture from powerful transmitters, American movies with sub-titles and Communist propaganda seduced a generation, able to understand and read, away from traditional Islamic Arab culture. But I also knew that there was a star of nationalism shining in the east in the shape of Nasser who was both 'modern' and Arab. Nasserism did not have overt signs in Morocco which was a kingdom and had moved away from French colonialism with little fuss, but the strength of a new Arab nationalism in spirit and politics became more obvious as we travelled eastward.

I liked Morocco and wish that we had stayed there longer. Perhaps it had something to do with race and I knew that the Berber kingdom had roots of power that went back hundreds of years. Despite periods when piracy and slaving of Europeans had made the Barbary Coast a place of terror, there had long been diplomatic relations and communication between the rulers of Morocco and Europe. The King of Morocco exchanged embassies with Louis XIV. France's colonial grip on the country in the 20th century had been relatively gentle. We experienced the results of this in the grave courtesy, dignity and shy friendliness that we met after crossing the border outside the suburbs of Ceuta, a mongrel city.

*   *

The formalities were quickly and efficiently over and we drove in the afternoon through olive and citrus groves to Chaouen and then up into the Rif mountains. We camped for the night in an old gravel quarry above the winding road through pine and fir trees in the clear mountain air. It was our first camp in Africa, and the first of so many that we made by the roadside away from any conveniences of our civilisation. We unpacked our folding chairs, table and cooking equipment. Later it was to become such a regular and automatic activity that in the fatigue after a long day we did it without words

49

and almost without thinking. Only when that chore had been completed would we look about and think about cooking or sightseeing.

Barbie prepared the vegetables and I started the stoves that first time as the sun set through the trees. Goats bleated their way past us, the leader with a bell clunking around its neck. Two following herdboys wearing what looked like long striped nightshirts stopped to watch us for a minute then were gone amongst the trees after flashing us a brief smile.

It was cool in the morning at 4,000 feet and the water in the plastic can that had stood outside was icy when I came to wash and shave. I remembered that the road through the Rif was closed by snow in winter. Driving on in the cool of morning, we saw a secondary road going down to a valley where there were farms and plantations spread out like a map. We stopped to photograph a hillside far below where tightly terraced vines and shining green wheat covered the sides almost to the crest of the mountain opposite. Dribbles of smoke rose from the homesteads hundreds of feet below.

We diverted to Al Hoceima, a new resort girdling a cove at the foot of giant yellow rock cliffs. A modern concrete hotel had been built on the beach and sticking onto the cliffs like leeches were a rash of square villas under construction. Down by the cove it was airless and the temperature rose above 90º F so we struggled sweatily into swim suits in the back before going for a swim and sunbathe beside the clear green water. At the far end of the beach locals swam and children screamed and played, while in front of the hotel its inhabitants lounged aristocratically beneath umbrellas. The women wore chaste one-piece costumes and the men were plump and stocky with chests covered with curly black hair and their gold-rimmed sunglasses studied Barbie's body in its brief bikini as we walked by, with public faces of disapproval.

Beyond Al Hoceima there was an old pirate island, Peñon de Alhucemos, which was a piece of rock covered with old, flat-topped buildings, completely walled around the edge. It was originally a Phoenician outpost and was to-day a fishing community, still owned by Spain. It looked like the last remains of an inundated city, a remnant of Atlantis. A small jetty projected from steps up to an ancient gate and it seemed to be the only way into its mysteriousness. In the siesta hour it was silent and I could see no movement.

I thought it would be pleasant to camp on the shore within sight of this ancient island and we followed a rough track. I found a way to the sea along a wide dry watercourse of sand and pebbles that ran past a small village. Tracks led out onto it where trucks went to pick up loads of sand and pebbles for building work, so I followed them before heading seawards. We hummed along on the hard-packed sand. The island came into view behind a low headland and on the near bank of the watercourse a stand of wind-twisted pines stood.

"That's the place!" I said with enthusiasm and aimed towards it. Within seconds, we were deep in mud beneath the innocent crust where water still oozed. All four wheels spun impotently in reverse and I felt the heavy hand of doom. Standing ankle deep in mud I looked back along our tracks and then across the sand to the sea where the mysterious island stood offshore. It was suddenly an evil island that had lured me to disaster.

"It's a long way to that village for help," Barbie said. "What are you going to do?"

"Let me think and have a look around," I said. A little distance away there was a darker patch of sand with what looked like weeds growing in it and I walked over. They were baby pine trees that had been washed down in some spring thaw flood from the mountains. To my relief, when I bent to pull one out, it came away easily.

"This is the answer," I called. "We must make a carpet of these little pines."

Barbie started pulling them while I dug channels behind the wheels. An hour later we stood triumphant beside two tracks back to the hard sand, black mud splashed up to our knees and elbows. Slowly, my heart beating, I let out the clutch and gently revved the engine. There was a brief low howl as the wheels spun and I eased the accelerator, thinking with an instant sick feeling that we would now have to unload all our gear. But as I lowered the engine speed, some of the wheels stopped spinning and caught on the little pines. "Come on, slowly," Barbie called beside me, watching the wheels. I peered out the window to keep in the track and suddenly Landie was moving easily on the sand.

We lit cigarettes with relief then walked down to the beach to wash in the sea. Barbie was about to take off her clothes for a quick swim when a look around told that we were not alone.

Standing by Landie was a tall Arab in a grey robe with two boys in pants with long shirts. With them they had four donkeys harnessed up together to a long rope. They were gravely examining the pine-filled tracks and the skid marks. In our bustle and confusion we had not noticed them coming.

"Oh, my God!" I exclaimed. "They've come all the way from the village to pull us out."

"Oh, no!" Barbie's voice was dismayed.

My meagre French could not express what I wished to say to them as they watched our faces with soft grave eyes. Maybe they could not understand French anyway. Barbie offered them cigarettes and I showed them a piece of paper money, but they shook their heads firmly. After rummaging in the back, I found a reserve tin of pilchards and this they accepted with dignity and a few slowly spoken sentences in Arabic. We all saluted each other and then we had to drive away, leaving them to plod slowly back to their village. Barbie was snuffling and my eyes felt hot.

Of course, we abandoned the island and drove on rather aimlessly. In compensation, we came to an excellent roadside camping place. On a whim, I followed a track into a shallow valley, and there on the far side of a thick blanket of eucalyptus trees there was an open space beside a rushing river. We were able to wash properly in the cold mountain water and, relaxed, cook and eat as the sun set. The air was filled with the sound of water and the scent of the trees.

In the morning we were drinking coffee when the rattle of a horse's hooves in the stones of the river bank surprised me. With creaking of leather from his polished saddle, a patrolling policeman descended. How had he found us, so early in the morning? We could communicate a little in French and I wondered if we were on some prohibited ground; but no, he indicated that we should finish our breakfast and he settled to wait for us. I offered him coffee, but he refused it with quiet dignity and asked if he could inspect the Landie, which he did quite thoroughly but without fuss. I asked if we had done anything wrong and he shook his head, saying something complicated about Algeria that I could not understand. I explained that we were heading towards Algeria and had come from Ceuta and he smiled and nodded. It was alright. He waited until we had packed up then climbed back on his horse. Both he and the mount were smartly groomed and a credit to the Moroccan police.

"What was that about, I wonder?" Barbie said as we drove away. "And why was he on about Algeria?"

*   *

That day we went on to Melilla, another Spanish enclave like Ceuta, a few square miles in extent. We had to go through the rigmarole of customs and immigration but it was a simple procedure. It was almost disconcerting to be back in Spain and 'Europe'. Most of the people in the busy streets were Spanish and the robes (I learned they were called *djellabas*) and veils we had begun to get used to were gone. Arabic script disappeared too. We stopped at the Hotel España which looked respectable but was cheap and Barbie wanted to bath. Apart from the showers near Cartagena, we had not bathed since England. Until you have missed it for a while, the turning on of a tap to watch water flowing, especially hot water, is commonplace. But in the real world of travelling in Africa it was becoming an extraordinary luxury. However, we could not get a hot bath and had to make do with a good wash and a change into clean clothes.

Feeling fresh in the cooler air of the late afternoon we wandered the streets to the town centre where there were several pavement cafes all remarkably full of well dressed people. We found two seats and crowded amongst the families and groups of men. A friendly older man with some English questioned us and enjoyed finding out why two young Britishers were in Melilla. In return he explained that it was a particular saint's day and there was to be a parade soon, now that the heat of the day was gone. While he told us about it, the thump of a drum began to echo and the bray of brass instruments came to us.

The procession, with two or three brass bands, took about an hour to pass: there were the strolling dignitaries, leaning back with chests puffed out and staring carefully to the front, the priests in their robes, the Saint held high by a group of young men in their vestments. And then came the schoolchildren in their ranks, platoons of the army or some other military force, firemen, ambulance men, all the services who wore uniforms. I loved the echoing music. The spectators looked for familiar faces amongst the procession and children looked up excitedly at the solemn faces of fathers pacing by.

Afterwards, we had a delicious sea-food dinner with iced *viño de casa* in a friendly restaurant with a bunch of amateurs playing folk music. I think they were enjoying their music more than the diners.

"We're not roughing it as much as I thought we would," Barbie said happily as we climbed the stairs in our hotel.

"Let's enjoy a bit of good living while we can," I said. "And everything is so cheap here."

In the morning, we were returned to normality. The heat built up rapidly in our cramped room and there was no water in the taps, even though we waited around until nearly ten o'clock before leaving. The streets wafted gently with that characteristic stench of dried sewage that seems peculiar to the Mediterranean summer.

By mid-afternoon we were in Oujda, a large Moroccan town not far from the border where the Moroccan post was deserted and this seemed ominous. A slim, pale-skinned official in immaculate khakis stamped our documents and wished us, "*Bon voyage.*" I did not like the strange atmosphere and was glad that Morocco did not require visas, so we could return if something was wrong. Two border guards lifted the barrier for us and they were wearing steel helmets and carried sub-machine guns.

The noise of our Landrover motor seemed loud in the silent baking heat in the empty no-mans-land. I began to feel distinctly nervous. Around a corner we suddenly came on the Algerian post. The barrier was up and a great milling crowd filled the roadway and car park. Battered black Citroën and Renault cars and taxis littered the forecourt and empty buses stood on one side. Piles of suitcases tied up with string and bundles wrapped in camel blankets lay about amongst squalling children and heavily robed women. At first it all seemed uncontrolled and I wondered if there was any authority present. Why didn't these people just walk through? Then Barbie touched my arm and pointed. Behind us but facing the crowd was an armoured car with a heavy machine gun mounted on the top. Husky young men in battle dress were perched on it.

"Just remember we're British," I said gaily. "Have to deal with these bloody natives, what?"

"Jolly good, old chap," Barbie said. "I'll guard the Landie."

I went into the door marked, *Entrée*, and came to a halt. There was pandemonium and I felt despair. The long hall was divided in the middle into entry and departure sections, but the barrier had been pushed aside. Everybody was trying to leave Algeria. Except me. The mob of several hundred people, mostly men, was literarily howling, repeatedly yelling for attention with monotonous shouts, waving papers and passports like flags at a procession. The officials behind the counter were spending more time shouting back at the mob than actually processing documents. The noise and the level of emotion and panic was physically nauseating. A tense young army sergeant sat just inside the door I had entered by, clutching the butt of a Bren gun which stood on a table before him. He trained it back and forth nervously as the noise swelled. I stood quite nonplussed, wondering what to do.

I caught the soldier's eye and shrugged, raising my eyebrows. He shrugged in reply, but waved the muzzle of the gun in the direction of the counter so I went up to it. After some minutes, one of the harassed immigration officials detached himself and came over to look at our documents that I had ready, passports opened to the Algerian visas. He sighed and I realised that it was with relief that he was dealing with sanity in a world gone mad. I expected to be given forms to fill in, but his hand picked up a rubber stamp, hovered for a moment then descended decisively. I pushed the carnet de passage for Landie to him and he smiled apologetically.

"*Pas de douane,*" he said, gesturing with his hands. No customs? He smiled again and pointed to the yelling mob. "*Ces't impossible!*" He returned the documents and waved me off with a little salute.

I returned his smile and salute and went back to Barbie.

"Now what?" she said despondently.

"Now we go," I said, grinning.

"I don't believe it."

A young soldier came over from the barrier and had a cursory look in the back. Barbie had bought a copy of *Time* magazine in Melilla that morning and he became agitated, holding it up and waving it around. Another soldier came over and my heart felt like lead again. What was this about? The two men argued over the magazine and then the senior asked brusquely why we had the magazine. I said we had been in Melilla that morning and bought it. What was the matter, we had not had time to read it yet. They studied the date on the cover and talked more before tearing it up. The older one apologised for his bad manners and waved me off.

"Well, well," I said. "That was worrying."

"There was something about Algeria in the cover-story," Barbie said. "There was a picture of the president and some other guy on the cover. But I hadn't read any of it yet."

The blazing heat outside smelled of freedom, but we were going alone against the stream. All those desperate people were trying to get out of Algeria, and we had no idea why. When I started Landie up and drove slowly through the women, children and old people waiting with the piles of luggage, the men on the armoured car gave me a brief disinterested glance. Our European appearance and a Union Jack on Landie had been a more powerful passport than any documents.

After some miles we came to a road block with an armoured car.

A tall, good looking soldier walked over. His uniform had razor sharp creases and there were bars on his shoulders. His boots had hardly a fleck of dust on them.

"Pardon," he said. "You are English?"

"Yes, we are both British," I said.

"How long will you remain in Algeria?"

"I don't know," I said. "It depends if we find good places for camping. Two weeks, three..." I smiled.

"You are journalists?"

I laughed. "No. We are travellers to Cairo."

"Ces't bon." He touched his hat. Then he gestured at Barbie's bare legs. She was wearing shorts. "Mademoiselle should wear a skirt. Showing legs is disrespectful."

I could feel Barbie's Aussie pride being pricked. "Why all those people?" I asked quickly, pointing back up the road.

He frowned. "They are so-called refugees. We will not embarrass the authorities of Morocco by allowing them to pass through the controls." His voice was cold.

"All those poor people," Barbie sighed.

"But why so many controls?" I asked.

"You do not know?" He seemed amazed. "We have a revolution. President Ben Bella has been replaced by Boumoudienne and the government is changed."

It was my turn to be amazed. A revolution, and we just happened to be travelling through. The officer patted my shoulder reassuringly: "It is not your affair," he said. "Travel peacefully and there will be no trouble for you. Obey all instructions from the police or army... Bon Voyage!"

A revolution! Barbie and I discussed it with excitement and wondered if it would really be alright, but concluded that we had no alternative but to carry on. A little further on there was a more serious road block. Tents had been pitched neatly by the side of the road and two armoured cars were parked beside them. A platoon of soldiers were standing around a sandbagged emplacement with a heavy machine gun. A sergeant looked us over and peered in the back before waving us through.

"That soldier didn't seem bothered," Barbie said. "Algeria is communist isn't it? Does it matter who is in charge?"

"As long as they don't start fighting each other. That would be terrible and very bad for us. But the army seems quite relaxed."

We were stopped several times in the next hour and learned how to distinguish between the army and the police. The army liked to look in the back but did not care about documents. The police liked to stare at passports but did not bother with what or who we could be carrying. When we reached the outskirts of Tlemcen I took a minor road up the mountain to the right to find somewhere to camp for the night.

"Do you think we should camp in the open with all the army around?" Barbie asked.

"I've no Algerian money," I said. "For some reason, I didn't change any in Ceuta."

An escarpment loomed in the late afternoon light above Tlemcen and we found a level place hidden from the road. I parked the Landie under a clump of eucalyptus trees and a clear spring ran from beneath some rocks. We looked out onto a wide valley with groves of olives and citrus stretching away from the city. Some women in long blue skirts and orange blouses, with jangly brass earrings at the side of their faces came by, herding a flock of sheep and goats. They turned away from us and soon we were alone, watching the sun set and the lights come on in the city. We ate omelettes cooked in olive oil and garlic, filled with fried onions and green pepper, and drank a bottle of sharp rosé wine. A cooling breeze rustled the leaves of the eucalyptus trees. It was rather fine there.

CHAPTER FIVE : 'LE GROS'

In the morning we drove slowly into Tlemcen, an ancient city with six hundred year old, crenellated red-claybrick perimeter walls and towers. Entering, we passed through a roadblock where our passports were checked and I had a sudden fear that we would have to explain where we had spent the night, but it seemed that our foreignness continued to be as good a passport as any although rifle barrels were poked into our gear in the back.

The banks were open but doing little business and I cashed travellers' cheques with no trouble. We filled up with petrol and bought food and wine in a little French-style grocery shop while the sanitary truck drove by washing the street with its spray of white water, filling the air with the smell of wet dust. The atmosphere of the city was relaxed and I liked it. The streets were lined by green-leafed trees and there were dignified buildings. The market bustled. We had a tiny cup of coffee at a stall beside the market and swarthy men in blue French-style working clothes watched us and some of them smiled at us when they heard us talking English to each other.

The road ran northeast towards the sea and the temperature climbed into the nineties by ten o'clock. Towards noon we were in the outskirts of Oran and a hot dry wind was blowing dust and litter about the shabby, pink colour-washed suburban houses. A few soldiers stood about at traffic junctions and the city was deserted and brooding. It was very hot and we had no reason to stop so we took the short length of autoroute past the airport, the tires singing on the unaccustomed smooth tarmac. Suddenly, we seemed to be in an industrial estate with no clear way out. Behind, at the airport, military Dakotas were running their engines blowing yellow dust into the brilliant sunlight. There were a few factories about, all deserted. I saw the office of Unilever Algerienne with stone-shattered windows.

"Pretty bloody dismal," I said. "I suppose we should go back to town." But before I could move a police jeep hummed up from behind and pulled up alongside.

"*Où est le route à Orleansville?*" I asked, getting in first.

"*Passeport?*" His face was expressionless. We had to go through a thorough check before he was satisfied and he pointed at the airfield: "*Photographie interdit.*"

"*Comprendre,*" I said nodding.

"*Bon.* You follow." He jumped into his jeep and drove off, and I followed.

"Now what?" she asked.

"Who knows?" I shrugged. I had become inured to the revolution, mainly because of the invariable correctness towards us. About two miles further back the jeep slowed at an obscure junction and the policeman's arm pointed down a rough side road. "Orleansville!" he shouted. "*Bon voyage!*"

The road was narrow and the tarred surface uneven and potholed. The countryside was rolling and cultivated for wheat with olive groves. There was much evidence of the recent Algerian War. Rusted barbed wire entanglements surrounded battered concrete pillboxes and there were many abandoned French colonial farmsteads, all with bullet pitted facades and some were blackened shells. There were few people about to begin with on this route and we travelled many miles without the harassment of police or military roadblocks. We thumped and rattled onwards in the heat, temperatures in the cab rising to 108ºF. After Relizane we entered the wide valley of the Cheliff River with prosperous farms on either side of the road. The wind dropped and the air cleared. For miles the road was lined by an avenue of trees.

Now there were *camions* loaded with vegetables and wheat straw bellowing along, forcing us off the narrow tarmac and we had not seen so much traffic since leaving Spain. Some of the farms had vineyards, the bunches of grapes beginning to mature on the vines. But the heat continued to oppress us, my eyes were sore, lids sticking, my hands slippery on the steering wheel. By mid afternoon I needed a break and we pulled up in the shade of an oak tree and we dozed in the back with the door open, waking up after a half-hour wet with sweat, our clothes sticking to our bodies all over.

The water in our plastic can was warm and had to be forced down and we had eaten nothing all day. I felt weak. "We must reach the sea to-night," I said.

"Too right," Barbie replied, mopping her face and neck.

The shadows were lengthening so that the sun struck through between the trunks of the avenue like golden swords.

Orleansville (re-named Ech Cheliff by 1993) seemed crowded with aimless people, hanging about its dusty and shabby centre. We stopped beside an open air café and the heat of the pavement burned through the soles of my sandals. The chairs of the café were broken and the paint chipped; the tables stained and dirty, buzzing with flies. Lines of men in blue denim work suits lounged in the shade of the buildings. But, thank the Lord, we were able to buy iced fizzy lemonade. I drank a litre, gulping and burping. What heaven!

At a petrol station I put my head under the tap and raised it to look into the eyes of a women in the back of a shiny, air-conditioned Mercedes with Moroccan number plates. She was swathed in a beige robe with fine embroidery around the neck and masked to her dark liquid eyes. I stood for some moments letting the water dry with tingling coolness and she let her eyes remain on mine. I had a sudden feeling of psychic fire before she looked down demurely and I sensed a smile behind the veil.

Barbie had been watching. "Feeling better?"

"I have often read about Arab girls' eyes above their mysterious veils," I said.

"And now you know." She grinned. "Let's get to the sea."

North of Orleansville we drove for miles through rolling hills where the wheat had been harvested leaving fields of stubble. We stopped for photographs and in the quiet heard the distant growl of a harvester at work. Here was the world of the Roman conquest when Africa fed the Empire.

The road descended to the sea through a spectacular gorge. The sun was setting as we emerged from the gaunt rock canyon and we were met by a most beautiful sight. It was as if nature had decided to reward us after eight hours of driving in the heat. Five hundred feet below us, a basin was carved into the cliffs, filled with blue sea, and the ancient port of Tenes was cradled around it. The sun was an orange ball and this light bathed the scene. Black silhouettes of fishing craft crawled back to harbour. We stopped and got out to admire and suddenly, to complete our pleasure, a high haunting chant of a muezzin called from the old town immediately below. It was magical. When the muezzin ceased, a motor scooter started up, its 'b r r r r r r r' echoed from the cliffs and I heard the babble of children. The spell was broken.

60

The road bypassed the old town and wound in hairpins up the eastern side of the basin. It was getting dark and I felt dazed with fatigue. Finding a place to stop became an anxiety, but I drove on automatically. It was after seven o'clock. Barbie, studying the Michelin map, said that there was a river running into what could be a cove and it might do. She peered into the dark on her side, hunting for a track. Suddenly, I saw a hand-painted sign in French: *Plage du Recreation - Movement Socialiste Algerienne pour Jeun et Jeunesse International.*

"My God! If ever there was an answer to a prayer. I don't believe it!" I exulted, as we drove down the track through black shapes of twisted olive trees and bent old pines. A dog barked somewhere nearby.

We bumped heavily down the track, past a block of silent clapboard shacks, and into a plantation of stunted Mediterranean pines. The air was filled with their clean resinous scent and the smell of the sea. I could hear the soft rush of small waves somewhere in the blackness. The headlights probed between the trees to show a wide shingle beach and the dim outline of a high cliff beyond. Three huge boulders provided natural shelter and I parked beside them. In the silence the 'rush-rush' of the waves was hypnotic. A light breeze stirred the perfume of the pines. "Fate led us by the nose to a perfect place," I said.

"Here come the comrades," Barbie warned. A torch was bobbing towards us and a deep voice spoke rapidly in Arabic from behind it. It was an authoritative voice and not friendly. I climbed out.

"*Anglais,*" I said gesturing at Landie and the light hovered over the registration plates, then came back to our faces.

"*Vous dèsirer campè?*" the anonymous voice asked.

"*Oui, si'l vous plait.*" I waited while the torch wandered over us and Landie again. I could not stand any problem now, and I wished I could see who was confronting us. It was an eerie and disturbing feeling, like being a naked slave in a market place.

At last: "*Ca va! Bien ici.*" The torch turned away and I had a glimpse of a giant white-clad figure. There was a flash of teeth in a dark face. "*Bienvenue a Bouchera.* Welcome."

We ate a tin of reserve food and crawled into the back to sleep like dead people.

*   *

61

I awoke to the growl and roar of huge Czechoslovakian earth-moving equipment. Where were we? The sun burned its way into Landie through the dusty windows. It was already hot and my eyes were sticky, my body damp. I listened to the thunder of diesel engines, the crash of tons of shingle loading into tip-trucks and the faint calls of men. We obviously could not stay in a gravel quarry but I had a sudden powerful desire to stop moving. We had been on the move daily since Cartagena, which seemed to be on a different planet. I struggled out of my cotton sleeping bag and pulled on shorts while Barbie watched with a jaundiced eye.

"I don't want to go on," she said in a faint voice. "I want to sleep. Please find a quiet place to camp." She pulled her pillow over her head.

Perched on one of the huge boulders beside us, a big man was sitting waiting. He wore a voluminous white cotton robe and a length of white cloth was twisted about his head. When I stumbled about, shaking the sleep from my head, he jumped down and came to me with a wide grin. A huge hand enveloped mine.

"Travail, travail! Grrrr-Grrr!" he shouted cheerfully, pulling me away. "À la bas!" he bellowed. Deep within the pines I discovered the little village of pre-fabricated wooden huts we had glimpsed the night before. The noise of machinery was subdued to a deep grumble and we stopped. The huts were well spaced in the pine plantation, the trees were trimmed with white painted boles to combat disease. The yellow stony ground was swept clean and scattered with fresh pine needles. Beyond the huts, the yellow rock sides of a cliff could be seen. It was a good place.

The giant explained that he was the Chef of the workers who lived in two of the huts and we could use one of the others for as long as we wished. His round face decorated with a clipped military moustache was split with a huge grin as he swung open the door. "Pour vous!" he declaimed. "Reste bien ici."

I could just make out his explosive pidgin French, sometimes mixed with a bit of German for some reason, and at first it was difficult but later we held long conversations. It is remarkable how people can get on once they get to know each other and can watch each other's faces and hands no matter how little language they have in common. Then, I was still unsure of his authority and protested that we had to keep going but this outraged him. "Non, non! Campè ici. Tranquil, dormè bien." He made swimming motions and pointed to the sea. He gestured at the main road, shaking his head: "Algiers not good. City no good, nicht gut. Here is good." He clapped me on the back, making me stagger. I grinned, "OK".

"*Ca va!*" he shouted and rushed away. A small army returned with him to help us unpack. There were three drivers of the big tip-trucks, two shy women we came to know well, and a quiet man in European clothes. I backed the Landie through the trees to the end hut while Barbie watched bemused. The white-robed giant supervised us all and within minutes the contents of Landie were inside the hut in neat stacks. They all took their leave politely.

"What happened?" Barbie asked finally, sitting on one of our campbeds, her hair sticking to her damp forehead.

"You said you wanted to stay here," I said, grinning. "I arranged it..."

She laughed. Then, looking at the unpacked equipment she asked: "For how long?"

"As long as we like. The Chef insists."

"He's nice. What's his name?"

"I don't know," I said. "Let's call him *Le Gros*, the big one."

The next many days were often an idyll. Although the country had just suffered a military coup and the terrible war with France was not long over, I don't think we could have found greater peace and kindness from strangers anywhere in the world. In Tenes, where we went shopping, the shopkeepers got to know us. The butcher reserved cuts of *carne anglais* for us, at the Alimentation Generale a selection of wines were always brought out for us as soon as we entered and vegetables were carefully selected so that we did not have to pick over the stock like the local housewives would. In return for the special attention, we stocked up on olive oil, rice, salt, beans, pasta, sugar and paraffin for several weeks ahead. People in the streets nodded gravely to us. Le Gros accompanied us on the first day to show us around and no doubt the whole town knew about the English couple who were staying at Oued Bouchera. If the shopkeepers put up their prices to us, I did not notice it for everything seemed very reasonable. We lived for less than ten shillings a day each which included plenty of wine to entertain our friends, reasonable quantities of luxury meat and all the stocking up of imperishables.

The magnificent impression of Tenes we received on the evening of our arrival was not spoiled by its daytime appearance. The town, sheltered by two great headlands and built partly on a defendable plateau above the sea, had been founded by Phoenicians and later became an enclave of Carthage until the Romans came and continued to use it as a port for grain exports. In the middle ages it was a fishing port and a resort of Barbary pirates. It was still a fishing village, unspoiled by tourists and cut off from the mainstream of Algeria. All the buildings seemed to be at least twenty or thirty years old, many much older, but they were in good repair. There were no bullet holes. Rich market gardens terraced against erosion, mostly local cooperatives, flourished where topsoil from the mountains had washed into the valleys and level alluvial patches.

Bouchera delighted us. The soaring rocky cliffs rose straight from the sea, and within the bay and shelter from the cliffs the sea was gentle. The quiet and freshness of our pine plantation and the kindly fellowship of our Arab friends living alongside us produced the tranquillity that Le Gros insisted we would find there. Of course, there was the background noise of the bulldozer and the tiptrucks during the day, but they were at the end of the road some hundreds of yards from the camp and shielded by the trees. Instead of being an annoyance, the sound became strangely comforting and in my memory later I thought of the distant growling as being an evocative part of the experience.

We learned the sketchy history of our friends early, and details were expanded over numerous cups of coffee and in the gatherings we had later. Le Gros had joined De Gaulle's Free French army as a boy in 1943 and had landed at Nice and been to Paris in the Liberation. He transferred to the French regular army and had risen to the rank of sergeant-major before the Algerian War, in which he had been a hero on the rebel side. He had a mysterious wife who lived somewhere in the interior. The other man in the group we called 'Comrade'. He was a delightful person, quiet and serious but with a dry sense of humour to counteract Le Gros' bearlike personality. He had escaped the Algerian War because he had graduated from an academy and been sent to East Germany by the rebel authority to become indoctrinated in Communism. Thereafter, he had been trained as a mechanical engineer in Belgium under the auspices of a trade-union organisation. He was in charge of maintaining the equipment.

His wife, Chadra, was a lovely young woman with big dark eyes and an eternal smile on her mouth with whom Barbie became especially friendly, and they had a toddling baby. I thought that Chadra was the most intelligent of our friends but she always deferred to her husband and had a kind of teasing relationship with

Le Gros as if he was a naughty and immature elder brother. To complete the group there was Lila, a Berber woman in her forties who was employed as some kind of official cook or 'housekeeper', preparing a big midday meal for the truck and 'dozer drivers who apparently lived at a depot some distance away. We called her 'Auntie' and she was a small stringy person, a cheerful little sparrow. She had blue tattoo marks on her pale face with dark eyes and long black hair pulled back on either side. She dressed in bright red and yellow cloths and wore big brass earrings. When strangers came, Chadra put on a veil, but Auntie's culture did not require that. We met the other truck drivers of course: tall slim men, some bearded and all moustached, grave and shy who greeted us with raised hands. I grew fond of them all, they were the salt of the earth. They quietly accepted us with a natural friendship that I have seldom experienced elsewhere.

Every morning, two or three long, crusty loaves of fresh pale brown bread were brought to us by Le Gros. The first morning I tried to pay, but that was greeted by gargantuan laughter. *"Non! Le Gouvernement ces't payer!"* He bellowed. It was free rations to the workers and we were getting our share. So we only cooked once a day, in the evening, and nibbled that delicious bread with cheese and tomatoes whenever we were hungry. After the first day when we lazed in a kind of daze, obviously suffering somewhat from mental exhaustion after days of excessive heat, driving onwards and the tensions of police and military checks, we were fit and healthy.

One day, bright-eyed Auntie announced that we would be treated to cous-cous. I had read of this traditional North African food but had no idea about it, so was much intrigued. Auntie agreed that I could watch her preparation and cooking. I asked if there was any way we could contribute and was told that a meat stew in addition to a vegetable sauce was considered a luxury. I insisted that we contribute a meat stew and Le Gros and Comrade agreed, deciding that we should have a 'party'. I knew that our friends were Moslems but both men had lived in European style for many years, so we went to Tenes to stock up with wine as well as buy a kilo of lean goat meat and fresh vegetables.

In the afternoon, Auntie set about her cous-cous. Over her open fire she placed a wide and shallow, conical iron cooking utensil, like an upside-down umbrella. A mountain of roughly-cracked wheat germs were poured into the pot, salt and water was added and it was constantly stirred. The secret, as I understood it, was to keep the wheat moist but not wet. Every now and again, Auntie swept her hand through the steaming cous-cous to judge its texture and add a slop of water from her jug. She was at it for about two or three hours, stirring, constantly tending the fire so that it was at the correct intensity and checking the moistness and softness of the wheat. When it was cooked it was a coarse dry porridge of remarkable nourishment, full of rich flavour and with none of the vitamins and minerals cooked out. Peasant foods always seem to be so much better tasting and more logically prepared than those created by 'scientific' methods.

We stewed our goat segments gently all afternoon too, adding chopped onions, lots of garlic, tomatoes, fresh local herbs and dollops of olive oil. It smelled delicious.

The evening was a great success. We were summoned by bellows from Le Gros as the sun was setting. In his hut, a table stood in the centre with boxes serving as chairs. A variety of plates were set on the table with a strange mix of utensils: spoons, a twisted fork here, a plastic measure there. Thick chipped glasses and tin mugs stood at each place setting. A paraffin lantern and two stubs of candles supplied the light and Chadra had her prized transistor radio out playing wailing Arab music from some local station. We all sat down and grinned at each other for some moments with delight and a tremendous feeling of simple friendship.

I put two bottles of local red wine on the table and there was an embarrassed silence. I thought I had made a fool of myself until Le Gros produced a gust of laughter. Making allowance for our European tastes, they had gone to the trouble of buying half a dozen litres of beer and with a grin Comrade lifted a pile of wet sacking to reveal the glistening dark bottles cooling beneath. The beer was opened first and the wine left to accompany the food. Talk broke out in a Babel of French, English, Arabic phrases, German and even Flemish-Dutch. Hands began to wave, shoulders moved and eyes flashed within nodding faces.

After the beer was gone I asked about the latest revolution.

"Hah! Ben Bella nicht gut. Capitalist!"

"In Europe we understood Ben Bella was a true socialist?"

"Non!" A sweeping gesture from Le Gros nearly had our plates on the floor. "Ben Bella like money too much. *Automobiles, le grande chateau, commercialiste. Boumedienne c'est bon: soldat de Revolution Algerienne, socialiste. Tres bon.*" To them it was as simple as that. Comrade assured me that the coup had been popular, which is why

66

the country was so quiet and we had been very lucky because of that. It was a sobering thought.

The cous-cous was served with our aromatic meat stew and a mountainous salad of chopped tomatoes, onions, radishes and cucumbers generously slopped with olive oil pressed in a nearby village. With each mouthful of the cous-cous I felt as if my stomach was blowing up like a balloon and a pleasant lassitude filled me. I watched my hosts carefully, and was glad to see that their appetites also quickly waned. We all lapsed in companionable silence until Chadra, with a mischievous grin, addressed Auntie in a stream of Arabic. The radio was turned up and the women began to dance.

It began as a slow, sinuous traditional dance without movement of the feet but with much expressive gestures of hands, heads and torsos. I was greatly touched by it and a wonderful happy feeling was with me. Outside, the slow 'hush-hush' of sea on the shingle blended with the breeze moaning in the pines. Inside, the flickering warm light shone on the innocently sensuous movements of the two women, the littered table with the remains of good simple food, Le Gros in his white djellaba, a heroic Roman figure, beat time to the music and Comrade sat with a soft smile on his lean dark face in the corner. The wail and thump of the traditional music was terribly nostalgic and sad there and stirred my emotions. I loved my companions who had given us uncomplicated honest friendship with such generosity.

"I never believed we would experience something like this," Barbie whispered to me, her eyes glistening. The music changed and the dancers speeded up, spinning about, with wild clapping from everybody before sinking down with averted faces, suddenly shy. We thumped the table with appreciation.

Le Gros leaned over with serious confidentiality: *"Le dans Algerienne traditional."* I nodded earnestly, *"Tres bien,"* I said. He slapped me on the shoulder, breaking into a grin and pointing at Barbie and me: *"Les Twist?"* The others clapped and laughed. *"Les Twist!"* they demanded.

Chadra began fiddling with her radio to find a European station and Auntie brought coffee while Comrade opened another bottle of wine. Le Gros wandered outside and returned with more beer, a litre of which cascaded down his throat and the evening became disorganised. Barbie and I rather clumsily demonstrated the twist which was roundly applauded. Every so often *les Twist* was mentioned after that and Le Gros tried to demonstrate it with Auntie to the Arab music from Algiers. The sight of that huge robed figure ponderously shuffling with the slim, tiny Auntie had us all rolling around shrieking in hysterics. Comrade decided that he and Chadra could jitterbug and as he danced he tried to reproduce a Glen Miller sound.

"What a turn-up!" Barbie wailed, eyes streaming. She went to fetch more wine from our hut and Le Gros had to try and demonstrate how Spaniards drink it, poured directly from the bottle on high. Comrade, his nostalgia awakened, gave an imitation of a German beer-drinking song and for a fleeting moment I thought of that other extraordinary evening crossing the Equator in the *Klostertor*.

But music for more of *le Twist* was now a challenge to revolutionary Algerian ingenuity. Comrade assembled several torches to test their batteries in the radio to see if he could get more power from it. Le Gros disappeared into the dark and we heard him banging about among the parked trucks and bulldozer with loud curses. He returned with a roll of fencing wire to serve as an aerial. *"Une grande antenna!"* he announced proudly and proceeded to lay a cat's cradle around the hut. Whether it was the batteries or the tangle of heavy-gauge wire, he eventually succeeded, and over a roar of static we received Radio Monte Carlo. "Now you twist!" yelled Comrade triumphantly and Barbie and I did so through four pop songs until they let us sit down again, running with sweat.

It was now Le Gros' turn and he seized Auntie and, copying our movements, did his version, limbs threshing and great body swaying. The inevitable happened, of course. His flapping robe caught the 'grand antenna' which knocked over the lantern which went out. Torches were switched on to enable the party to continue and Le Gros was now indomitable. He had to tie a torch to a roof beam to act like an electric light. Like an agile polar bear he was up on the table, his great sandalled feet shuffling the plates to one side. But one foot went into the salad bowl and slipped on squashed tomatoes. With a horrible cry he fell onto the table, and the whole thing gave way with a groan of wooden joints. To a background of hissing Rolling Stones, the plastic plates clattered over the floor and the huge iron cous-cous pot landed like an eastern gong. Le Gros was bellowing with rage. The pain in my stomach muscles was like fire as I rolled in my chair and Comrade had slipped to the floor doubled up with laughter. "I've wet myself!" Barbie moaned, tears streaming.

But, Chadra and Auntie were not amused. Like two witches they abused the felled giant, laughing now amidst his wreckage. That made Auntie pick up a broom with which she began beating him over the head and shoulders until he got up and lumbered into the night, howling with laughter.

We tried to help clear up, but Comrade urged us out, putting a half-empty bottle of wine into my hands. "That was gut, ja?" he said, grinning. "Bouchera not like this ever before, before you came..." He shook with a spasm of laughter and turned back to placate the women.

We walked back amongst the pines where shafts of moonlight filtered through. Barbie put a hand on my arm and we stopped to listen. There was the distant sound of splashing and a voice raised in song. In the dark waters of the bay there was a flash of white foam.

"He's swimming," I said, awe in my voice. "What a man..." Barbie said, her voice ready to giggle again.

The next day, Le Gros ordered his people around with irritated bellows in the distance and we kept away, swimming in the sea and lazing. But in the evening he and Comrade came over to drink coffee in a routine that was to become established. They told us stories of the war and their experiences of life and asked many questions about England, what we thought about the future of Europe or Africa and what we hoped to experience on our long journey southward. Comrade, a sincere Communist with a gentle faith in the goodness of man, was particularly interested in the progress of socialism in Britain and I realised my inadequacy in trying to give him honest answers. There was general agreement in our talking about the inherent cynicism and professional dishonesty of politicians of any nationality and ideology. Kings and tribal chiefs in olden days had no need to resort to the propaganda and lies of to-day since they had no newspapers or radios. Artists were the only true antidote to politicians in modern Civilisation they believed. I had never before spent time with people like them: Arab socialists who had matured through long civil war and revolution.

Our gradually increasing intimacy was a warm pleasure. Barbie was with Chadra and Auntie for many hours during the days while I read or went for walks on the beach thinking. It was the first time on the journey that we had time for idleness and reflection and it had a powerful effect on me. Until then, all mental energy had been devoted to preparation and then the daily practicalities of the beginnings of the odyssey with all its strangeness and small tensions.

Barbie and I had to get used to each other's company and adjust to travelling intimately together in our lonely bubble.

One day Le Gros rode to where we were reading under the pines on his *petrolette* motor scooter and told us a story of the Algerian war. The reminiscence began because he had to explain why he had ridden a few hundred yards instead of walking. His leg often pained him badly and, put into English, the story of his leg went something like this:

"At the time of our War of Independence I was a soldier, of course. It was a hard war because we had not enough food and ammunition and we had to hide in the mountains while *les Francais* lived in their cantonments and slept with soft girls. In all of *La Guerre* I only had three girls and it was no good; just quick like a school-boy.

"I do not care about politics. I fought because it was right to fight and the French should not have come back after the German War as if nothing had happened, especially because of Vichy, and it was the British and Americans who liberated Algeria. We had no respect for France. We, the Arabs, had changed much and if the French had returned with understanding ready to help make a new country, then the Colons would still be here on their fine estates." He laughed. "To-day we would all be capitalists and not socialists!

"But now it is over and the Colons have gone to France and many people are unhappy. And in my body there are big wounds that pain me when I become fatigued, or the weather is changing." He got up and demonstrated, pulling his billowing djellaba this way and that. On one shoulder there was a dark twisted hole and a scar running down his back. His left knee-cap had been smashed and around it were great nobs and slashes of scar tissue. He slapped his knee, "It is here that I pain to-day, the weather will change, you will see.

"I was a sergeant in our nationalist army and my company was based in the mountains around Algiers from where we made raids on the suburbs and ambushed the roads. Many of the French were young and inexperienced and we had an easy time. So perhaps we became careless. Anyway, one afternoon we were in ambush on the road from Blida to l'Arba and we shot up a convoy beautifully. It was finished and the trucks were burning. I led my men back to the hills by our usual route until we came to cross a small motor road five kilometres away and I thought we were safe. But there must have been an experienced French officer around and a jeep was waiting for us. Its machine-gun sprayed us and although I jumped in a ditch, four of my men were killed. I heard the motor move and was thankful, but as they drove away they threw hand-grenades behind to keep us down. One exploded not two metres from me.

"Then began my nightmares. I was lying on my stomach. One piece of the grenade ran up my back and remained in the shoulder. The other penetrated my knee from the back and remained beside the knee-cap. The pain was so bad that I do not remember after the first shock, except that I was screaming like a baby. Of my patrol of twelve men there was only one unharmed and he went to an Arab village for help after dark. We were hidden there for some days. My wounds were cleaned and sewn with ordinary needle and cotton, but there was no antiseptics or drugs so I was frightened of gangrene. I lay thinking that my leg would have to be cut off.

"But we had an organisation to look after our wounded and on the third night people came. My shoulder had terrible pain with the metal inside, but my knee was poisoned. If someone came near my bed I began to scream in case he should shake the bed. So perhaps you can imagine how it was to go inside the back of a donkey cart with bags of grain on top? I had to smoke *kif* and drink much brandy, but even then I think I was mad. A cloth was tied into my mouth. Before dawn we came to a farm near Algiers and stopped there two days before we could go through the 'pipe'. A raid was organised on an electricity station and six of us were taken on a motor truck to the west of the city. Cloth was tied in my mouth again. There we were dropped down a sewer manhole and carried on stretchers into the Arab section of town where there was a secret hospital. All I remember of those days was dreaming that sewer germs were in my leg. But our Arab doctors saved my leg, as you can see. Only, it is painful sometimes, like to-day."

The three of us sat quietly for some time gazing over the wide bay and the clean rocks of the cliffs topped with pine trees.

"Of course," he went on. "I don't complain about those matters. That was *La Geurre* and I was a professional soldier since 1943. What was *merde* was the French secret police and their torturing for information. They used to catch young men and girls, take off their clothes and force them to sit with greased Coca-Cola bottles stuck up their private places and their legs pulled out straight." Barbie made a disgusted sound of shock. "It's true. And many, many other bad things. Soldiers never suffer that way in war. It is civilian people who suffer worst." He got up and went away on his petrolette.

71

The weather did change that night and a cold damp wind blew from the north sending big waves crashing onto our beach.

*　　*

The next day there was no growling of engines and we slept late. When I went down to wash in the sea clad only in my towel, I found cars parked and crowds of people picnicking. Young men and women were playing volleyball, radios were wailing Arab music, children ran and called. It was a holiday week-end, maybe a celebration of the end of the emergency. We hibernated by our hut, intimidated by the onslaught, suddenly realising how we had changed in the days since we had arrived at Bouchera and how the company of our friends had made city holiday makers appear strident and artificial. We discussed this feeling that we had begun to move in a world where simplicity was real and complexity of civilisation was alien.

I thought that it was probably a normal resentment of the strangers moving in to what we had come to think of as our private patch. But it was not that simple and, later in the journey, this feeling was reinforced. It began at Bouchera in the company of Le Gros and his comrades. Frequently we were forced to deal with complex urban society, of course, but we became less happy in those conditions. Until then I had always enjoyed the bustle and vital excitement of city life as well as the countryside and the wilderness. Naturally, there were things to be enjoyed in the cities, but we became increasingly uneasy and generally unhappy within them. My attitudes and tastes were changing and simplifying: the first major introspectively observed effect of our journeying.

In the afternoon, a subdued and polite Le Gros arrived at our hut together with a suave gentleman in a black sport shirt, immaculate dark slacks and shiny leather sandals over white socks. Inevitably, he wore sunglasses and his hair was neatly cropped. We were inspected gravely while Le Gros made warning signs behind his back. The scrutiny complete, the gentleman introduced himself in good English: "I am the sub-Prefect of this District. I understand from the *Chef du Travail* here that you are camping?"

I nodded and smiled and put on a posh voice. "A lovely place, very beautiful and tranquil. The *Chef* has been extremely helpful."

"Good," he said. "I'm glad you enjoy our country. However, you will have to move on. The Algiers branch of the Socialist Youth Movement is bringing war orphans here to-morrow."

"Naturally we will move," I said, feeling sudden, quite unreasonable resentment.

He made a little bow. "*Monsieur... Madame.*" He moved off and Le Gros made a comical grimace with his mouth behind his back.

"And you too," Barbie said quietly and wandered down to the beach to sit by herself, staring at the sea.

To get away from the camp and explore a little, I decided to drive across the bay to where I could see what looked like a café and some houses beneath the opposite headland. The gravel was hard-packed at first then became heavy going and I slipped Landie into low range. We began to churn along with the engine constantly on the point of stalling. Adrenalin ran through me and I was reminded of getting stuck in the mud near Al Hoceima and feared the humiliation of having to go back and ask for help. We eventually crawled out at the other end, engine and gear-box smelling of hot oil, and drove back on the main road while I thought about the deceptiveness of terrain surfaces. I was still learning.

In fact we did not have to move on immediately because our hut was not needed for at least another week and we could have stayed there to the bitter end, which is what Le Gros dearly wished us to do. He made uncomplimentary remarks about superiors in general and Algerian senior officials who aped the ways of *Les Francais*, even muttering about capitalists.

But the arrival of young schoolteacher-organisers changed the atmosphere. They came in a battered Citroën 2CV and a camion filled with tents and tatty army-surplus sleeping bags. After unloading the truck they explored and were delighted to find us there. They thought they were very 'hip' and were keen on what they had heard about the 'swinging' life of London and Paris and so they were also anxious that we stayed on, for quite different reasons. Our hut was designated as the expedition store-room so that we would not have to move out of it, and they brought their perishable foods and packed them at one side. We were persuaded to remain but after two days we had enough.

This new group consisted of four young men, sharp and lively, full of nervous energy, and two chirpy girls who were to look after the youngest children. The girls and one of the men spoke good English and so we were interrogated for hours about London, the lifestyle of young people, the Beatles and mini-skirts. They were insatiable and although Barbie in particular found this stimulating at first, it palled. When I told Le Gros that we had to go, he was mournful and protested but it was clear that he understood. He watched how we had been mobbed with a cynical little grin.

On the last night we decided to invite all of them along to dinner to respond to the many kindnesses and went into Tenes to stock up. I asked if our old friends would eat peppery food which they said they would enjoy, so we prepared a vast curry and rice. The party was not a success. The young people from Algiers and the 'old guard' were like oil and water and had little to say to each other in their barely disguised mutual contempt. Our old friends dressed conservatively, Chadra wearing her veil, and were subdued while the young group outdid themselves in blue jeans and bright shirts, laughing and showing off. The two groups separated themselves at the table we had rigged up and the 'old guard' talked amongst themselves quietly all evening, barely touching the wine we had provided. From time to time they smiled at us in reassurance and Chadra took Barbie away for a long low-voiced conversation.

The youth group brought across a battery-powered record-player and a stack of scratchy French pop music and proceeded to get high on the wine. They twisted away, outdoing each other, and Barbie had no chance to sit down. One of the young men told me with passion that he would come with us to Egypt, because he desperately wanted to feel the excitement of the new Arab-socialist society being created there by Nasser. It was all innocent high spirits and one-upmanship, of course, but I sank into silence. Chadra and Auntie took our plates and cooking pots away to wash up and Le Gros and Comrade led me outside for an emotional farewell. I had to endure a great bear-hug from Le Gros. I watched them return to their huts. Later, in the sudden quiet, Barbie and I finished the wine before falling into our campbeds.

*   *

On the way to Algiers we stopped briefly near Cherchell where there were Roman ruins and washed Landie in a clear stream which ran across the road. It was a fine coast with many rocky coves, vegetable gardens in the hollows and forested mountains coming down to the sea. I imagined it was something like the French Riviera or Costa

Brava had been many years ago, before they became fashionable and built over for tourism.

We stopped in Algiers to change money and collect mail at the Credit Lyonnaise. Reading letters from home, it was almost a surprise to realise that there was another world that still continued to march in parallel time. Algiers was noisy, full of bustle, thousands of people, a big city. We wandered about a little, looking into shop windows and watching the confident people in smart clothes. We felt like Martians.

After a simple lunch in a restaurant which cost as much as two days' good food at Bouchera, we headed out towards the Kabyle Mountains. We had intended to spend some days in Algiers, do some sightseeing, wallow in a hot bath, maybe take in the local entertainment that the young group had insisted we should, but we drove on after a minimum of almost casual discussion.

PART TWO : ALGIERS - PORT SAID

CHAPTER SIX : *ROMAN EMPIRE*

From the heat of the coast at Algiers we began climbing in to the Kabyle Mountains. Vineyards and fruit orchards gave way to rugged hills with pine forests. There were also areas where the hillsides were covered by bushes with small tough leaves to withstand the dry heat of summer. I saw some with flowers similar to the proteas of the Cape of Good Hope and was sure that they belonged to the same botanical family.

As we slowly climbed higher and admired the view from our winding road, I realised that the north-west corner of Africa had many similar characteristics to the south-west corner. I checked the latitudes later and noted that both Algiers and Cape Town lie close to 35º north and south respectively. It was as if Africa was a great mirror lying across the Equator and the geography at its extremities was the same. I thought of the Sahara and Kalahari deserts at the same distance from the Equator, and the vast rainforests in the centre, dividing the continent. The idea of the African geographical mirror occupied my mind for the first time that day, and its possible effects on the higher mammals and mankind. It has tempered much of my thinking since then.

Before and after the town of Tizi-Ouzou we passed through road blocks, but they were courteous and friendly. At the village of Azazga, where we stopped to buy fruit, there was a man sitting on a bench outside a house and he was wearing canary yellow and pale blue baggy clothes with a turban on his head. His face was pink, like a northern European, his eyes were a bright clear blue and he sported a magnificent grey moustache. I thought that he must be a Frenchman from Alsace that had gone 'native' and then remembered that I had read that in the Kabyle there were pure descendants of the Vandals who had settled the region in the 5th century. The Eastern Roman

Empire had chased them away from Carthage and the coast in 533 AD, and the Arabs had conquered Algeria by 670 AD. Despite this, remnants of the Vandals had kept their racial integrity in the Kabyle down to the present. I was delighted to see evidence of this. We both noticed other people in colourful clothing, old men with thick beards of fine hair and a solid stockiness of bodies and squareness of heads that was quite different to Arabs. It seemed remarkable to find such clear racial differences in a small pocket of a country that had been inhabited by other civilised peoples for so long. I wondered how long they could keep themselves separate and follow a distinctive old culture in the modern socialist society that had been born in Algeria.

Shortly after Azazga, the road deteriorated to a narrow bumpy track scarcely wide enough for one vehicle and it wound around the rugged mountains. We came to another road block at Yakouren and a young army officer who spoke good English was glad to chat. I asked him why there were still so many checks on the road and he said that there were rebel groups in the Kabyle who resented the latest socialist regime. He wanted to know where we were going to sleep since it was getting late and I said we were heading for Bougie.

In fact, we camped in the overgrown yard of an abandoned farmstead high in the mountains, surrounded by dripping pine trees when thick mist formed at sunset. The cold and damp was a welcome change and it was cosy to snuggle under blankets. From the time we stopped until after breakfast the next morning no vehicle passed on that lonely road. Mist hung in the mountains as we set off next morning and we passed a number of old stone forts. I supposed that the road we were following was an ancient pass, in use for many hundreds of years. I wondered whether the forts were defensive ones built by descendants of Vandals or offensive outposts of Arabs. I supposed they had been used by both sides from time to time. There were also concrete bunkers from the recent war.

*   *

Of course, I knew that North Africa had been an important and populous part of the Roman Empire ever since they had conquered the colonies of Phoenicia which became the independent trading empire of Carthage. The island that had led me astray into bogging down poor Landie had been Roman, and Tenes was another important port. After leaving Bouchera we had seen our first Roman

77

ruins at Cherchell. Now we were entering country which increasingly exhibited its Roman relics. Bougie was an ancient port serving the fertile Soummam valley and we passed it by to drive along the beautiful Corniche Kabyle with cliffs, sandy coves and pockets of bright cultivation amongst the mountains sweeping to the sea.

We stopped at a fishing village to buy fresh bread and mouth-watering goat cheese from the highlands, and picnicked. It was an exhilarating drive on the road carved from the cliffs with a fresh vista of mountain and sea around each sharp bend and it reminded me once again of the Cape of Good Hope. Again, I supposed that the French Riviera had been like that a hundred years or more ago before wealthy people travelled there as tourists from the cold north.

We left the sea to drive up the deep Kebir valley to Constantine. The country was becoming increasingly dry and gaunt, yellow rock showing through the sparse vegetation. We stopped to photograph a primitive village beside an almost-dry river winding through a gorge with high cliffs. The people had built simple huts and could have been nomads who brought their sheep and goats down to the river during the summer.

The city of Constantine lay on two levels in rugged country and we got quite lost in it, driving around seeking any kind of direction. Like Orleansville and Oran it had a shabby and exhausted feel to it from the aftermath of war, with many shops boarded up and paint flaking from buildings, and I was glad to get directions for the main route N20 to Tunis. We left the mountains of Algeria behind there.

In the late afternoon, I was driving automatically with inner thoughts rotating in my mind when Barbie caught my attention. "Hey, Den, look! Nomads' tents."

I braked and we got out. On the side of a bare earth hillside there was a collection of dark brown tents. They were pitched in the classical sprawling Sahara style, stretched over poles, that I first saw illustrated in my primary school geography books. There they were, exactly as I had imagined them but had never expected to see in reality. And camels were nearby. A small black figure was a herdboy. The tents were made of great pieces of cloth, clearly defined in varying shades of brown. We grinned at each other.

"The Sahara and veiled Tuareg desert sheiks," I said. Barbie grinned and nodded, "Great isn't it?" Further on we saw another group of tents with horses and camels and people. We camped in an open field that night, like the nomads.

78

We had problems the next day. Firstly, we had lost count of the days and we should have stopped in Constantine to change money. It was a Saturday and the banks were closed. At Bouchera I had topped up Landie's main fuel tank from the reserve cans filled so cheaply at Ceuta and we were running low. At the last Algerian town, Souk-Ahras, where I discovered the banks were shut, I did some careful calculations. Our fuel consumption, driving over the Kabyle, had been higher than average and the bad condition of the Algerian roads which had not been maintained since the French colonial days did not help. Though we had left the mountains, the road still twisted and turned a lot and followed the gradients of the rolling hills exactly so that I had to change gear frequently and jog along behind donkey carts or slow-moving old trucks. The map indicated that Tunisian roads were better but I did not know for certain. In theory we should reach Beja, the first main Tunisian town with a certainty of banks and petrol. But, the deciding factor was that it was the week-end. If we were to be stuck until Monday, I would prefer to be out of Algeria, certainly away from Souk-Ahras which was a dreary town with nothing to recommend it, and if we camped somewhere by the roadside we would have to eat from our reserve tins without any fresh food.

"Let's take a chance," Barbie said, and that was it.

The border crossing was difficult and I began to feel that it was a doomed day. Entering Algeria at the time of the coup and the dreadful panicking crowds, we had been passed through without a customs check. I had been relieved then, but now we reaped the cost. Landie's carnet had not been stamped and we had not completed any currency declarations. Thank God our visas and passport stamps were in order. But the customs officials were not helpful. I explained exactly what had happened to three different men with varying numbers of stripes on their shoulders but each, after listening gravely with expressionless faces, merely shrugged and went off to deal with other travellers, leaving me standing at the counter.

I spoke to the immigration officer, who smiled and seemed sympathetic, but he could afford to do that. It was not his problem. Eventually, I headed for the exit to explain to Barbie what was happening and this precipitated an unexpected reaction. There was a shout and the armed door-guard grabbed me by the arm and roughly pushed me back to the counter.

"Why you go?" one of the customs men who spoke the best English shouted in my face. "Why you try to run away? Hey? What you do?" The guard shook my arm.

I felt cold and sick in my stomach. I smiled weakly. "I want to tell my friend that there is a problem. She is waiting in the Landrover."

"What problem? You make problem. You break laws of currency; you have no legal carnet for Landrover. Is your problem!" His spittle was on my face and I smelt his garlic breath. I was now quite frightened. He rattled off in Arabic at another policeman who went out to reappear with an apprehensive Barbie. The whole room was now occupied with us and I felt all those eyes of officials and travellers on us. I sensed the other travellers' relief that it was some strange Europeans that were in trouble and not them. "It's all about not going through customs in that riot when we came in..." I began explaining quietly to Barbie, but I was given another shake.

"You don't talk!" my tormentor yelled and we both stood like statues. Time was suspended and my mind ran through all kinds of horrific possibilities: thrown into cells until Monday, Landie confiscated, huge fines to pay. It was the end of it all. How could we get help from the British consulate in Algiers? I had no cash at all anyway.

The closing of a door at the side echoed in the bare hall and I became aware of a man in a civilian suit talking to the angry customs officer who delivered a spate of Arabic, waving his hands and jabbing his fingers in my direction. Calm eyes ran themselves over the two of us. I heard Barbie snuffling and guessed that she was ready to dissolve into feminine tears. There was a moment of silence and then we were taken into an office to stand before the civilian-suited man's desk.

"Why did you try to run away from the officials?" he asked after a suitably intimidating pause. The voice was calm and authoritative and I was greatly relieved that he spoke good English. I explained, as quietly and humbly as I could, why I had tried to leave the hall and why we did not have correct documents. He took our passports and studied them carefully, page by page, right through to the back cover. He looked at the dates on the entry stamps again and checked with a calender, before staring at us, tapping the passports on the desk.

I suddenly realised that he believed every word of my story and his problem was how to get rid of us without having to apologise or lose face. How could he acknowledge the possibility that the customs officials at our entry point had been in such disarray with political chaos looming that they had abandoned their duties?

"Monsieur," I began, improvising with simple truth as I spoke, which is much easier than trying to concoct a story. "The officers at the post where we entered were very kind to us. There was a terrible problem with so many people in a panic and the army was there with tanks and machine-guns. Because we were foreigners, your officials were very kind and we were grateful to them. I thought that Algeria was very civilised in its conduct of long-distance travellers." I tried a little smile.

His face remained stern but he was a man of superior intelligence and I saw his lips twitch as he fought a smile of amusement. I knew we had won. He dropped his eyes to the documents and sighed. "*Bon*," he said quietly. "We shall continue to be civilised.... But you will have to submit to a thorough check by the officers." Apologetically, he shrugged. It was the necessary punishment.

"I understand, Monsieur", I said.

At the counter, the carnet was stamped with a flourish and we were herded out by the armed guard and the uniformed customs officer. He ordered us to empty Landie completely which we did grimly, in silence. It was very hot, well over 100ºF, and a wind blew dust around, adding to my depression. When every piece of our gear was out, the only time between Cartagena and Mombasa, the officer turned away and went back into the hall without a word. A half hour later, Barbie was still using four-letter words and strange Aussie phrases.

*   *

The entry into Tunisia was brisk and efficient. I made sure that every possible document had stamps and initials on it.

The road surface improved dramatically and the first farms and small villages we passed through were brighter and clearly more prosperous. We stopped beside the road where a raised concrete irrigation canal ran away into the distance through citrus trees and we went over to bathe our faces and I splashed water over my head and shoulders. What relief!

The immediate difference between Algeria, which had suffered their recent war, and Tunisia, which had experienced steady prosperity for twenty years, was marked. Although Algeria had been a much wealthier country before independence and was to be so again later because of petroleum that was found, the war had clearly set the country back ten years and degraded the people. This set me to wondering about a theme that was to recur repeatedly; in the lives of ordinary people was the price of poverty and drastic degeneration of everyday standards acceptable in order to have the privilege of so-called political 'freedom'? 'Freedom' was a word that was being trumpeted brazenly a great deal in Africa at the time, and it was partly to see the results of it that I was undertaking my journey.

Who were the people benefiting from this magical 'freedom'? It was obviously not the ordinary masses.

Were one set of rulers better than another, only because they were of the same nationality as many of the people? Often, the people were not homogenous and a national leader, or government elite, did not speak the same language or have the same religion as all the people. I did not know any answers then and these problems were only beginning. The endless road blocks, checking of documents, heavy policing and deployment of the military around the battered towns of Algeria were new to Africa then and it was the first time I had come across the need to control ordinary people in that way. In South Africa, where the *apartheid* laws were being rigorously applied at that time, there was more apparent 'freedom' than in Algeria.

I had been living and working in Nigeria both before and after independence not four years before, and politicians and press had thundered on about the tremendous benefits the masses would acquire. In Nigeria, the immediate results had been a noticeable decline of bureaucratic efficiency combined with an increase in corruption. I saw that Algeria was not fully comparable because when there is civil war everything and everybody suffers. But they had already had one coup with the military used against the general populace and if I was an ordinary Algerian, I would be feeling insecure and unhappy about life.

Who were really benefiting from independence? Was it not the politicians who suddenly had power, and the civil servants and army officers who suddenly got promotion in great jumps up the scale without having to bother about qualifications or having to gain experience and wait for opportunity? Political independence from a colonial authority was good for the educated and vocal elite who had everything to gain, like school sixth-formers ousting the teaching staff, but I was beginning to see that it did not necessarily have

82

advantages for people out of work, deeply insecure and being pushed around like sheep.

What had happened after the Romans left? I guessed that local chieftains and city factions had warred and the people were miserable.

Meantime, my relief at escaping from serious trouble at the Algerian border post and pleasure at evidence of prosperous stability in Tunisia was disturbed by increasing worry about petrol. Every time we approached a village I slowed and gazed at the needle in the gauge, hovering over the 'empty' mark. If we were going to run out, I wanted it to happen in a village and not miles from any source of help. I drove steadily, making sure that I did not accelerate or brake suddenly. Each kilometre post beside the road was a countdown to succour at Beja, the first town of importance. Our relief at reaching it was profound.

Beja was the pleasantest town since Oujda in Morocco. The streets were clean and most buildings freshly painted. In the suburbs houses had blue trimmings around doors and windows which gave an impression of cool freshness. With the petrol needle firmly stuck at 'empty', I penetrated hesitatingly to the town centre where we seemed to be drawn by some good-luck charm to a small hotel in a side-street just off the main square. There seemed no reason not to park in the street outside and I went into the dark lobby. The concierge was reading a newspaper and greeted me with a smile. I was put at ease immediately: he had a room with bath, it was cheap (about the equivalent of £1.50 for the night for two of us), in the morning the manager would change money and he would advance me enough for dinner in exchange for my passport. All was in order! Suddenly, the doom of the leaving of Algeria flew away. I went back to Barbie and my grinning face told the story.

We toiled up to the third floor where a tall-ceilinged, simple room with three beds led to French windows and a balcony with wrought-iron balustrade. The bathroom contained a huge cast-iron bath with big brass taps.

"Look at this bath," Barbie called. "I'm going straight into it. Do you realise we haven't washed all over in fresh water since that cungy campsite of yours near Cartagena?"

That was weeks ago. "You're right," I said. "Towns have some advantages, after all."

"Nice towns like this. Isn't it a nice town?" Her voice sounded hollow and strange in the big empty rooms.

While Barbie bathed and washed our clothes, I stood on the balcony. As the rays of the sun became golden and slanted across the houses directly opposite, the air cooled. From the square came the echoes of traffic and below there were children laughing and calling to one another. A French door opposite opened and three girls came out onto their balcony. I waved at them which caused them to dissolve into giggles and go back into their room. I was sorry about that and retired into ours to lie on a bed and wait for the seal to finish plunging about in our giant bath.

In the evening, feeling quite strangely clean with skin dry and smooth we ate a pleasant dinner in a nearby restaurant with a litre of rough pink Tunisian wine and wandered in the square with other townspeople taking the cool air. Couples walked arm-in-arm with children scampering about and some had older relatives pottering along behind. Down another side street I heard music and we unconsciously followed it until we turned a corner and found a theatre. There were posters by the box office advertising a folklore concert and the sounds of live music and singing came loudly from behind ill-fitting doors. I pushed at one and it swung open so we crept inside.

It was an open air theatre or cinema packed with a rapt audience sitting on crowded rows of metal chairs and standing around the edges. On the small stage above us a Berber orchestra was playing a fast compulsive rhythm on a variety of drums, tambourines and cymbals backed by the keening wail of traditional wind instruments. The music had an extraordinarily strong emotional effect on me, and I almost gasped with pleasure.

The drummers and a chorus of men and women at either end of the stage were singing, their voices pitched high to match the wooden flutes in their various sizes. Before the orchestra, a chorus line was dancing wildly to the rapid rhythm. The girls wore scanty bright green and red costumes, picked out in gold, their heads were covered with filmy scarves and they held others in their hands which were flung about as they danced. The atmosphere was electric, every eye and ear strained to pick up every nuance of sight and sound. I found myself breathing with open mouth, almost panting. It was an incredibly powerful impression of passion and excitement. Incongruously, my mind flashed to snapshots of memory of a Zulu war-dance in Natal and Ibo singers and dancers in Nigeria when I had experienced similar raw emotional power from a traditional performance. These Berbers of North Africa would join the others in my memories. No contrived modern music and dance could compete with the raw power of performances of musical folklore of Africa.

Of course, we had caught the tail-end of the concert otherwise we could not have got through the door without paying, and after ten minutes it was over. The crowd pouring out after us was made up mostly of young men and older couples. There were no young women or girls and I assumed that the Berber dancing would be unsuitable for unmarried Arab girls to watch. Barbie received a scattered barrage of laughing taunts and suggestive-sounding remarks in Arabic so we hurried back to the main square and our hotel.

"That's what I can't stand about Arab men," she said furiously. "They're so bloody rude to women. It's bad enough in Italy or Spain where if you're with another man they only look. That was really awful."

"I suppose they were all sexually excited by the singing and dancing. I found it fantastic, didn't you?"

"Sure, but I hated those boys yelling at me, calling things I didn't understand but can guess at. It spoiled the evening for me. They didn't care whether I was with you or not..."

I understood what Barbie felt, but as I went to sleep I was filled with the wild vigour of the dancing we had watched and the gut-wrenching, keening sound of the music.

In the morning, the hotel manager changed a traveller's cheque for me, we bought petrol and by noon we were checked into a similar cheap and simple hotel in the great city of Tunis, sixty miles from Beja. We walked about in the vicinity of the hotel and picked up some brochures from a tourist office. Tunis was impressive and there was quite a lot of new construction going on. In the afternoon, we drove out to Carthage along the arrow straight causeway over flat swampy land to the sea. It was Sunday and there were crowds of locals in the cafes or strolling about in the seashore suburbs. Fine villas hid behind walls with palms and pines in their gardens.

"Maybe we should have stopped in one of the guest houses along here," Barbie suggested. "But I suppose they are expensive."

I was disappointed by Carthage because the ruins and ancient sites were badly signposted and seemed to be treated with little respect. I supposed that I had expected a sort of special park or open-air museum, but the ruins of the ancient Roman city stood about without any demarcation, merging incongruously with the modern luxury villas and terraces of shops and cafes. There were no guides or information that we could find. We walked amidst fluted columns and crumbling walls with litter on the uneven stony grounds and it had no atmosphere.

"Well, I don't know," I said. "There's no way to tell which is which. I wonder where the early Phoenician city was. I know that the Romans razed it, but I would like to know where the site was."

"Maybe we could arrange a guided tour, but there doesn't seem to be anything like that." Barbie said.

"I saw a *syndicat d'initiative* office but it was closed."

It was hot, not quite as bad as in the interior and we were now acclimatised, but airless behind the barriers of ornamental trees and buildings so we sought a café for Coca-Colas. The locals were mostly dressed in European clothes and none of the women wore veils. I noticed a couple of cars with French registrations. The waiter was cheerful and easy-going and we could have been on the French Riviera and I felt cheated somehow.

On the way back I saw a battered little sign pointing off the road to the Roman port and followed it to a place where we could park. There was a circular depression covered with coarse dry grass like straw and some lumps of masonry lying about. Again there was no information and I regretted the lack of a proper guide book.

"Silted up a long time ago," I remarked. "And quite a long way from the sea. But its amazing to think that one of the most powerful ancient maritime nations based its fleet here and Hannibal sailed from here to try and conquer Rome. After the Romans beat Carthage they used it as a trading base for hundreds of years."

"I suppose if they had more foreign tourists they would make something of it," Barbie said.

We stayed in Tunis another couple of days. I had Landie serviced at the Rover and Triumph car agents and we collected Libyan visas at the consulate.

The consul wanted to meet me for some reason and I was ushered into a large room with tall windows opening to receive a breeze from the Mediterranean. He was an urbane man and spoke excellent pedantic English. He told me that he had studied at the University of London in the early 1950s and had worked for the British thereafter during the United Nations mandate of his country before independence. He was interested in our 'great trek' across Africa in a friendly way and I think he just wished to chat in English as a diversion. We drank a small cup of excellent coffee and smoked his fine Egyptian cigarettes. I did not think he had many British passports coming to his desk. Anyway, his curiosity about us ensured that we got the visas in a couple of hours instead of days.

In the morning and at lunch time we bought magnificent filled sandwiches from the perambulating hawkers. They went up and down the streets with their trolleys set up with bundles of unleavened bread and small metal trays stocked with a variety of pickled and fresh salads, olives, cheeses, fish and dried sausages. The hawker would slit the bread down the centre, then fill the pouch with whatever you selected from his array, sousing it with olive oil when it was filled.

We walked through the huge central covered souk with massive dressed-stone entrance guarded by carved lions. Like all markets and bazaars, the interior was an exciting throng. Hundreds of stalls in a maze of alleys offered everything from beaten ornamental brass, textiles and clothes, leatherware, utilitarian domestic hardware, vegetables and fruits, meat and dry groceries. "We could stock up here for the next six months," Barbie said. "Just look at all the different kinds of lentils and beans and dried fruits." Bowls overflowed and sacks spilled dribbles in caves of plenty. An oil shop had six or seven different grades of olive oil and forty-five gallon drums of sunflower and cotton seed oil. The richness of the Mediterranean world was there.

We bought some souvenirs. I chose a finely worked camel leather cushion and a brass ashtray. Then, in the textile section, we both bought cloths designed as body wraps. Mine were a convenient length and width to go around the waist, like an East African *kikoyi*, but Barbie's were wider to go from above the breasts to below the knee.

"Good," I said. "Now I don't have to use a towel as a loin cloth, I've got the proper thing." We were pleased with ourselves.

In the evenings we ate at a simple restaurant near our hotel called The Little Hut which had good French food at reasonable prices. The omelettes were especially good with a variety of fillings. Students came in to read books over cups of coffee or talk as they sipped beer or wine.

Tunis was a good city for us, sophisticated and free of tensions. The efficiency of the garage, who kept Landie for a day, and the friendliness of the Libyan consul allowed me to relax. Barbie attracted interest because she did not have long skirts, but she did not complain of insulting behaviour.

At Bouchera I had developed a minor but annoyingly irritating urogenital infection and in Tunis I sought a doctor. The concierge directed me to a 'European' doctor who turned out to be an elderly Italian who lived and had his empty consulting room in an old apartment block reached up gloomy stairs. He spoke very little English and was unsympathetic. He scribbled a prescription for me which a chemist later said he could not supply because the drug was obsolete and virtually unknown. I bought some vitamin C to supplement the multivitamin tablets we took daily and decided to trust to luck. My problem was not debilitating.

*   *

From Tunis we headed for Monastir where there were the beginnings of a new tourist industry. Hotels were under construction around a pleasant sheltered bay with rocky outcrops relieving the gently shelving beach. A replica of an old castle was nearing completion, its bare golden colour of freshly masoned stone contrasting strangely with its ancient shape. I supposed it would weather and mature as the years passed, but it looked quite false and tawdry in its new rawness. Baby date palms had been planted in rows but there was no other vegetation.

We drove on to the site of ancient Thapsus at the end of a point of land, Ras Dimasse, which probed eastward. The land was flat and stony with low scrubby bushes and coarse grass cropped by goats. The road was a dirt track and I drove on until I could go no further where our way was blocked by a low wall of worn and jumbled stone. The sun was setting behind us and the colours were golden tinged, the sea a rich purple. Facing that sea and backed by the rough wall we made our camp on that flat promontory, feeling naked without the cover of any trees. A boy came by with some goats and questioned us in a strange schoolboy French. He hung around until his goats had moved some distance away and he had to leave us with a grin and shouted remarks. I looked more carefully at the stones on the wall and saw that some had remnants of carvings and two or three were round portions of fluted columns.

"We're camping in the ruins of ancient Roman Thapsus, I think," I called to Barbie.

She had been wandering about and came back with some flakes of carved stone. "You must be right," she said. "It's a good place, I feel free." She faced the sea not more than a hundred yards

88

away. I wonder what part of the Roman town this was, where we are now?"

I did feel excitement there, even though there were no monuments. The ancients were closer than they ever could be at Carthage. We cooked over our Primus stoves, sheltered from the evening breeze in the lee of the ancient stones, and speculated about the people who lived there, in that very spot, two thousand years ago. It was a warm feeling there, a friendly feeling and the huge sky and empty scene was peaceful and at ease. We slept well and nothing disturbed us.

In the morning we returned through a string of rural villages to Monastir, passing streets of old houses being levelled and rebuilt to house hordes of tourists for the 1970s and the booming future. Women and children were swimming, the women chastely covered with petticoats or nightgown-like garments and the children dressed in torn underwear. We joined them in the warm sea and I thought of the masses of umbrellas and suntan-oiled bodies in smart gear that would push these locals away in years to come.

Heading south later that day the sun blazed onto a rocky landscape that gently undulated in a series of low hills. Mirages fluttered on the ribbon of tarmac. Passing through a scattered settlement with an avenue of tall eucalyptus trees we came across our first roadblock in Tunisia. Automatically, Barbie began unlocking the safe beneath her seat to get out our passports, but they were traffic policemen and I had been travelling too fast. They warned me to go slowly through towns and sent us on with a salute and, *"Bon voyage!"*. Not much of a town, I thought to myself, driving on sleepily in the intense heat of noon along the ruler straight road. Not far from there, however, I kept noticing a blurred lump ahead which seemed to hover in the mirage above the road where it touched the sky. As we rose and fell, it came and went, until with closer approach it solidified.

It was a vast ruin, a great amphitheatre built of weathered stone blocks, climbing several arcaded levels into the sky. Around its base there was a scattering of small square houses and hovels. Bemused by this extraordinary sight in the midst of a yellow plain, I disengaged the gear and allowed Landie to coast to a stop and switched off the engine. We sat, awed, staring up at the massive ramparts of the ancient building deposited there by long-gone civilisation. Hot wind whistled and swept up little twists of dust, the engine ticked as it cooled.

"What is it?" Barbie asked, wonderingly.

We got out and walked through the grand entrance. Inside there was an elliptical arena several hundred feet long and layers of seats rose up around the edges to the centuries-battered arcaded heights. Our feet scrunched loudly on the gravel and my ears sang in the sheltered silence. I heard trumpets echoing and the roar of a crowd. Horses' hooves pounded and the wheels of chariots racketed. A provincial tribune's voice of declamation was raised in indistinct rhetoric. We walked about. A crow and pigeons flew across the gaping space.

"Romans gathered here maybe eighteen centuries ago," I said quietly. "And it still stands alone in nowhere...."

Outside again I went for my camera and I photographed the ancient pile with a smiling boy and his donkey before it. We found a battered and dusty signboard that named the place. It was the Roman coliseum at El Djem. I had not read of it nor heard about it, but I found it most strangely powerful. The ruins of Carthage, famous to any schoolboy in the Western world and beyond, had been a grave disappointment in their setting of modern suburbia. El Djem in its majestic isolation provided the mystery and majesty I had been seeking.

The seaside city of Sfax was surrounded by olive groves, citrus and date orchards, small vineyards and irrigated fields of wheat, maize and rice. The town was deserted because we entered it at noon when all good people were indoors out of the baking heat. The banks and shops were closed and there seemed no reason not to drive onwards. Three hours later we were in another seaside town, Gabes, driving along a handsome esplanade lined with a terrace of cream and white-washed French colonial style buildings relieved by date palms. The country we were passing through was flat and featureless and we had no desire to put up in a hotel in a dull provincial city. We kept going, heading for Djerba Island.

As the sun lowered and the landscape became golden we left the main road and drove along straight roads in bad repair, past salt flats and pockets of cultivation, through the small town of Zarzis with robed men sitting in a café to take their evening ease. We stopped off the road on the mainland where a causeway led to Djerba.

It was low-lying there, the calm water lapping gently onto the crusty brown surface of the shore, sparkled by crystals of salt. Not a person or vehicle travelled the road the whole evening while we cooked a simple meal and watched the sky change to purple and black over our heads. In the morning I shaved with sea water and cut myself and without any shade the temperature was in the 90s F by eight o'clock. The humidity drifting off the sea made us feel sticky and dirty. But we had been looking forward to Djerba, Homer's 'Land of the Lotus Eaters', and set off across the causeway in good spirits.

CHAPTER SEVEN : *LOTUS EATERS*

Djerba Island was completely flat and sandy with vast groves of palms and some cultivation around a few simple villages. It was somewhat square in shape, about fifteen miles a side. We followed the bumpy tarred road down the centre, following the signs to the only town, Houmt Souk, which was a sprawl of neat flat-roofed buildings all glaringly whitewashed.

There was a square in the centre with shops and a couple of pavement cafes, shaded by leafy trees trained into umbrella shapes. Off the square was a delightful old covered market, the Souk. Because the town was on the island, at the end of the road, it was quiet without through traffic and had a charmingly relaxed and friendly atmosphere. The older people dressed in traditional Arab clothes and, except for the hours after noon when the heat was immense, there were always men sitting in the cafes drinking little cups of coffee, talking or playing some complicated game of chequers. There were not many young people around; I supposed Houmt Souk was not lively and enterprising enough for them and they would tend to migrate to Tunis or the busier towns to the north.

We called at a tourist *Information*, but the people there were not very helpful. Tourism was obviously in its infancy and not much was available; the posters on the wall advertised Tunis and Hammamet and the beach at Monastir. Not that we were looking for 'tourism', but we wanted to spend a few days camping beside a fine beach if it were possible. The young woman directed us to the police station where we could get a permit.

The idea of a permit to camp seemed alien to me and I felt irritated. We had been camping by the side of the road without a thought until then, apart from the idyll of Bouchera. So I went into the police station anxiously because I did want us to have another fine break there and the ambience of the town had attracted me.

"What the hell do we need a permit for?" I muttered.

92

In the station, the two uniformed policemen were not very interested in our arrival, hot and dirty, clad in rumpled clothes. They spoke in rapid French and I gathered that there were a few designated camping places and we had to specify which one we wanted before a permit could be issued. I started by explaining that we wished to know what was suitable, that we were travellers and did not know Djerba, but that was met by the same story, repeated slowly in simpler language for the stupid foreigners. I asked for a map or some information, but this was countered with shrugs.

"What the hell?" I said angrily to Barbie. "We're going in circles."

"Ask them to give us a permit for anywhere, for their choice," she suggested, and we tried that with the same response.

I became angry then and gave up trying to speak in French, giving a harangue about the hopelessness of authority that prescribed designated campsites for tourists but refused to say where they were or do anything to help. My raised voice brought a superior out of an office and a discussion followed between them which eventually produced a permit, sulkily written out. Our designated campsite was Plage de Sidi Mahres, wherever that was.

"I suppose they've got regulations about foreign tourists but don't know what to do with them," Barbie said. "There don't seem to be any around. I wonder how many campers come here."

"I know," I sighed. "We have to be unusual, otherwise others would have forced them to be better organised. I just hate it when people in authority say you have to do something then make it impossible for you to do it. It's pure Kafka... Let's do some shopping."

"How about a meal?"

"Why not?"

We bought fresh food for the next couple of days as the market stalls were closing for midday, then wandered beyond the main square where there were a couple of shops with tourist goods. One had a sign in French, Arabic and English. 'Du Pays Ulysse - Arts of Djerba Island', it proclaimed.

"See," Barbie said. "There must be some foreign tourists coming here. There must be a hotel somewhere."

I pointed to the sign: "It's time that I got out Homer's Odyssey and had a reading every evening. We've reached his countries."

Around a corner there was a small restaurant with tables on the pavement under big umbrellas and we sat gratefully. We were the only customers and quickly received the full attention of a small middle-aged French woman with dyed red hair and thickly rouged face. She suggested fried fish and salads and iced white wine. It was excellent and, without asking, a second carafe of wine arrived so we were soon laughing and joking about life in general and the incompetent infant tourism industry of Djerba. By the time we finished, it was bakingly hot and the food and wine made us feel like exhausted pythons. Strolling back to the square, the sky sat heavily on our heads, the shops were shuttered and our sandals scratched loudly on the gravel in the silence.

We drove slowly along the perimeter road girdling the eastern shore of the island, searching for the idyllic campsite. Wherever we came near the sea there was no shelter and the beach was in full view of the road. But the white sand and the beauty of the limitless pale blue sea beneath the silver blaze of the sun drew us on with promises. After about eight miles there was a sign to the Hotel Ulysses and we drove down the side track which ended at a raw new tourist hotel, not finished properly, fenced around with a high chainlink barrier.

"That's the tourism that they want," I said. "All foreigners nicely tucked away in their hotel away from the locals. I wonder how it will all develop in the future."

Onwards, and I was beginning to feel desperation despite the good feeling from the wine. And then suddenly it was there. A gap appeared in a line of rough scrub and palms between the road and the sea, and on impulse I drove through it onto a flat area that had been used as a quarry for road making material. Rocks stood out in the shallow sea sheltering a small intimate sandy bay and there were scattered palms beside the beach. The line of scrub isolated us from the road. "This is it!", we cried and ran about. Later, looking at a map in a brochure Barbie had picked up, I saw that we had chosen a place marked Plage de la Seguia and hoped that no policeman would come checking if we were in the right place. There were no signs, so we could plead ignorance. In fact, we were never troubled at all.

We pitched the tent under a scrawny palm and used it as a support for guys which would also serve as washing lines. We had a lot of washing to do. It was also an opportunity to partly empty the Landie and do some tidying, the first time since Bouchera. After the 'inspection' at the Algerian border there had been chaos in the back. I found my small leather suitcase of books and stationery and was able to write proper letters home and be prepared for reading Homer's *Odyssey*.

Having unpacked and tidied, we went for a drive back to town to fill our fresh water jerrycans, the first time since leaving England. Usually, we had managed well enough by topping up an ordinary two-gallon plastic can that lived with the cooking gear, ready to hand. We debated whether our scattered goods were safe and decided that they were. Provided we were away from towns, we never worried about ordinary camping gear and never had anything stolen. On the way back, I took another track through the scrub to our site and found a salt pan. With Landie empty and feeling light, I raced around it, skidding in tight corners. "Wheee!" I called and laughed. Djerba felt so good; we were free!

A donkey came to join us as we cooked and stayed nearby all the days we were there. Later, over a glass of wine, I started our ritual of a reading from the *Odyssey* most evenings. Naturally, I chose the description of the Island of the Lotus-eaters, recognised by scholars as being Djerba:

> "Nine days I drifted on the teeming sea
> before dangerous high winds. Upon the tenth
> we came to the coastline of the Lotos Eaters,
> who live upon that flower. We landed there
> to take on water. All ships' companies
> mustered alongside for the mid-day meal.
>
> .... Lotos Eaters,
> who showed no will to do us harm, only
> offering the sweet Lotos to our friends -
> but those who ate this honeyed plant, the Lotos,
> never cared to report, nor to return:"

"We haven't had any lotus to eat that I know," I said when we were going to bed. "But it feels like it. I'm ready not to return."

The stars were clearly shining, massed against the absolute black of the moonless night. There were no artificial lights anywhere, but there was a sense of ease and comfort about us, nothing to fear or cause anxiety. Small waves swished slowly on our private beach and I heard the donkey shift her feet nearby as I drifted away.

*   *

The rising sun woke us and I lay on my comfortable campbed feeling a warm, light breeze tickling the hairs of my arms. The green canvas of our tent-awning shifted slightly as the air caught it. The donkey praised the sun with a sudden, "hee-haw!"

I climbed out and used the loin-cloth bought in the Tunis souk for the first time, wandering the few yards to the beach to squat, staring along the golden path of reflected sun, drawing at a cigarette, feeling that already-warm breeze on my nakedness. We had complete solitude, nowhere in sight was there any being on two legs. There can be few more ecstatic simple pleasures of nature than to be up at dawn, in a warm dry place by the sea, sharing it with no stranger.

Barbie ran by me, her body already tanned a rich colour by the days at Bouchera. She splashed into the clear shallow water of our private bay, calling to me. I dropped my loin cloth on the white sand and followed into the milk-warm sea, tasting the cleansing sharpness of sea-salts as I plunged. And that was another ecstasy of simple pleasures.

We rearranged our camp, making a little compound by lining up the petrol and water jerrycans and the boxes of spare food and cooking gear. We swept the sand and set out our folding table and chairs neatly. It felt snug and secure. Barbie set to on the washing. Our cotton sleeping sheets and towels as well as clothes were soon flapping gently on the guy ropes; another comfortable feeling of domesticity. We ate a lunch of bread and salads and snoozed for a while, lazily, not caring about time.

After another quick dip in the milk-warm sea we walked to a nearby fishing village, not far away. There was a lighthouse on the point behind palm trees and boats drawn up on their beach, but it was too early for people to be about. A scrawny dog barked and I thought of that old cliché: 'mad dogs and Englishmen...'

When we returned, we got into Landie and drove south, further along the perimeter road until palms and vegetation were left behind and we were confronted by low-lying land covered by coarse tussocky small-leaved bushes interspersed by areas of glaring salt flats. A rough track wound away along the edge of the sea and I followed it. Mirages danced and specks became two wandering camels who allowed us to come quite close. It was all so romantic and our spirits were never higher. We stopped and pulled off our outer clothes for yet another quick plunge into that limpid sea, laughing and splashing, playing like teenagers. When we stopped to dry off, sitting on the narrow sandy shelf above the beach, there was a sailing craft passing by with lateen sail rig and the crew waving and there were faint shouts on the wind.

We looked at each other and grinned. "Do you think they watched every thing we did?" asked Barbie. "We must have looked naked from a distance."

"I'm sure we've made their day," I said. "Two foreigners behaving in an improper way." But I was not bothered, the distance across the neutral water removed any embarrassment. Nothing could trouble me on the Lotus Island. Barbie felt the same, for she waved and I thought I caught the white flash of movement in reply. Was it friendly or derisive? We were too far away to see, and a moment of unease was instantly gone. Did it matter?

Further along the track through the dusty grey ground-cover a dark shape sat above the silver of the mirage and as we came closer it resolved into a massive square stone fortress, confidently squatting at the end of what had become a tongue of sand reaching towards the dim white line of the mainland. It was maybe five miles to the road behind us and apart from the camels and little birds flitting over the low scrub nothing had moved on land. The lateen sail of the fishing boat was lost to the northwards. The great fort stood foursquare on the scrubby sand-flats, eternally guarding the entrance to the Golfe de Bou Grara that separated Djerba from the mainland like some tireless, sightless giant.

I stopped and we stared at it, wondering about ancient days of rival fleets and pirates, and who had built and manned it when its importance was great. The utter loneliness of today was suddenly eerie when confronted with its stark power and the proof of long-gone activity there. I took photographs while Barbie studied the brochure she had picked up in the tourist office.

"It's called the Bordj Castile," she said. "Built in the 13th century by the King of Aragon. That's the north-east of Spain around Barcelona, isn't it? I wonder why it was built here."

"I'm fascinated," I said slowly, still staring and imagining lonely garrisons. "I suppose Djerba must have been occupied during the Crusades. Southern Spain was still a Moorish colony."

At the centre of the western wall, there was a breach and we climbed over tumbled stones to stand inside in the echoing stillness. A flicker on some rubble showed where a lizard had dived into hiding. Apart from the breach, the ten feet thick walls had no cracks and stood solid after six or seven hundred years. I looked for signs of barrack rooms or stairways to the rampart high above, but any woodwork had long rotted to dust or been taken away. There were the remains of a well.

"All of this stone must have been brought here, by sea I suppose," I said, quite awed by it all. "Shiploads and shiploads of it. It must have taken years to build."

"It makes me think of El Cid again," Barbie said. "That movie was about those days. Think of the horses and those great sexy men, and the trumpets and drums."

Disease, loneliness and squabbling too, I thought. And harsh discipline to keep order so far from home. And some desperate battles no doubt. I climbed back over the tumbled stones and walked away to look at it from afar, because it had more nobility and power from a distance, brooding over the horizontal line of land and sea.

Driving back to camp I tried racing along some smooth salt flats and the tires sang as the speed built up. A mirage kept coming and going, lifting the hazy green line of palms with their feathery heads up into the sky like a low-lying cloud. The scattered white houses of the small village of Aghir floated within the gliding palms. I stopped to photograph it with a long lens because it was so encompassing, right across the view, caused by the billiard-table flatness of the land. Further on, Landie's tires began sinking below the crust of salt and we slowed with a jerk. I swerved away towards the tussocky grassy-scrub as Barbie looked at me with alarm, imagining another desperate digging- out and there were no little pine trees there, washed down from the mountains to make a track for our wheels.

We discovered that our friend, the donkey, had brought flies which liked the shade of our awning. Barbie reckoned they were almost as bad as the renowned Aussie fly. After dinner, we both suffered diarrhoea, and Barbie was vomiting which I was sure was the result of eating salads well treated by the 100°F heat and the flies. I buried the remains of our salad vegetables and dosed ourselves with chlorodyne.

In the middle of the night while I was having a disturbed dream I was woken by Barbie shaking me to become instantly aware that we had been hit by a storm. The canvas of the awning was flogging and the fronds of our palm tree above were thrashing. Close by, waves were breaking on the beach and I tasted salt spray on my lips.

"I thought you'd never wake up," Barbie shouted. "Are you still feeling crook? We'd better do something."

By the light of our torches we rescued some pieces of clothing and cardboard boxes and weighed everything down with the jerrycans. I moved Landie so that our camp was sheltered by her bulk, although that made it worse in a way by causing gusts which carried sand. But I needed Landie as an anchor to which to fasten additional guy ropes. For fifteen minutes or so, scattered heavy drops of rain were carried almost horizontal and made quite loud metallic pings on Landie's body. If it really poured, I thought, everything would be thoroughly soaked, despite Landie's shelter. We huddled together, smoking cigarettes, listening to the roar of wind and the crash of waves. Distant lightning lit the scene with purple flickers but I did not hear thunder. Gradually the wind died to a strong breeze and we crawled back to bed.

In the morning the flies had gone, blown far away I hoped, and the air was sparkling clear. Barbie still complained of nausea although my stomach had surmounted the assault of unfriendly microbes. We were both listless and feeling the effects of lack of sleep and food-poisoning. We plunged into our private bathing bay and were somewhat revived, splashing and floating about; revelling in the clean coolness under the silver-blaze of sun.

While I read that morning, Barbie thoroughly cleaned our cooking utensils and had another turn-out of clothes, hanging bedding on the ropes to air after the storm and washing so that we spent the morning clad only in our wrappers from the Tunis souk. By noon all was crisply dry and sorted and she dressed in a different outfit and after shampooing her hair put on some make-up.

"How about a drink at a tourist hotel?" she suggested. "Shake off this mood."

"Wanting the 'real' world are you?" I teased. "But I'm still feeling a bit low."

"Aw, come on, Den. We haven't had a civilised drink since Spain. I'll shout."

I roused myself, dressed and brushed my hair neatly and disentangled Landie from the awning. On the way, Barbie read from the brochure she had picked up. "It says here that they are going to open a Club Mediterranee here, somewhere on this coast. There'll be camel expeditions and camping out in the desert and all that."

"Doesn't fill me with excitement," I said. "I bet they'll take them around the middle of the island in circles so they think they've gone a hundred miles. I wonder if they'll take them down to our castle."

We found a second hotel nearer to us than the one we saw on the first day. It was the Hotel Aldjazira and as we entered the lobby I did not feel the pleasure I was seeking. Maybe it was the thought of the forecasted contrived world of Club Med that was threatening Djerba's simple peace. The hotel was clean and modern and characterless, all squared off and straight lines and glass. We could have been at a beach resort in South Africa, or Australia. It was the world of northern Europeans translated to a hot climate. I heard the humming of air-conditioners. I felt awkward as we went out onto the terrace beside a big swimming pool and found a table amongst a crowd of rather fat people, many with blonde hair and blue eyes. German seemed the predominant language and the golden children splashing and shouting in the pool seemed to be of a particularly alien race. It was so strange to feel ill-at-ease amongst my own kind and I thought about how we had become strangers to all except ourselves.

I had so adjusted to the Arabs we travelled amongst that they seemed quite normal although I neither understood their language nor shared their religion and culture. It was also something to do with wealth too, I realised. Living close to the land, camping roughly, shopping in markets and local stalls, dealing with strange officialdom, the total absence of other Europeans in the world in which we travelled, we were living a simple nomadic life where money beyond our immediate means had no effect. That we had still hundreds of pounds worth of traveller's cheques locked up in Landie's safe made no difference to our lifestyle. On the terrace of the package-tour hotel there was the startling wealth of middle-class Germany and Scandinavia, and the means to use it. In fact the hotel was there for the express purpose of consuming their wealth. Whiffs of expensive cigar smoke drifted by, tables were piled with bottles of imported beer. A menu fixed to a little chrome stand advertised poolside snacks at a price equivalent to two or three full days eating for us. I wondered what the local staff thought about it all. I thought that they saw these affluent foreigners as Martians to be looted.

The picture of that sailing boat with its berobed fishermen watching us fooling around on the beach returned to roost. I may have got used to living close to the land and accepted the world of Arab people, but I had not fully adjusted my own behaviour to them. We had been as guilty of offence in our own way as any package tourists.

I pondered the problem of the clash in cultures that we had talked about, especially sexual customs, and this was to be raised again as we crossed North Africa. Arab morals and standards of behaviour in public clashed thoroughly with ours. And it was not because Barbie and I both came from 'colonial' lands where recreation on beaches and outdoors in a perennially warm climate had formed our ways. Our Western Civilisation standards had been similar to the Arabs years ago, but in the 20th century, because of the two world wars, we had changed so that not only were women emancipated but we had taken our private lives into the public domain.

I thought of pictures of the crowded beaches of Blackpool in the 1930s when the millions of working class British had begun taking seaside holidays. The idea of all those strangers crowded together intimately, changing behind towels, beginning the enormous revolution in public behaviour which was reinforced by the coarsening and levelling of years of war; men living on the soil of the land, homes blown apart, city centres razed, families all over Europe existing in massed poverty and degradation. It had not been many years before the days when we were playing on the beaches of Djerba. I thought of couples necking and hugging on the grass of Hyde Park and draping themselves with rugs to cover more intimate love-making. Girls had begun bathing without bras on some beaches of the French Riviera by then, creating salacious delight in the weekly picture magazines.

How could the ancient civilisation of the Arabs with their particular emphasis on respectable women covering themselves so thoroughly in public cope with this? I thought about the sharp division of disapproval that had formed between the 'old guard', as I thought of them, at Bouchera and the bright young communists who wanted to be 'swinging' even if they were so proud of their socialist ideals. I realised, probably for the first time, that East European Communism would be more culturally and politically disruptive in African societies than the old paternalistic European colonial governments which were just then packing their handfuls of administrators off home.

When would it be realised that the liberal-socialism of European culture and Western Civilisation was alien and dangerous to Africa? It was so fashionable and politically correct in the second half of our 20th century. But that was a European intellectual view. And European intellectuals with their left-wing liberalism knew best

101

for all the teeming millions of the planet, didn't they? This arrogance increasingly angered me as we moved on through Africa. I was not surprised that Nasser was building a huge movement with a new and modern Arab-Moslem nationalism.

The French colonials had not 'liberated' those young Algerian schoolteachers at Bouchera and interfered with their culture. We had seen how they were sadly distanced from an older generation who had actually fought physically and dangerously for their 'freedom' from colonial 'tyranny'. It was Communist-inspired social and economic dogma that had divided Algerian-Arab society.

Only a hundred British colonial officers governed the Sudan, two and a half million square kilometres, before WWII. Colonial systems had not reached down to how you behaved on a beach under a hot sun. No wonder European girls were harassed and sometimes raped in North Africa. And what would happen when all those 'swinging' Europeans came to the Club Med on Djerba? I was sure there would have to be high fences.

These almost naked, perfectly respectable family groups of Germans and Swedes on the hotel terrace about us made it obvious to me and made me think about it all, because Barbie and I had dressed up smartly to go and have our 'civilised' drink, as if we were local Arabs.

"Hey, Den!" Barbie snapped her fingers at me. "What will you drink? Have anything, I said it's my shout."

"Sorry, Barbie," I said, pulling myself together. "I'll have an iced Hamburg schnapps and a cold lager to chase it down."

"Hey, are you sure they have that?" She looked up at the hovering waiter, but he was nodding while he made a note on his pad. "O.K., I'll have a double Bacardi and Coke with lots of ice. And do you have English Benson and Hedges cigarettes?"

We were jolly for a while there with the drinks, and had another round. But when the lunch gong sounded and the overweight middle-aged people and the young couples, the women in bikinis, took their golden children in to the neat tables with gay cloths and laid-out cutlery, we fell silent.

Barbie sighed: "I suppose we don't really belong do we?"

Back at our campsite, the flies had returned and we did not have any fresh bread or cheese to eat. The breeze had dropped and the sun hammered down. I stripped off my clean clothes, pulled my loin cloth around me and lay down. Muzzy from the drinks and my empty stomach queasy, I soon fell asleep with my hands over my face to stop the flies crawling into my mouth and eyes.

Sounds of people laughing and calling woke me. We had been invaded by a group of locals, young men and teenagers, some were splashing about in our bay, others were playing informal volley-ball further along. Some distance beyond the volley-ball players there was a blue Hillman Minx with 'GB' and 'CD' plates and a smart little family tent. What was clearly an Englishman sat in a folding chair smoking a pipe watching two small children playing in the shallows wearing bright plastic blow-up rings tied to their necks. I shook my head to clear it and wandered down to the sea to splash water on my face. What had happened?

It was Sunday, of course, which was celebrated in the European fashion in Tunisia, and in our disassociation from the real world, we had forgotten. We often got caught out by the days of the week. I looked for Barbie and saw her perched on a low dune with a dark figure next to her. She was in her brief bikini and he was in shorts that he had used for swimming. I grinned. Barbie had found an admirer which was not surprising considering the total non-availability of decent Arab girls for casual encounters. What did surprise me was that the whole volley-ball gang was not clustered around the honeypot. I wandered over and the young man jerked away when he saw me, looking very embarrassed. I stifled a smile, pretending that I had not noticed that his hand had been gently caressing Barbie's smooth brown thigh.

"Hi, Den," she said. "This is Abdul. I'm sure he fancies me a lot, but we don't have much language. I think he wants to carry me off on a camel and be very naughty, but he's smaller than me. Shall I carry him do you think?"

I smiled. "I'm sure his lust would overcome his pride." I saw that he was not out of his teens and was looking even more disconcerted as we talked, shifting away and calling out to his friends. "I'll leave you to discuss your tactics and talk to the new arrivals."

"Yea, they came about an hour ago. Pommies, I think."

The pipe smoker greeted me and introduced me to his Scottish wife who crawled out of the tent. They were a pleasant couple, he in his early forties and she mid-thirties I supposed. I sat with them and had a cup of tea while we chatted amiably. He was on the staff of the British mission to Libya in Tripoli, military I guessed, and they were due for a spot of local leave so had come to Djerba for some Lotus-eating. Tripoli was often short of good quality fresh vegetables and meat, the local wine was poor and the imported very expensive. So Djerba was just the place for a week's rest. I asked why we did not see more people like themselves enjoying informal camping holidays; there had to be fair-sized expatriate communities in Tunis and Tripoli and we had loved the scenery and people all the way from Morocco. The only problems had been the unfortunate incidents at the Algerian borders and we had avoided the cities as much as possible.

"Well, you know what most expat people tend to be like," he said. "Holidays are an opportunity to rush back home or take a ferry to the French or Italian Rivieras. We have always enjoyed camping and where is there a better spot...?" He waved his arm. "Of course, you and your lady know that, you're doing it in real earnest aren't you? Going on down south are you?"

Barbie's admirer departed when I got back to our camp, smiling shyly at me, and the volley-ball gang trooped away as the sun was lowering. Their chatter and laughter faded amongst the palms behind us and we were left with the swishing of the sea and the occasional sound of children from the English camp. The donkey brayed her pleasure at the quiet after being disturbed by the rowdy humans all afternoon. We walked down the beach together towards the distant fishing village where the boats were pulled up on the beach and watched the sun descend behind a frieze of palms. Djerba had so much magic.

We made a curry with the last of our goat-meat bought in Houmt Souk, because it was going off somewhat, and added the rest of our onions to be stewed thoroughly.

"The last time we made a curry was the night before we left Bouchera, using up all the bits and pieces," Barbie said. "We've got to replenish to-morrow, shall we stay another few days? It's really so nice here."

"I'm easy. Let's decide to-morrow. Maybe your lover will return?"

"Oy! Come on. He was only a boy really, and very sweet."

"When I was fifteen I used to drool over pin-up girls," I teased. "I'm sure he knew very well what he wanted from you."

"Yeah, I can guess what you were up to while you drooled." She stared at the pot bubbling on the Primus. "It's very sad, this business of no friendships between girls and boys in Arab countries. Although it really pisses me off, I can understand why they are so

104

offensively interested in European girls. That friend of mine that was raped on the beach at Tangier I told you about: well, to the Arab boys she had to be available, wandering around without any males and dressed in European fashion. That Abdul was sweet, but I could tell he was very turned on.... And if you and the Pommie family weren't here I could have been in trouble with that volley-ball lot."

Next morning, after our 'wake-up' dip in the sea, this time wearing swimsuits because of our neighbours, we drove the ten miles into Houmt Souk. I took some of my best photographs of the whole of the trip that morning, wandering about the Souk and the few shops and cafes. We spent time in the 'Arts of Djerba' shop and bought a couple of souvenirs. Barbie wanted a typical Arab music record like the Berber music we had heard at the open air concert in Beja, but they only had a few Egyptian 'pop' music seven-singles. We admired the beaten and etched brass wares and the woven camel blankets. I bought one of them. Sweat was running from me after walking around and photographing and we had a cold Fanta in one of the cafes before food shopping.

Fresh food had not been a problem so far. There was always meat of some kind and tomatoes and onions. Meat kept for two days if it was sealed in a plastic container, and even three days at a pinch if we curried it. But we had learned our lesson with greens, and only bought to eat immediately after thorough washing or cooking. Eggs were a great stand-by, and bread. In Morocco and Algeria the cheeses had been superb. Our stock of instant coffee and powdered milk from England was standing up well and lasted all the way to Egypt. We took a multi-vitamin pill every morning with our coffee. Bearing in mind what the English fellow from Tripoli had told me, we stocked up with wine and cigarettes in Houmt Souk. Cooking paraffin from England, topped up in Tenes, was also lasting well and we started the Primus stoves going with petrol.

Back at our camp we changed and floated about in the healing balm of the sea while the neighbours' children splashed about, sensibly clad in cotton vests and sun-hats.

"Maybe we should move on," Barbie said. "These Poms are all right, but it's not the same, is it?" She was right, suddenly it wasn't the same.

So, we packed up the camp and loaded Landie carefully, not knowing when we would next have a sort-out. We lunched on crisp fresh baguettes, tomatoes and lettuce washed in the sea, and had a last swim. The shade temperature had been 108°F at ten o'clock that morning and climbed to 112°F by noon. It was very humid, surrounded by sea, and the combination was cruel. I was glad that we were acclimatised by then, otherwise I know that we would have been ill with it.

But the white sand, the palms, the sea and being able to bathe whenever we wanted had been a great pleasure at Djerba. That and the solitude and the ease, the tang of history and the delightful old town still hardly touched by alien tourists.

I drove them, all three wailing, to the ships,
tied them down under the rowing benches,
and called the rest: "All hands aboard;
come, clear the beach and no one taste
the Lotos, or you lose your hope of home.

HOMER, 6th century BC.

CHAPTER EIGHT : *MORE ROMAN EMPIRE*

Apart from leaving our Lotus-eating island, where we had lived a free beachcombing life for a few days, there was a more imperative feeling of change as we drove the short distance to Ben Gardane on the border. We were leaving the relatively well-populated lands of ex-French North Africa where, even in war-damaged Algeria, all the services and administration that we would normally expect were available, even if efficiency and standards were not up to Europe. To use a word that could be misinterpreted, we had been travelling through 'civilised' countries.

We were entering Libya and starting the portion of our journey which traversed the shores of Africa where the Sahara desert and the Mediterranean lapped at each other directly. Now, there were no intervening mountains to catch and distribute rainfall which created vegetation and the resource for a reasonable spread of civilised men. It was not that I did not think of Libya as being civilised. Of course it was. The same sophisticated Arab race inhabited Libya as did Tunisia and Algeria. Greeks and Romans had set up colonies and it had been a valuable part of the Roman Empire for centuries. A Libyan had been Emperor of Rome, lived in a palace in York and probably died there. In recent time, Italy had distributed modern technology and established systems of communication and commerce that were integrated with Europe just as the French had in their colonies.

However, when entering Libya I had the feeling that we had left 'civilisation' behind, by which I meant that we had left behind the networks of towns and organised society. 'Civilisation' in Libya could only be found in isolated pockets separated by hundreds of miles of desert. I did not think that we had left behind culture or achievement, but I did think that we were entering land that was a very great and awful wilderness. On the other side of the Sahara to the south in what we had just recently begun to call, 'Black Africa', one might say that there was a lack of those material attributes of civilisation which also existed only in isolated pockets. But there was a tremendous difference.

In 'Black Africa' there were always people. In many parts they were not what some might then have called 'civilised' and they might have been illiterate and subject to poverty in materials or manufactured goods. They might not speak a written language and their concepts of law and religion might be generally different to ours. But always we could be sure that they were part of the same humanity; we all belonged to a thoughtful and helpful species whose instinct was to succour a genuine traveller come in friendship. In 'Black Africa' it was always possible to receive some kind of help and assistance.

In Libya, help and assistance were thinly spread and non-existent away from the thread of a road on which we travelled. In those days, its vast petroleum resources were only beginning to be exploited and the infrastructure had not been improved much since the end of World War II. The population was small, about 1.5M, and the government was old-fashioned and conservative. It was, of course, ripening for Colonel Ghadaffi's revolution, fuelled by the oil wealth still to be realised.

At Ben Gardane, on the Tunisian side of the border, there were a number of camels with people covered up in robes and headgear. We had already seen our first large sand dunes. There was a street of shanties shimmering in the heat of afternoon with dust and rubbish blowing in the wind. We were mobbed by people from rough stalls and shops who wanted to sell as a variety of goods, not tourist souvenirs or fresh foods but cheap household hardware and dried and tinned food. We had a little Tunisian currency left and I spent it on some tins, cigarettes and bits and pieces.

We had not seen anything like it before. That small commercial slum-town in nowhere emphasised my thoughts, as if saying to me that hereafter there was nothing and we could buy nothing. Indeed, we had no negotiable currency of any kind at that point and my map told me that there was no town on the Libyan side. I asked a boy who had persistently followed us around why the shacky shops were there and he said it was because many Libyans came to work in Tunisia and it was their last chance to buy many things cheaply.

The Libyan customs and immigration hall seemed to be anxious to strengthen the feelings that I had been exploring. Again there was a small mob of people clamouring at the counters and tired and exasperated officers trying to deal with them; helping some, returning the abuse of others, ignoring those who must have annoyed them. I stood in the entrance with a twinge of despair. Were we going to have the same treatment as we had in Algeria? There was a difference, though, this mob was not trying to flee a revolution, these people were clamouring to return home after working in neighbouring Tunisia. There were not that many jobs then in Libya before the petroleum boom.

At the counter I found no forms to fill in and the immigrants were waving tattered cardboard identity cards of some kind. Those that were having attention and being passed through appeared to be those whose cards were in good order and who were able to satisfy the officers' brief interrogation. Thereafter, their suitcases and bundles were opened and probed. It was then that I realised that the mob, mostly men, were returning Libyan workers, and the routine for them was different.

From a corner, a languid Arab in uniform drifted to me. He was smoking a pipe and wore a smart moustache. His uniform had a distinct Italian look to it; darker khaki than the Frenchified Algerians and Tunisians, narrow peak to his cap, insignia on his shoulders that looked like some entwined vine. "English?" he asked me, and I nodded gratefully.

"You fill in those forms, please," He said pointing to a window sill where I could see a small pile of brown paper. When I picked them up, faded and tattered round the edges, I was surprised to see that they were in Italian and Arabic and it took me some time to interpret them. When I had obtained the gist, I returned to the officer who was back in the corner of the hall, puffing contentedly on his briar pipe.

"Excuse me please,"I said. "These forms are for 'Exit to Sudan'. Sudan? Am I right? Maybe there are other forms? And they are in Italian, is that O.K.?"

He smiled gently, his eyes crinkling. "Don't worry so much, Mister Englishman. Write on the top 'Entry from Tunisia' and fill in the details of name, passport, visa, vehicle. Those are the same whether you come or go to here or there, isn't it so?" I nodded. "We don't have many foreigners coming here." he explained.

I filled in the forms, bubbling with laughter inside at this sensible lesson in practical bureaucracy, re-writing whatever I thought needed it. The senior officer wandered over when I went over to the counter to check me through himself. He looked at the visas carefully then wielded a rubber stamp. When I showed him the vehicle carnet, he searched around for the customs department rubber stamp and wielded that too. He gave me an ironical salute and another gentle smile, waving me away to the door.

There was no town on the Libyan side, and we drove away along a thin strip of tarred road with sand and gravel spreading to the horizon. Later we came to where the road went around a wide salt flat with rocky mounds and I drove off the road and we camped. A couple of buses drove past as the sun was setting, carrying the returning workers I supposed, but otherwise we were alone in the Sahara wilderness.

*   *

Nearing Tripoli the road was bounded by an avenue of tall old eucalyptus trees, planted by the Italians. We passed villages and there was cultivation of maize, vegetables and what looked like sugar-cane. Suddenly there was a line of stopped vehicles and we edged past slowly to find that there had been an accident between a truck and two camels. The dead beasts were sprawled on the road with twisted necks and I saw smears of rich red blood matting their brown coats. Bundles of farm produce were scattered about. The driver of the truck was backed against his cab waving his arms about at a group of locals in robes who were abusing him.

Tripoli was a shabby city sprawled on flat land along the sea. There were few cars and we found our way easily to the commercial centre by following our noses until the buildings became more substantial and 'European-looking' with balconies or columns on their facades. I caught sight of Barclays Bank and turned down a side street to park.

Inside there was a large hall with numerous clerks sitting at tables piled with documents. We picked up mail and I went through the interminable routine of changing travellers cheques which seemed to need the attention of four or five different people for calculating and checking. But the clerks were courteous, smiling at my impatience. Back at Landie, we found that urchins had been scratching at our Union Jack stickers, trying to prize them off. This seemed a particular violation to me. It was getting very hot and a dry wind was blowing from the desert, carrying a haze of dust.

We sat in a café to read our mail and I suddenly felt depressed and miserable, far from home. I made some thoughtless, hurtful remark to Barbie and she was quickly in tears and angry with me, lashing back. We sat silently together for a while, locked in mutual misery of homesickness and foolish antagonism, unable to tell each other what was really troubling us.

"Let's get away," Barbie said eventually. "There must be some shops on the outskirts."

Streets heading eastward landed us on a deserted seafront boulevard and we spun along new, wide tarmac until we found ourselves confronted by high barbed wire fences leading away inland. Low white buildings lurked and there was a US flag waving gaily over the gates. A big sign proclaimed: *WHEELUS BASE : US AIR FORCE.*

"Ice-cream, Coca Cola, Bourbon whiskey, Lucky Strike cigarettes, air conditioning..." I murmured looking at an armed and smartly uniformed guard watching us. "Yuck!" Barbie said and I grinned.

We found a road that headed inland and took it through suburbia of bungalows and villas sitting in sandy compounds decorated by straggly oleanders and cassia trees. Casuarina pines, palms and eucalyptus provided an air of luxury in the baking dry heat. A row of market stalls by the road served the little patch of professional, official and expatriate homes and we stopped to buy fresh produce. There were onions and tomatoes and a sort of frizzy cabbage. I tried to explain eggs to an elderly Arab who squatted in his djellaba on a small stool and we had a comical interlude as I demonstrated the shape with my hands and drew pictures in the dust. He watched my antics gravely, shrugging his shoulders at each new effort. Finally, Barbie made a cock-crowing noise and flapped her arms and we all laughed with relief.

A basket of a dozen or so was produced from within the covered stall by a boy and we bought them all. "*Ovos, ovos,*" the stall-owner repeated, chuckling to himself. I had not thought of using the Italian word.

After leaving the city behind, I stopped off the road and we had a snooze.

A hundred miles along a ragged potholed road we came to Homs, a quiet dusty town shaded by eucalyptus and palm trees. It stood on one side of a shallow bay and on the other were the ruins of the important Roman city of Leptis Magna. A rusted sign showed the way down a track to the ruins and we followed it, going on to the end until it stopped near a clump of isolated scrub which made a good place to camp the night. From there we looked out over the sea, quite close, and the pale columns and jumble of the excavated ruins.

We sat on our folding chairs and had a cup of coffee as the air cooled from oven heat to gentle balm and the sun declined behind us. We would explore the ruins in the morning. As sunset approached it was enough to sit quietly, talking, relaxing after a rushed two days of contrasts, officialdom and blazing heat.

Passing through Homs we had noticed a hotel and on a whim decided we would go there for dinner. It was a good choice. The hotel itself was a simple concrete building with verandah and balcony above without the decoration and style of its equivalent in Tunisia or Algeria. The owner welcomed us for he did not receive many visitors, especially from Europe. He was a middle-aged Italian who spoke explosive English and was happy, laughing and joking with us.

We drank cold beers while a meal was rustled up and discussed our changing situation after the temporary euphoria of Djerba. I knew that the entering of Libya had become a kind of watershed for us both, and I was aware of my feelings of insecurity now that we were facing the reality of wilderness travel. No doubt, Barbie sensed this and had her own worries. But neither of us were confident enough of ourselves or of each other to be able to lay these matters out. We bickered during the next weeks in occasional bursts of bad humour, taking our deeper inner concerns out on each other in trivial irritations. I cannot remember any particular problem we may have wrangled about although I clearly remember the excitements, the landscapes, the physical trials and the pleasure of relief from them, and the people we met.

When the meal came it was good and food instantly changed our mood. We were in senseless bad humour when we were hungry and tired, which we often were, and that is natural. We were too inexperienced then to understand and make allowances. After all, we had neither of us undertaken anything like the loneliness of the extraordinary expedition we were engaged on and had no previous knowledge of those particular stresses with only our own tentative relationship to sustain us. It was in Libya where we found ourselves far away from some holiday adventure which we were both perfectly able to manage. The true immensity of the task we had set ourselves suddenly began sinking in and we were probably too young and proud to admit fears and apprehension to each other.

In those days there were no other bands and groups of trans-continental travellers to meet and exchange experiences with, wind-down and find relief in sharing information and worries. There were no *Rough Guides* and *Shoestring* books full of information for overlanding travellers to consult and to explain where to meet up with others of our kind. There *were* no other 'travellers' of our kind! We were alone, and that had its severe emotional toll.

Many years later, I watched young people with plenty of company and mutual support, get into prolonged and painful estrangements during weeks of rough travel in Africa. I have met young people, both men and women, resourceful and holding down responsible jobs in Germany, England or America, who had been abandoned by travelling companions, even close friends of long standing, in places like Niamey or Nairobi with little money and with documents rapidly running out of validity, steeped in misery and despair. I often thought at those later times how well Barbie and I coped with much greater stresses in our day.

Reading the biographies of the great pioneering explorers in Africa, such as Burton, Speke or Grant, one can be astonished at how badly these experienced and intelligent men treated each other in the loneliness of wilderness away from their own people. Until one has had an experience approximating something like theirs, one cannot comprehend subjectively how such people could behave in that way whilst engaged in such uplifting and noble enterprise. The nonpareil African explorer, David Livingstone, never got on with his companions and had a notorious history of petty dispute and unfair behaviour. His last great journeys were solitary. Stanley, Baker, Thompson, Selous, Mungo Park and a host of others travelled without friends by choice, hiring local help when they needed it.

Sitting on the upstairs terrace of the square concrete hotel in Homs, we had tender meat of unknown origin with a rich Italian sauce made with onions, tomato paste, garlic and olive oil which the owner served us personally. There was a mound of rice and an onion and tomato salad, followed by ice-cream. We were introduced to the local wine: a sharp, acidic rose served very cold.

Our new friend told us that he was going through hard times since independence because most Europeans had left. There was much talk about petroleum and some fields were being exploited but they were to the east in the hinterland of Cyrenaica and did not influence his trade. His family had been settled in the region by the Mussolini regime in the 1930s when there had been bustle and development, but it was all over now. He had been a prisoner-of-war in British hands and had been treated well. He was hanging on in the hope that tourists might eventually come to see the famous ruins of Leptis, but he was fearful of political rumblings which suggested radical changes.

"The young people are not satisfied with King Idris. They say he is a puppet of the Americans and will give away the oil of the country." He shrugged. "The young are looking to Nasser who kicked out the British and French. What can we do? Nothing, except pray for peace..."

He brought another bottle of the sharp rose wine and drank a glass or two with us. There were one or two vineyards still producing wine in the jebels of Cyrenaica where Italians had introduced their know-how, but he did not know how long it would go on. The quality was not good now, certainly too poor to export and with reduced local demand he thought production would cease. Those Arabs that drank wine were wealthy sophisticates and would not drink the local products and now that his compatriots had mostly left he guessed that many agricultural products would fade away.

"Our Italian government made cooperatives to encourage development of farming and brought poor peasants from southern Italy and Sicily who understood this hard country, giving them land to farm which was desert before. The work was hard but our people knew that and we made something. Until 1940 Libya was exporting food to Italy. Yes, it's true." He shrugged and looked away. "Now, we are going backwards and the young Arabs only want money from oil to finance socialism and what they call development of the people. But they don't know what that is. It is just words that politicians use. They are the people who will give away the oil wealth, exchanging it for buildings, aeroplanes, power stations and machines they don't need. Every country should support its people with food. Here we used to do that, but not any more."

We had seen what looked like big deserted warehouses every twenty miles or so beside the road, invariably surrounded by gnarled old eucalyptus trees and I asked about them.

"Yes," he said. "They were the cooperative agricultural depots from our colonial times. Not many people know that we took Tripolitania and Cyrenaica from the Turks. They think it was all because of Mussolini. But in 1912 we liberated this place from the Turks who were very corrupt and kept all the people down."

After the ice-cream, coffee came, and glasses of strong rough Italian brandy and we were merry when we returned to our campsite

114

in the moonlight behind the columns of temples to Roman gods. I was sure that there were friendly ghosts seeing us safely to bed.

A hot, dry wind was blowing from the interior as we drank coffee for breakfast and packed up our camp. The temperature was over 100°F before eight o'clock; a pattern that was normal throughout our traverse of the Sahara. After all, it was the peak of summer.

Leptis Magna was the home of Septimus Severus, the only African Emperor of Rome. His natural language was Punic, the language of the Carthaginians. He became Emperor in 190 AD and is recorded as dying in England, at York, where he built a palace. He repaired Hadrian's Wall thus preserving the *Pax Romana* in Britain. He also patronised Leptis Magna and elevated it to a standard above that of other provincial ports and market towns. Behind Leptis in those far-off days there was savannah for grazing and sufficient rainfall to promote orchards, vineyards, olive groves and fields of wheat.

There were irrigation systems and terracing for soil conservation. Over-cultivation, excessive grazing and the subsequent spread of the Sahara had converted the prosperous littoral to desert. I wondered how effective the Italian colonial efforts would have been to turn the clock back by the introduction of government-assisted Italian peasants. Whatever the success had been in the short time that had been invested before the war, it was now obviously lost. The native Arabs were nomadic herders by tradition, not natural agriculturalists. I presumed that perhaps they would be lucky with their oil and import food from somewhere else.

Wearing a straw hat but rapidly becoming wet with sweat I swarmed over the ruins of the ancient city. The excavated portion was enclosed by a fence and we picked up a brochure at the gate. The extent of the city was several times that which we could see and we had been camping the night on the accumulated detritus above an inner suburb: no wonder I felt the brush of ancient ghosts.

We walked the paved streets and through the theatre, forum, temples and along the quay walls of the port. I was particularly interested in the port which was silted above sea level like that at Carthage. A small promontory protected the entrance to the harbour and a *pharos* had stood on its end. The harbour itself had been excavated by archaeologists and along one side the massive stone quays were backed by the regular outlines of warehouses and merchants' storehouses.

It was eerie walking the quays, trying to imagine the press of shipping, maybe tied up two and three abreast when the main harvest was being exported. In the stores, apart from grain, great amphorae of wine and olive oil would be stacked awaiting shipment, and no doubt there were bales of goats' hair and sheep's wool. Perhaps there was a local textile industry exporting cloth.

We sat on a high level in the theatre, constructed in conventional hemispherical Roman style facing the stage, and tried to cool down. It was very hot amongst the ruins and the light reflected from the pale stone and white marble burned my eyes, already smarting from sweat. With a better guide-book and cooler weather, it would have been good to have spent many hours wandering the city, quite deserted but for the two of us. I thought that in Roman days there must have been many cloth awnings in use to provide shade in the summer which would have provided a gay sight. Daily routine would have started at dawn with a siesta period of several hours followed by activity until quite late at night.

There was much statuary in the theatre, some whole figures, others broken so that heads grinned from stacks at ground level and limbs lay entwined in piles. Some of the whole pieces seemed particularly sensuous and I wondered whether that was typical of the period or of the place. I could imagine Leptis having its own decadence; it must have been wealthy with a large slave population from interior tribes. There were the strains of remnant Phoenician culture with its Biblical curses on Sodom and Gomorrah.

"Pretty sexy, some of those statues of young guys," Barbie commented. There was a sculpture of a large rampant penis. "Do you think that was its real size or supposed to be larger than life?" she asked, grinning. There was other phallic artistry about.

I felt quite dehydrated after a couple of hours of sightseeing and Barbie had retired to Landie to rest in its shade where the temperature was 118ºF. We drove into Homs to drink several cool Fantas before resuming our journey. Luckily, it was not far to Misurata where the road ran close to the sea and there we bathed and refreshed ourselves.

*   *

We travelled far in the next two days. The road was terrible, mostly untended since before the war. Poor Landie crashed into potholes that could not be avoided and the verges were ragged where the sand had blown away from the covering of tar. Occasionally we met a truck travelling between Tripoli and Benghazi and had to leave the road and find a place to return without too great a shock. I feared for our tires and was glad that they were new. I restricted our speed to less than 50 mph. and we rumbled and crashed onwards hour after weary hour. The air that circulated through the cab was like the draught from a furnace and our skin looked like a reptile's, covered with a sheen of salt dust from sweat that dried the instant it was forced from our pores.

About every 150 miles there was an outpost of civilisation where a tiny community existed to serve the few travellers. Battered, hand-operated petrol and diesel pumps stood beside concrete buildings that had survived the desert war and at these modern oases for mechanical camels we gulped warm and fizzing Fantas and Cokes.

I tried drinking the well water at one of these stops while an Arab boy watched with a grin of anticipation. It was a shock to my taste buds, a warm solution of bitter metallic salts, mostly magnesium, which I almost vomited out again. Without being asked, the boy opened another Fanta and offered it to me.

Between Misurata and Sirte we traversed land that was spread flatly into the hazed distance and it had the appearance of salt flats that might be swampy when some rain fell in winter. The wind blew strongly along that stretch and the sky became pale blue-grey with a silver glow where the terrible sun lurked. Troops of baby tornadoes stalked the landscape and fine white dust blew across the road and coated the inside of Landie. We gritted our teeth and went on, eyes smarting and heads ringing. Near Sirte, sand-dunes encroached and we saw nomads' tents again, a tattered collection drawn up in a line facing away from that devastating wind from the burning interior. If the temperature reached 120ºF close to the sea at noon, what could it have been 500 miles into the centre of the Sahara?

Sirte was an old town sheltering within windblown and sun grilled eucalyptus and palms. The eucalyptus had certainly been a modern boon to the towns of the desert. There was the ruin of a castle there and we were lucky to be able to camp in a small plantation of eucalyptus outside the town. While I prepared dinner, Barbie went off for a walk by herself and found the rocky seashore where she had a refreshing swim, but I was not feeling well and could not eat much.

*   *

117

We breakfasted on Fantas and were off early, stopping at the first opportunity by the sea for a quick dip. And then on, on, on; thumping into potholes, cooking pots and jerrycans rattling in the back, the metal body drumming; furnace air blowing through the cab, Barbie lounging back with her bare feet propped up on the dashboard to catch the wind through the ventilating ports below the windscreen.

El Agheila had been famous during the war. We stopped to photograph the battered ruin of an Italian fortification; the brave concrete walls had a particularly impotent look in the middle of nowhere with drifts of yellow-white sand building up all around in miniature dunes. There were sandblasted petrol drums and other metal detritus scattered around. We got out to stretch tense limbs and rest from the bucketing of our vehicle and the blast of the oven's breath. My ears rang.

Another of the Fanta stops that day was at the Marble Arch built by Mussolini at the boundary between Tripolitania and Cyrenaica. We had been driving along a dead-straight road with drifting white sand across it when it suddenly came into sight over a low ridge. I had heard of it because it had been a famous landmark in the war and my first astonishment at seeing this tall monumental concrete tower bestriding the road changed to recognition because there was nothing else that it could be. We stopped to photograph it, standing there in the middle of the desert, no buildings in sight, no sensible reason for its existence, many miles from the nearest settlement. What an extraordinary folly! I can admire outrageous monuments whether they are artistically pleasing or not, because I enjoy evidence of eccentric extravagance, but there was something particularly sad about Marble Arch standing there alone in the stark wilderness.

The only reason for its existence was that a straight line had been drawn on the map there, dividing two administrative entities. In past centuries there had been two distinct nations based on the fertility of the land around Tripoli and on the mountains of Cyrenaica, separated by the Gulf of Sirte and the desolation of its shore. Modern Italian administrative neatness required lines on the map and thus Marble Arch stood there, lonely and meaningless. On the eastern side there was a small huddle of shacks which we only saw after passing through the concrete arch. A battered Esso petrol sign lay on the ground beside its broken pole. A shell-blasted concrete bunker stood to one side and a concrete building that had lost part of its walls served as a kiosk where we thirstily gulped fizzy orange water. A couple of young Arabs manned the post and laughed and joked but we could not understand them. I hoped that they had reasonable recompense for living there in that awful wilderness beside the sad giant of a memorial to an imperial dream.

Later, a strange dark cloud on the horizon slowly grew as we progressed across an endless gravel plain. The sky was blindingly clear and there was no reason for the uniform monster growing out of the earth and spreading across the horizon. We speculated about it for a quarter of an hour until eventually we had to agree that it was smoke, impossible as that might seem. It was smoke. In the midst of total emptiness, a silver painted oil tank-farm stood beside the road within a high security fence. Several of the giant tanks were ablaze, orange flames licking over their edges, thick black smoke towering up several thousand feet in the still air before drifting away in a pall.

We stopped in the shadow of the cloud, thankful for the relief from the blaze of sun and sprawled on the cool sand resting. We brought out a Primus stove and made coffee; it was so strange to be sitting under the giant umbrella of the artificial black cloud. There was utter silence, we could see no people, nobody was fighting the fires. I concluded that there were no means to fight them, so they were being left to burn out. What colossal waste, and what an ominous and powerful phenomenon of man's folly in that vast desert where nature seemed to prevent natural life. I thought I understood how strange it must have been for soldiers in the war to have fought backwards and forwards across Libya, striking each other with high explosive, causing fires like the one we silently watched and killing one another against the infinity of the desert backdrop. Great fires, terribly destructive modern machines of war, growling engines and the voices of many men belong in the cities of civilisation, not in boundless deserts.

"I don't think I've ever seen anything quite so weird as this," I said, lying on my back and staring at the roiling edges of the smoke cloud a thousand feet above.

Barbie touched my arm, "Here comes something just as strange," she said pointing behind us. I rolled over and there was a brightly painted red truck fitted out with valves and shiny pipework driving slowly along beneath an electric power line that I had not noticed until then.

"A funny fire-engine," I said, beginning to laugh. "What on earth is it doing?" But it wasn't a fire engine, it was a vehicle specially designed to drive along hosing the dust from the insulators on the power line to prevent electric short-outs. It droned nearer, the hose hissing regularly as an operator aimed the jet at the ceramic insulators with practised efficiency. They took no notice of us, who must have appeared equally strange to them. They seemed oblivious to the destruction of wealth in the tank farm.

Driving off, we saw a sign proclaiming that the installation was the Esso crude-oil terminal of Marsa Brega and later we were told that the fire was sabotage by left-wing nationalists opposed to the conservative regime of King Idris and American exploitation of the oil fields.

We camped that evening on a flat plain of hard brown gravel some distance from the road. Faced with flatness to the horizon I drove about bemused until Barbie asked me what I was doing.

"I can't decide where to stop," I said seriously. "It's all the same."

"I think you're going mad," she said laughing. "Just stop anywhere. Stop here!" So I did, and we sat on our folding chairs watching the red ball of the sun come down to rest on the ruler-straight black line of the western edge of the world.

Before it became dark we suddenly realised we were not alone. A solitary man came walking up to us, clad in the inevitable flowing djellaba of his people. I could not think what he was doing there until I saw a camel and some sheep in the distance from the direction he had come. He greeted me in Arabic and we replied in our own way and then he made the gestures of smoking. Barbie gave him a cigarette and lit it for him. He was tall and thin with a lined face, and he stood there pulling deeply at the cigarette until it was down to a stub. He made a hand gesture of thanks and set off directly back to his flock. He had not said a word while he stood there and smoked the gift in our presence rather than merely accepting it and walking off. It was a perfect lesson in natural courtesy.

I wondered what his sheep were eating and where they found water to drink.

*   *

The next day we passed through Benghazi. It was a smaller version of Tripoli and had nothing to attract us except the twin-domed Italian cathedral which we photographed. By now we had found cities to be anathema and they seemed to excite our tensions and irritations. We

120

both had an unspoken desire to keep to the wilderness and get the trial of the desert journey over.

At Tokra, the site of another ancient Roman settlement, we branched off the road after stopping for Fanta and a rest. There was a working well in the centre of the village with men sitting about it under the shade of a cluster of tall eucalyptus. They were dressed in djellabas with coloured stripes and turban-like headdresses, absolute models for traditional Biblical illustrations. I took photographs of them while they watched me gravely, turning their heads away when I aimed my camera. A teenage boy squirmed with embarrassment when I took his picture, grinning at me with engaging shyness and a cute young girl smiled at me from a red-framed doorway.

Driving inland, climbing into the mountainous country of Jebel el Akhdar, it was like returning to Algeria with scrubby grey-green bushes on the rocky hillsides. Peasant settlements with cultivation appeared and there were camels and goats. On top of the plateau we passed by the town of Barce which was in ruins having been ravaged by an earthquake in recent years. Nearby, a new town, El Merj, was struggling to emerge with modern constructions on a stony hillside. I noticed more of the Italian cooperative agricultural depots further along which the hotelier at Homs had described to us. Their shabby walls were pink or ochre-washed and they were roofed with mellowed orange roman tiles. I thought they blended well with the landscape although they obviously could not suit new Arab nationalism. The ones I saw were abandoned and falling into ruin.

We took the wrong road but eventually found our way to Cyrene, the great and famous Roman city, originally founded by Greek colonists in the 7th century BC, standing on the edge of a high escarpment overlooking the Mediterranean. Not only were we visiting important places of ancient civilisation with links to our Christian heritage, but for both Barbie and I there were personal connections. Marble Arch had reminded me of listening to radio news, seeing film newsreels and the gossip and chatter of adults in my boyhood during the war. From Cyrene onwards, these places of contemporary nostalgia and emotion increased in number. I had an uncle and other relatives and family friends who had served in the British and South African armies in Egypt and Libya in 1942, and Barbie had similar connections with people who had been with the Australian forces. The difference between us was that I had been old enough to understand and remember the events and the people at that time, whereas Barbie had been a baby.

I could clearly remember listening to an uncle excitedly reminiscing with a cousin in the family circle about a rest break at Cyrene after the Battle of Halfaya Pass: how beautiful it had been up in the mountains with trees and farms about the great ruins and how they had gone down to the sea for swimming expeditions. Stopped there ourselves beside the marching lines of fluted columns surrounded by sweet smelling pine trees, in the cool of their shade, I understood how those soldiers must have experienced the contrast.

The Roman city of Cyrene spread along the very edge of the escarpment and the layout had been created in a grand design to use every advantage of the location. Terraces with temples were placed so that the people could gather or stroll in leisure time enjoying the aesthetic pleasures of a thoughtfully conceived artificial environment and the unobstructed grand views of the landscape below. The clarity of planning and architecture to make the most pleasing arrangement on a commanding site was impressive. A medieval town would have sprawled like an ants' nest with charm but no form, a modern town might have had form but no charm. I was absorbed in the thought that no branch of civilisation since those days could have come as close to the perfection of Greco-Roman Cyrene in that place.

Why have we lost that magical and inspired aesthetic sense of the classical civilisations, I thought? In replacement, what have we contributed? Nothing but hasty conceptions whose transient attractions are lost within a few years and the ever-increasing complexity of trivial technology rapidly superseded. In the modern village of Cyrene, also perched on the escarpment edge, we thirstily drank yet another warm, sickly-sweet Fanta while gazing at the Venus Pool in the grounds of a delicate little temple whose columns adorned an ancient terrace a quarter mile away. Cyrene had been laid low in a Jewish revolt in 130 AD, after more than six centuries of dominance over the prosperous plateau.

From the heights, the motor road twisted until an intermediate level was reached, guarded by a shell-pocked Italian fort which reminded me of the duality of the emotional experience I was undergoing. The black ribbon of tar snaked down to the narrow littoral plain where the vegetation became sparse again without the rain squeezed out of the atmosphere by the plateau above. A new concrete-box hotel, built in the hope of tourists, stood near the beach and on impulse I drove to it and enquired. They had plenty of free rooms, but the price was far too high for us.

I drove a couple of miles on to Apollonia, a ruined Greek port city that the Romans had taken over and enlarged. We swam off a sandy beach near the marble columns and tumbled walls of that town, more than two millennia old, and then returned up the hairpin road to Cyrene. We bought a couple of bottles of the acidic rose wine of Cyrenaica in a grocery shop and set up camp within a pine plantation littered with lumps of ancient carved stone and pieces of fluted columns. What grand building had once stood where we were camping?

I was filled with exultation there and we had a jolly time with the wine of the land and the first cool air at evening for weeks, not since the Kabyle mountains where the descendants of Vandals lived. The sharp aroma of pine trees seemed so clean and alive after the dry dead dust of the limitless Sahara. I could feel the mind of an Athenian merchant 2500 years ago, a Roman back from a long hard journey at the time of Christ, or a soul-weary South African soldier in 1942: colonials of three civilisations. Later, I whirled about 'throwing the discus' with bits of Roman stone beneath the canopy of firs, revelling in the relief from featureless desert. Barbie laughed and protested and our voices were loud in the deserted woodland.

We explored the massive extent of the ruined city the next day, taking several photographs. Unlike Leptis, we could enjoy the ruins in the bracing air of the plateau, occasionally shaded by eucalyptus trees. Nearby was the source of modern comfort in a simple Arab café where we had two cups of coffee on an empty stomach, so strong that my head swam and my feet floated.

Below again, we stopped for a more leisurely look at the ancient port of Apollonia where Greek, Egyptian and Roman ships had berthed to load riches of the land. Unlike Leptis and Carthage, the harbour had not been silted up in the last many centuries, but had sunk out of sight. Offshore of Apollonia there were treasures still to be salvaged by archaeologists.

A few years before, I had been given a fine photographic picture book of a trans-African journey produced by the Swiss photographer, Emil Schulthess, who had become something of a hero to me. He had begun his book with a picture of the Greek columns standing by the sea at Apollonia, and I took precisely the same photograph that morning, laying a personal ghost.

CHAPTER NINE : *WAVELL, AUCHINLECK, MONTGOMERY AND ROMMEL.*

From the heights of Cyrenaica to the city of Alexandria we traversed the coast road which produced a roll-call of names which were familiar to me as a boy: Derna, Gazala, Tobruk, Bardia, Halfaya Pass, Soloum, Sidi Barrani, Mersa Matrouh, El Daba, El Alamein. We had already passed through Tripoli, 'Marble Arch', El Agheila and Benghazi. Those names were engraved in my memory during 1942 and 1943 when I was eight and nine years old and it is the particular burden of my generation to have had the names of battles retained so vividly during childhood.

Living in South Africa at that time, it was these North African battles which were etched on my young mind. I do not recall the same detail of names of battles in Normandy, the Pacific or Russia, apart from the major ones, but I remembered every little place along the coast of Egypt and Libya. Of course, the reason is plain: I had an uncle, whose sons were more like brothers than cousins, serving as a platoon commander in the 2nd Battalion, Royal Natal Carbineers, 1st South African Infantry Division, 30 Corps, British 8th Army.

There were my mother's cousins in other regiments, including the daughter of my great-aunt who was a sergeant in the S.A. Women's Army Corps in Cairo. The husband of a cousin on my father's side was a captain in a British yeomanry artillery regiment in Egypt. Around that time, my father's brother, a regular Group-Captain in the RAF, was in India. An aunt was a commissioned staff-nurse in the S.A. Medical Corps and another uncle was a Major in the same service. Of particular interest to a young boy, my father's handy-man, a tall Zulu named Maxwell whom I admired, went 'Up North' as a sergeant in the South African Artillery. A schoolmaster who had a particularly strong influence on me had been wounded and invalided from the South African 1st Brigade fighting the Italians in Abyssinia and Somaliland. Every time I listened to the radio news in the company of my parents or other adults there was a special tension when North Africa was mentioned.

At our boarding-school there were a number of boys who had been sent to South Africa by several arms of the British government and military establishments. They were known as 'the refugees'. Most were oriented to the Indian Ocean or northern Africa. We had boys whose parents were incarcerated in Singapore, whose fathers had served in Malaya, the Persian Gulf or were based in Ceylon. One of my 'best friends' had a father who was a wing-commander in the RAF and was an administrative military chief at Asmara in Eritrea.

Europe was immeasurably further away than North Africa to us boarding-school boys. Most of us had fathers, uncles, other older relatives involved. There were occasions when the headmaster would call a boy out of class or from the dormitory with a quiet and considerate voice and we always knew that it was bad news from North Africa. Either the boy came back, tearful but silent, or he was bundled off home. Somehow, by an unexplained intuition, we understood and the one who was the victim of those far events was treated with a strange rough compassion. I find it difficult at this distance to explain how we handled these matters, but I do know it was instinctive. Nobody told us what to do. In these days when disaster strikes, such behaviour may be notable and is agonized over for days in sentimental national television news and documentary programmes. Nowadays, professional 'counsellors' swarm around victims of a motorway accident. Then, it was commonplace and unremarked. It was assumed. All over Europe and wherever people were sending men and women to fight in that terrible war it was the same. It was always that way.

In adult conversation there was anxiety as to what would happen if the Germans swept through to Cairo and the Suez Canal. At one time, a Japanese fleet was poised to invade Ceylon and threatened Madagascar and the eastern African coast. Durban, where we lived at that time, was a great maritime staging post for armies coming or going to Egypt, India and the Far East. Japanese naval reconnaissance planes flew over at one time and submarines sank many Allied ships off the South African coast. Some of my sharp visual memories were of the huge convoys of ships anchored in the Bay of Natal offshore of the suburb where we lived.

I remember my Uncle Walter returning from 'Up North' and giving out souvenirs to his two sons and to me as he told their stories. It was he who had enjoyed some days of rest and fun at Cyrene. I still have cap badges and insignia from several armies, spent bullets and a prized German bayonet and Afrika Korps water-bottle. I remember him telling us about the exhilaration of the tremendous artillery bombardment that commenced at 21.40 hours on 23rd October 1942, the beginning of the Alamein offensive that was the 'turning of the tide' in Africa. He was one of the few who fought their way out of the second siege of Tobruk, was nearly killed by a near-miss artillery shell and later had a kidney removed in Alexandria. Uncle Walter enjoyed being 'Up North' and the carefree life of a soldier, adventuring in the desert with comrades. He was proud to have fought in Montgomery's victorious 8th Army. He died early at the age of forty-seven after collapsing on a golf course.

VE Day was exciting and a sharp memory is listening with our respected school-teacher, Jack Rethman the veteran of the Abyssinian Campaign, to a hissing shortwave radio broadcasting from Brazzaville in the French Congo which was playing the *Marseillaise* with hysterical French announcements fading in and out. He turned to us with an excited grin and said,

"I'm not sure, but I think the war is over." Someone asked, "What's it really going to be like without the war, Sir?" He shrugged and made a distracted grimace.

These thoughts, and others much like them and much fresher then, were often in my mind during the next part of our journey.

*   *

The desert resumed its bleak emptiness and pale heat after we descended from the heights of Cyrenaica. We followed the coast where there were patches of cultivation and palm groves flourishing in the valleys coming down to the sea. At the foot of these coastal hills, the pleasant town of Derna nestled. We stopped briefly and I surmised that winter rainfall on the heights above must seep through in perennial springs and be preserved to irrigate the gardens.

After Derna, it was gravel plains again broken by a sea of low sand ridges extending to the dusty horizon, shimmering under the vertical sun. Some tussocky coarse grass grew on the ridges of sand and I supposed camels and goats could survive in that country if they knew where to find water when needed. We approached Tobruk in the afternoon. The town rested around the western curve of a bay which formed the roadstead of this important port, scene of two famous sieges in the war.

Approaching from the west, there was a view that made a strong impression on me. Beyond the bay in which the town lay, the coast continued in a straight line of vertical yellow cliffs with flat ground inland. Over the line of the cliffs there was a strange change in the light, presumably caused by the relatively cooler humid air welling up from the sea. Over the land the air was pale and hazy, an image of the fierce heat that prevailed. Immediately above the cliffs and continuing out to sea, the colour of the sky was a deep blue right down to the northern horizon. There was no wind and in the silence when I stopped to gaze at the phenomenon the whole scene seemed to vibrate with strangeness.

Tobruk was a town in transit from a war-ravaged Italian port to a modern base for oil exploration in the interior. There were new buildings going up in apparent haphazard style amongst the remnants of the old town, some of whose buildings still carried the scars of bombardment and street fighting. We found a new concrete hotel which had a room free and it was the centre of social activity. A rather eccentric expatriate Englishwoman was in charge and she engaged us in conversation after an amazing really hot bath, the first since leaving England (the baths in Beja and Tunis had not been much more than luke-warm). The food in the hotel diningroom was mediocre English, in the style of stewed meat and two veg.

The next day Barbie did not move from the hotel, catching up on washing, diaries, letters and so on. My minor infection which had began at Bouchera had to have proper attention and I asked the English manageress if there was a reliable doctor in town. She directed me to the government clinic. I went along in some trepidation and joined the few local people on a bench in the waiting room.

When my turn came, I was interviewed in a large room with bits and pieces of equipment laid out and an ominous operating table with lights suspended over it. The doctor was a tall Libyan not much older than myself who spoke immaculate English since he had been trained in London. He quickly put me at my ease and after examining me gave me a penicillin injection. I had to pull my shorts down to expose my bottom and the three or four nurses and assistants gave me a reassuring smile. He asked which company I was working for and when I explained what we were doing he was fascinated, asking me about it. I told him that I had stayed in digs in Hastings earlier that year with a Libyan student whom I had got to know well.

"Most of us go to Britain for further education," he told me. "We get grants and encouragement. My father could afford to send me, but even so I was looked after very well. Of course, the British supervision of Libya is finished now and we are independent, but our educated classes think highly of Britain. You know the war history of this region I'm sure?"

"Very well. I had relatives here in 1942. I couldn't forget Libya when I was a school boy because of my name." When I told it to him, he shook my hand and laughed. "You will always be welcome in our country."

I was given a prescription to present at the dispensary where I was handed an envelope full of concentrated vitamin C tablets and an ampoule of penicillin which I was strictly instructed to take to the district dispensary at Um Sa'ad at the border before leaving the country.

In the evening there was a cocktail party in the bar-lounge area for Norwegian engineers and oil experts and we sat on the verandah chatting to Tunisian and Libyan young men who were engaged as manual workers, jeep drivers and handymen. They spoke English, the *lingua franca* of the petroleum industry, and we drank a few beers with them. We were told about the hazards of driving into the desert to the well-heads and exploration sites which some of them had to do as a routine every week to carry mail, visiting Europeans and essential bits and pieces summoned by radio. The vehicles they drove were Landrovers equipped with special wide-profiles and tires made in France with an interesting and unique wavy tread. It was the first and last time that I saw that design of sand tire and I was intrigued by them.

"Do the tires work well in soft sand?" I asked.

"Oh yes. The tires are very good. They are designed for low air pressures and we never get stuck. It is not tires that are a problem. It is driving for many hours with four wheels. Landrovers are not so good for that; they overheat and we have engine troubles."

"What about my Landrover? Would it be alright to cross the Sahara?" I asked. They had inspected Landie earlier.

They shook their heads in unison and grinned. A Tunisian said: "You have ordinary tires, good for mud and hard ground. No good for soft sand, and you have a heavy load. Too much weight is the assassin of jeeps."

A Libyan told me quite definitely: "To cross the Sahara you should go through from Algeria to West Africa where there is a route used by many people. It goes by way of Tamanrasset."

"I know people who have travelled that way," the Tunisian confirmed.

"I understand that route," I said. "But I did not want to go to West Africa and through the Congo, because there is a civil war there now and it's dangerous. If we were stopped in the Congo we could not go on. And we could be shot at."

"What will you do?" they asked.

"We plan to go down the Nile to Aswan, by ship to Wadi Halfa and then cross the desert to Khartoum. I know that trucks and jeeps go that way. After Khartoum there are ships that go up the Nile."

They nodded, but one of the Libyans repeated his warning, talking seriously. "Do not try to cross anywhere in Libya, your Landrover will not survive without special tires and you will die. Even if there were more of you together, I would not advise it."

The Tunisian was thinking. "I heard that the ships do not go from Aswan to Wadi Halfa because they build a big dam. You have to take a desert road." I knew of the dam construction and assumed that there had to be an alternative to the steamer terminus if it was being interfered with. My 'Bible', the AA book on Trans-African Highways, noted that the new high dam was under construction four miles upstream from Aswan, but confirmed that the Wadi Halfa steamer service left from Shellal, above the dam.

Of course, I had never had any intention of striking off into the blue, but this warning was supported by an article in an Egyptian paper that the Englishwoman gave me to read and it was a horrifying story. She also told me that she had heard rumours about the Nile steamers being suspended.

During the Easter holidays, only a few months previously, a party of Germans from their embassy in Cairo had decided to visit Siwa Oasis which had been a famous Afrika Korps depot. They had set off in a convoy of two VW kombis and two VW cars, well kitted out and thoughtfully provisioned in good German style of efficiency. They had met heavy sand and one of the kombis had succumbed to overheating and clutch trouble. They had towed it for a while before abandoning it. When the second kombi packed up, they turned round. The clutches on the last two VWs then failed and some began walking. They had all died and their bodies had been found by the

129

Egyptian army scattered along the line of the route. It was a horrible and chilling story and I dreamed about it in a variety of recurring nightmares for some days.

I did not like the doubts about the Nile shipping services and these rumours and stories nagged at me. I wrote home from Tobruk saying that I might have to find another way to East Africa.

*   *

We visited the war memorials and graveyards around Tobruk. The British Knightsbridge Cemetery was the largest, a few miles into the desert. Under the harsh cloudless sky the whole scene was in tones of pale ochre and yellow, the colours of the sand and rock of the landscape, and the cut stone of the perimeter walls, the walkways and the rows of immaculately placed gravestones in geometric harmony. A few palm trees had been placed strategically to provide perspective.

Our sandalled feet scraped loudly on the stone and gravel under the dome of sky as we wandered the neat rows of identical stones as if taking our ease in some strange garden on a planet where there was no vegetation. On each stone there was carved identification: the regimental badge, religious symbol and the name, rank and number of the bundle of shattered bones and dust that lay beneath. Many were unidentified by name but their origin was known, probably by the racial characteristics or the tattered remnants of uniforms, for this was a graveyard of thousands of men from all over the British Empire.

The cemetery was in sections: British, Australian, South African, New Zealand, Indian, scatterings of Rhodesians, East Africans, Sudanese. There were Christian crosses, Jewish stars, Moslem crescents and Hindu symbols. There were the insignia of many famous British regiments and others venerated only in the far-flung Imperial distances. My eyes sought out South African graves and Barbie was away amongst the Australians. I saw Cape Town Highlanders, Regiment De la Rey, Natal Field Artillery, Umvoti Mounted Rifles, Royal Durban Light Infantry, Imperial Light Horse, Native Military Corps, Duke of Edinburgh's Own Rifles, South African Engineers, Regiment President Steyn, Royal Natal Carbineers (my uncle's regiment), Transvaal Scottish, South African Air Force, South African Naval Forces, South African Artillery (was my boyhood friend Sergeant Maxwell there somewhere? He had not come back to see us after the campaign as he promised he would...)

Burdened by the blasting heat of noon sun and mentally exhausted by comprehending this evidence of human slaughter in a stone and sand wilderness, I wandered to a stop and sat on a gravestone to smoke a cigarette. My eyes strayed to the stone opposite, which was embellished with one of the few personal epitaphs:

> N/1446 L/Corporal J. Hoala. Native Military Corps.
> 20th November 1942.
> "Always remembered where the Maluti breezes blow."

I stared at it and there were goose pimples on my heat-scaled arms and suddenly tears joined the sweat around my eyes. Corporal Hoala was a black soldier in the South African army and I knew the lonely Maluti Mountains on the border country between Lesotho and the Orange Free State. I had an extraordinarily powerful feeling of nostalgia and sadness, maybe far more than if I had found the known grave of a relative or family friend, for that epitaph was so unexpected and so suddenly evocative. (Who had caused it to be engraved on the stone?) In contrast to the dust all about, I instantly smelled the scent of sun warmed grasses and veld-flowers and heard the frail piping of highveld birds. I could see the moving red shapes of cattle against the background of rugged green mountains with pale sandstone cliffs. I could see an African herdboy clad in a blanket against the cool wind, wielding a stick as he called to his cattle.

I cried unashamedly for my homeland and this baSotho man dead there in a White man's war so far away. I was twisted with a spasm of my own homesickness and loneliness.

I was drawing on a cigarette when Barbie came to me. Her eyes were red too. "All those good Aussie boys," she said, voice breaking. It was quiet. Then: "Found some 'yippees' have you?"

I pointed to Corporal Hoala and she read silently. We walked back to Landie and drove away without talking for a while.

To the east of Tobruk about a mile inland of the cliffs which had created the strange division of light and air when we arrived there was a black stone square, a castle keep standing bold on the yellow sand. We drove to it and entered its fastness. It was the German memorial. There were no graves, and I did not discover what had happened to the thousands of young German bodies. I was sure that they could not all have been taken home, so had they just been bulldozed into mass graves?

On the interior walls of the castle keep their names had been inscribed in Gothic script, lines after immaculate lines of them. Our footsteps and voices echoed eerily within that Germanic construction, so compact and alien there.

Elsewhere, we admired the Roman-style memorial to Italian dead, a column to celebrate the sacrifice of Czechoslovakians, memorials to Poles and the Free French.

That evening we had another amazing hot bath and clad in clean clothes I went down to sit on the verandah of the bare concrete hotel and ordered a cold beer. I had finished it and was beginning to wonder why Barbie was so late, because we were both used to our rough nomadic life and did not take long to change and dress. I was about to go up to the bedrooms when she appeared and sat down abruptly.

"A beer?" I asked smiling. "You were a long time."

"I'll have something stronger if they have it," she said and I felt her tension. I fetched a large bacardi from the bar and when she had a gulp, she explained.

"You see that greasy fat bastard leering at us," she said pointing with her chin. There was a big man in some form of uniform sitting with friends in the inner room and his thick-lipped mouth was grinning beneath a moustache. He was staring at us both and I felt the impact of his strange smirk which seemed directed at me. He seemed aware of our conversation and to be amused in a superior way. I nodded to Barbie.

"He came knocking at the door and I thought it was you so I opened up dressed in panties and bra. He pushed his way in and showed me some kind of badge, telling me to keep quiet. He said he was the chief of police and if I didn't let him have a quick fuck he'd have you arrested and put in jail and then he could have me whenever he wanted... Jesus, it was awful..."

I could not speak. The blood drained from my head and I felt sick with the sudden shock.

"Oh, Barbie, I'm so sorry." I said, after some time, taking her hand.

I felt foolish and unmanned. I held her hand and could say nothing. She explained that she had recovered from the immediate surprise and had begun to struggle and shout and had got rid of him by promising to be available next day.

The incident laid a pall over the evening and we were both depressed by this attack on our integrity. I had not had the direct experience, but the sharing of it and the insult to the both of us was a heavy hand that could not be easily pushed aside. We ate little of the dinner and had several expensive whisky drinks afterwards. A Libyan who was falling-down drunk joined us and rambled away about how much money he was earning and what he was going to do when he got back home to Tripoli. He boasted that he had been to Malta and had Christian girlfriends. Barbie became morosely angry.

We left Tobruk next morning. For us, it had become an evil place with misery and much old death.

*   *

Bardia was another of those well-known wartime names at the seaward end of the escarpment broached by the Halfaya Pass and overlooking the Gulf of Soloum. Bardia was empty, a shattered town of shell-blasted and bullet-pocked buildings standing on the edge of a cliff with the blue sea far below. We wandered about amongst the forlorn roofless houses with tumbledown walls. I photographed a church with hibiscus in bloom with bright blood-red flowers beside it and we saw a donkey which survived there. Why was the town abandoned altogether, I wondered? The church showed that Italians had lived there and made a prosperous living in 1940 so why had it not been revived?

Beyond, a new tarred road descended the pass through rusting barbed wire and bits of discarded metal and tar-drums to the flat yellow lands that spread away to the dusty silver-grey horizon. The air over the sea was also silver, the cliffs that made miniature weather systems at Tobruk were shaved away there.

On the outskirts of the small settlement of Um Sa'ad, which the Italians used to call Fort Capuzzo, there was a sign directing us to the medical clinic and I drove up to it with my ampoule of penicillin. Within a small concrete hut with corrugated iron roof a middle-aged man was dozing in a chair tipped back against the wall. He rubbed his eyes and smiled amiably at me. He was dressed in a djellaba over neatly creased but shabby trousers and a turban cloth was wound about his head. He did not look like a doctor or nurse and greeted me in Arabic. Somewhat confused, I handed over the precious penicillin and the scrawled note which went with it. He read the note and looked up brightly, nodding to me.

Expecting him to indicate that I should wait while he went to find the nurse, I was surprised when he went to a cupboard and brought out an enamel bowl, hypodermic and a bottle of methylated spirits. He was the man in charge. The hypodermic was put into the bowl where meths was poured over it, the sweet smell instantly filling the room. He lit a spirit lamp and held the needle in the flame before waiting for it to cool, his eyes roving over me. When he was ready, he filled the syringe from my ampoule and gestured for me to take my shorts down. The meths on my naked skin was sharply cool but the needle was blunt and the injection hurt. I thanked him profusely and offered him a cigarette, but he quietly shook his head, still smiling. He waved me off and came out to raise his hand as we drove away.

"That seemed quick and easy," Barbie said. "I thought you would be hours, probably waiting in a queue."

"The place is deserted as you see," I said. "The whole experience was strange. I really don't know if he really was the nurse-in-charge, the caretaker or even a passerby. But it was all quite efficient, and he was friendly and professional."

We were approaching the border posts and Barbie pointed. "I wonder how professional that bloody lot will be."

I was expecting the usual delays and problems at the Egyptian border and was not disappointed. There was a huddle of dirty sheds and kiosks in the middle of nowhere. It took two hours to get through, this time not because of revolution or anarchic bureaucracy, but because of an excess of zeal. The documents were treated with massive importance and I was questioned minutely on my entries.

Particularly, I had to explain my planned movements in great detail and how we were to leave Egypt to two different officials and when I explained that we were going through Aswan to the Sudan there was a conference between them. I had no Sudanese visa, but because of my British passport did not need one then, and this seemed to worry them.

In the end, because our Egyptian visas were impeccable, and we both still had substantial amounts of money which they meticulously counted and noted, they let us through. I was warned with ponderous gravity that I would be imprisoned if I tried to sell Landie. I did not understand the fuss they were making and they did not explain their concern. I had become inured to hours of delay at the North African borders for this reason or that and no alarm note was sounded.

Drinking the inevitable Fantas and Cokes at a dirty petrol station with oil-stained sand all about after passing through the border, we met the first European overland travellers since leaving the ferry at Ceuta. It was a group of young French people with a battered black Citroën car piled high with boxes and cans. It had French number plates. There were three young men and a girl and they were sat about in the dust drinking wine from bottles and being merry. We greeted each other and chatted for a while. The duty on wine was so strict going into Libya that they were going to stay there the night and get drunk instead of trying to smuggle the wine. The boys teased Barbie, saying that she should join them for a good time while their girl stood apart from them and eyed me. I wondered if they had been having personality problems.

They said they were from Beirut and they were taking the long way home. Because of the problems of Israel they had to take a ferry from Beirut to Alexandria, via Cyprus. They were deeply sun-tanned and dressed in blue jeans and dark shirts with bright scarves or neckerchiefs. The girl was petite and slim but her bottom was deliciously well-rounded and she clearly wore no bra. With surprise at the strength of my feelings of desire for this first strange European girl after weeks of travelling, I understood the hunger of Arab men towards the apparent availability of European women, who must appear to be wild and free. They offered us mouthfuls of wine from their bottles, but it was hot and acidic. Barbie gave me a signal that she did not want to stay and drink.

"Those French boys were keen for a change-around weren't they?" Barbie said. "I don't know that I could have handled them."

"I must admit I fancied the girl," I replied, driving off. "She was rather sexy."

"I noticed. But I think she had had enough from those three for a while so you would have been out of luck."

"They reminded me of that bunch of Swiss boys on the ferry to Ceuta," I said wistfully. "They seemed so much more carefree than us."

"Come on, Den! I seem to remember you throwing the discus all naked in the pine forest at Cyrene. Telling me you were training for the Olympic games in 500 BC or something," Barbie replied. She smiled, but not about that laughter-filled evening. "Remember, we're going a lot further than those Swiss, or that Froggie lot."

We camped that night near Mersa Matruh after driving past Sidi Barrani, two more wartime names which made no impression on me because the desert had become so monotonous. I stopped to take photographs, but could see nothing to make an interesting composition, so just shot off a couple of frames at gravel and sand ridges pocked with dried tussocks.

The next day we were at El Alamein. I was again disappointed at first, trying to find evidence of the great battles that had been fought in that area and the residue of the two famous armies that had faced each other there for months in 1942. There was a railway line and a couple of battered sheds at the El Alamein station, but that was all. We both felt cheated, gazing at yet another panorama of the endless Sahara, no different to the unchanging view for the last hundreds of miles.

"It makes me wish we had stopped for a day at Bardia to get a real feeling for it all," I said. "We could have camped in the ruined church and there seemed to be a bit of a harbour down below the cliffs which we never bothered to explore. We could have swum in the sea and had a good rest. What a pity." I thought about it. "We had no food, of course..."

There was a cemetery further on and we wandered there for an hour or so, but it did not have the fresh impact of Knightsbridge outside Tobruk. Somehow I had the naive idea that there would have been some directions, some indication of where the final front had been, some layout of the positions occupied by this and that division: perhaps directions to Montgomery's or Rommel's headquarters. But, of course, the Egyptians had little interest and we were the only pilgrims we had come across. Tourism along the edge of the Sahara was hardly booming.

Heading eastward again, my thoughts were inevitably occupied with the next phase of the journey because we were only sixty miles from Alexandria, when a low altar-like structure appeared on the right hand. I looked at it idly and was about to pass by when I noticed the springbok-head insignia of the South African army and pulled over in a flurry of dust. I looked about, but there was nothing else in sight: just yellow sand and tufts of dried tumbleweed as always, stretching away to the next low crest of the rolling dunes. I got out and read the inscription cut into the pale stone.

SUID-AFRIKANERS HET HIER GEDURENDE HULLE TREK VAN ITALIAANS-SOMALILAND NA DUITSLAND UITGESPAN EN OOK GEVEG 1939-1945

There was English on the other side, but I preferred to read these remarkable words in Afrikaans. The extraordinary simplicity and under-statement on this simple altar-stone monument in the middle of nowhere in the Egyptian desert was so certainly right for South Africa that it was like a blinding flash. South Africa had placed its national memorial away from the others. And then, whoever had designed it had, probably unwittingly, caused the wording to be almost excessively opposite to that on all the others.

The Australian, British, French, Polish, Czechoslovakian, German, Italian had proclaimed the glory and heroism of their youth, the supreme sacrifice of the fresh bloom of their manhood. The simple words on the lonely South African monument were mocking in their strange simplicity and rejection of glorification. I stood rooted there, my thoughts in a whirl, feeling sad and proud, and wondering who was responsible, and whether in a hundred years anybody would understand the significance, and whether anybody would give a damn.

"Hey, Den, that's 'yippee' language. What does it mean?" Barbie brought me to earth. I waited, then grinned before translating it for her.

" 'South Africans, during their trek from Italian-Somaliland to Germany, outspanned here, and also fought.' Outspan means to make camp when you were travelling in the bush with ox-waggons. To unharness the oxen and set up camp." We were silent while Barbie thought about it.

"Well, it's different," she said eventually.

I felt reluctant to leave, taking a photograph and walking about, looking at the distance, trying to understand it all and get a 'feel' for those months of high drama, savouring the words on the simple, squat memorial beside the road. Some years later, I wrote to the head of the South African Army to enquire about it and received a factual reply from a major-general responsible for welfare. The stone had been placed in that precise spot because it was at the junction of the main road and what was called the 'Springbok Road' which led to the headquarters of the 1st S.A. Infantry Division.

We drove down a track nearby and 'outspanned' right beside the sea that afternoon. We ate tinned sardines and biscuits for dinner because we had run out of fresh food. I supposed that soldiers might have sat eating in that exact place twenty-three years before, but tinned sardines would probably have been a luxury. I kept thinking of the inscription on the monument and thinking of the men who had been there, where we were sitting on our folding chairs looking at the sea.

We bathed and the water was milky pale blue-green, like a vegetable soup, although there were no waves to disturb it. I found the opaque milky sea-water quite disturbing and did not go far in. Later, I tried our portable radio and by some other freak of the day picked up the British Forces Network broadcasting on VHF from Cyprus, which lay about 400 miles over the horizon to the north-east. Some weird aberration was occurring in the atmosphere that evening.

I had switched to VHF by accident and we were amazed to listen to a sharp and clear English voice introducing pop music that we had not heard for weeks, not since Bouchera and Le Gros' marvellous aerial. The Seekers had Barbie going on about Australia and I listened to her chatter while half my mind remained focussed on the outspanning of South Africans on their long trek, so far from home, facing unknown futures.

*   *

The next morning Barbie complained that she had not been sleeping well and had developed a rash. We were coming to the end of a particularly arduous stretch of travelling and I thought that maybe some days in Alexandria and Cairo, behaving something like ordinary tourists, would be a necessary change for both of us and brighten us up. I also wondered how much that unpleasant incident at Tobruk might have affected her. Barbie was not someone to reveal her inner worries and liked to be proudly self-sufficient, but nobody has these shocks to personal integrity and intimate privacy without severe damage to self-esteem.

In retrospect I doubt if I gave Barbie as much attention at that time as I should have and it had been something of a shock to me as well. I was filled with the excitement of getting to the great cities of Egypt, and was also apprehensive and getting quite worried about the problems that would accompany penetrating them after so many days of physical freedom, with a different set of simpler concerns in the grand traverse of the Sahara.

On the road east from Alamein, we soon approached civilisation. Fruit orchards, sugar-cane and maize fields showed where irrigation schemes were established and there were bustling small towns. They were rough towns, strips of new construction followed the old potholed road. Men were digging trenches beside

138

the road to install water mains and there were gangs at work laying new tar. For the first time in weeks we were held up by traffic. We ate fresh unleavened bread filled with chopped tomatoes and onions doused in rich olive oil and drank iced mineral water bought from a kiosk in one anonymous town. I filled Landie's near-empty tank with petrol which soon had the engine overheating and knocking, coughing and spluttering for a minute after switching off the ignition. Egyptian petrol was poor quality, it even burned badly with oily smoke when used in my cigarette lighter.

In early afternoon we entered the built up streets of the great and ancient city of Alexandria.

CHAPTER TEN : *THE NILE*

There was inevitable anti-climax driving into Alexandria that afternoon of 29th July 1965. We had set off from London forty five days before and had travelled across Europe and the whole of North Africa, including a traverse of the Sahara Desert littoral. We had reached one of the two most important staging posts of our grand journey. The other would be Mombasa.

We had got used to each other and had proven our ability to travel rough and lonely roads through countries whose culture and languages were different to ours. Despite those incidents which had gnawed at our psychic strength, nothing had gone seriously wrong and we had a lot of fun. We were seasoned. But, the arrival in Alexandria was the beginning of the next great jump, so as anti-climax worked in one direction, there was an opposite growth of excited expectations and anticipated worries. It was the expectations which became so thoroughly dashed.

The city itself was huge by African standards, perhaps four times as large as Algiers and twice as populous as Johannesburg. Agriculture and villages on the outskirts were a preparation, but the division between city and desert countryside was stark. Suddenly, the city was there: closely built up streets, factories and warehouses, apartment buildings, rows of shops, more vehicles than we had seen anywhere since Melilla and teeming masses of people.

The city was dirty and the buildings decrepit. The clamour and noise after weeks of desert was a shock, but the dirt and the ruined appearance of smoking workshops and tenements appalled. We stared, wide-eyed, not at magnificence and glory but at degradation and squalor. What had happened to this city? Why were the rows of Mediterranean style tenements with balconies and wrought iron decorations falling apart, paint long gone, plaster scaling away, windows broken, dust blowing, rubbish and broken cars stacked in the streets, urchins begging and squabbling? It was clear from the buildings that it had been wealthy and powerful and well-ordered, had grown with planning and style, pride and consciousness of its standing, but it seemed to be dying from some lingering cancer.

I was so used to a continuous and inevitable march of progress in South Africa where cities were vital and expanding: new buildings, new suburbs, new factories, new highways, new government housing for Blacks, higher skyscrapers, bigger harbours, endless boom. Britain was also on the advance, London was being cleaned up, new motorways being opened, welfare plans developing, fresh culture of the 'swinging sixties' was spreading. Decay in Zaragossa and Cartagena had been understood, but there seemed no reason for Alexandria. I had never seen a whole city in internal decay before starting on our grand safari.

I understood the evidence of Civil War in Spain and the war in Algeria and assumed that growth and polish would be reinstated. I found the cancer of the inner city of Alexandria shocking. I felt instinctive revulsion like having to gaze on some pathetic person mutilated by a loathsome disease. Alexandria was diseased and I had no understanding of how a city becomes ill like that. Barbie and I kept repeating monotonously, "I can't believe it; I can't believe it."

Bemused, I let Landie go ahead along the main route by which we had entered and we penetrated to the sea front where there was a boulevard that seemed majestic in contrast to the streets we had been following. The blue of the sea and clear sky was a reminder that we had not entered some weird nightmare. The apartment blocks along the front were more ornate and although their facades were scabbed and scarred they seemed in better repair. Obviously we had to find a cheap hotel and we did need somewhere that was clean and decent; there was no point in coming in from the desert to stay in some filthy slum where our Landie would be vandalised and our visit would be miserable.

I drove on down the boulevard and quite quickly approached the end of this more prosperous-seeming zone, so I abruptly turned into a street towards the centre again, feeling sudden despair at where we were going to stay. I slowed to a crawl, concentrating my mind on this immediate practical problem. There was a banging on the side of Landie. A young man in a pyjama suit was running alongside shouting and I stopped.

"Please, Sir. Please, Sir!" he gasped. "You English, yes? You want place to sleep? I show you ... " He was badly cross-eyed and his crooked gaze swept over the interior of the cab.

141

"Hold on, Den. I don't like the look of him," Barbie said, but I listened to him offering what seemed to be a room in a private apartment. "Shall we have a look?" I asked Barbie and she shrugged with bad humour. "The whole place is just irk. And we don't need to be taken for a ride..."

I got out. "I'll have a look, you guard Landie." Barbie shrugged again and I followed the boy into an apartment block that seemed in good repair. Within, there was one of those old-fashioned lifts with rattling iron doors, but it worked and the cross-eyed boy and I crawled up three floors. We left the lift into a landing which seemed respectable and French-style middle-class. The floor was polished and a pot-plant sat on a carved table. The boy pressed a bell-push and we were admitted into a reception room where a middle-aged man in a grey business suit with white shirt and pale silk tie was talking to a dumpy little woman in a dark shiny dress with a black scarf tied around her head. Her black, beady eyes looked me over with obvious distaste from bruised sockets and there were hairs on her upper lip. The room was furnished with a stylish over-upholstered suite clothed with machine-embroidered shawls and plush cloths in oriental colours covered the occasional tables. It looked like the home of a lawyer or doctor. A young man with friendly eyes and a smartly trimmed moustache in crisply ironed slacks and shirt took charge and spoke to me in French and then broken English while the older couple watched with what seemed superior contempt.

It was obvious that this family were forced to let out a room, probably one of the children's who had left home, but it was an activity that they hated; especially if it involved foreigners in dirty clothes coming in from nowhere. But the younger man was pleasant enough and he showed me a room with two beds and its own balcony. There were two bathrooms and we would share one with him. He confirmed that the room being let out was that of his sisters who were in Cairo. The rent was reasonable by English bed-and-breakfast standards, less than a pound each per day, so I agreed. The cross-eyed boy came down and helped with our bags. Landie, I was assured would be safe in the street in that precinct.

Unfortunately, as we were struggling into the room with our bags the lady of the house came out onto the landing and whatever resentments I had sparked were stoked by the sight of Barbie in a pair of shorts. She began babbling angrily and her son came out to translate.

142

"My mother asks if you are married?" he wanted to know and I said that we were not, without thinking, which produced a torrent of angry language while we stood with our luggage about us. I could feel Barbie's Aussie hackles rising fast.

"Obviously we are not welcome," I said coldly to the son and picked up my bags and turned to the lift and this caused more discussion. "Please," the son said and we waited. Eventually, the old woman left the scene although we could hear her fuming to herself. We were ushered into the bedroom and were given apologies: the mother was a strict Moslem and old-fashioned, she did not understand the modern ways of Europeans travelling long distances. He smiled and shrugged. But Barbie was angry and I was disconcerted.

After weeks of freedom on the road, the heavy respectability of this stuffy apartment in a decaying city depressed us. I stood on the verandah, letting the sweat dry and stared at an old man sitting on a reclining chair in the balcony opposite with washing flapping about his head. He seemed to be asleep, like a cat put out while the mistress goes shopping.

Barbie occupied herself with an unconscious need to prove her respectability, unpacking her case and putting out toilet things and personal bits and pieces neatly, grumbling to herself. She disappeared into the bathroom to wash clothes and shower so I got out the information about travelling through the Sudan and studied it before dozing off for a while.

From my base at Hastings I had followed up the information I had gathered far back in the early planning days at home in South Africa. I had written to the Sudanese embassy in London and received pamphlets and instructions and our Egyptian visas were issued on applications that described my purpose in travelling southwards through the Sudan to Uganda and Kenya.

I thought I knew exactly what was involved in driving down to Aswan, taking in the sights and history of the great Nile Civilisation, then catching a ship from Shellal to Wadi Halfa from where there was a recognised and reasonably well-travelled desert road to Khartoum following the railway line. From Khartoum there were steamers up the White Nile to Juba from where there were good roads in the dry season into Uganda. I had gone over the route, considered the climatic cycles, studied the costs and made all the necessary contacts. The final timing of the whole expedition had been made in order to journey up the Nile at the proper time of year. I had the Nile steamers' timetables and details of the costs.

The journey from Cairo to Uganda was a major expedition on its own, but it was not a dangerous pioneering route, provided each portion was settled and the links were clear. The infrastructure had been established by the British colonial administration at the beginning of the 20th century. My information told me that if we did not wish to drive across the Nubian Desert from Wadi Halfa to Khartoum, we could hire an open railway truck, put Landie aboard and travel that way. It was only a matter of cost and personal desire. We might be delayed a few days or even a week or two making the connections here or there, but I did not see that as a problem, especially not by the time we had reached Alexandria because we were experienced in desert travel together.

So, armed with passports, travellers cheques and the correspondence with the Sudanese authorities, I set off later that afternoon satisfied that we would set the ball rolling, get the latest steamer schedules and probably buy our tickets. My depression at our reception in Alexandria lifted and we were both in better spirits, talking about the marvels we would be going to see at Luxor, Abu Simbel and Aswan. This was probably going to be the most culturally exciting stage of our long journey across Africa. I had bought books on the Nile Civilisations in London so that we could read about the exciting ruins as we travelled in leisurely fashion southwards. Barbie and I had talked a lot about it all.

The state tourist bureau was a smart modern office manned by bright cheerful staff. Posters of temples and giant statues decorated the walls. There was bustle and we were attended to by a plump young woman who spoke English with an air of competence and efficiency.

"And so, what do wish to do in Egypt?" she asked, and I began an elaborate explanation of my plans. As I talked, her smile faded and she looked increasingly distracted.

"You have letters from the Sudanese Embassy?" she interrupted, and I passed them over. There was a particular letter dated 21st May 1965 from the Consul in the London Embassy which gave me all the necessary information I had requested about the procedure for travelling up the Nile from Egypt. It told me to get all my tickets and reservations from the Sudan Railways Office in Kasr el Nil Street, Cairo, and our clearances from the Sudan Embassy in Garden City, Cairo. It could not be more detailed or helpful.

We waited while she read them slowly with a worried expression before getting up abruptly. "One moment," she said sharply and dived into an interior office. Barbie collected some brochures that were lying about, street maps of Alexandria and Cairo, while I felt approaching doom. I mentally recalculated the expected cost of the steamer and rail tickets for ourselves and Landie for the hundredth time. I wondered if the prices had been substantially increased in the last three months. The rumours that I had picked up in Tobruk were suddenly recalled in my mind.

The woman returned with a uniformed man who seemed to be her superior.

"I'm very sorry," she said. "You have been badly misinformed. It is not possible to travel beyond Aswan at this time. We do not understand these letters, they are not correct in any way."

A sick feeling started in my stomach, were we going to be delayed and for how long? What extra cost would be involved? "What is the problem?" I asked. "Is the new dam construction interfering with the departure of ships, are the ships out of order?"

She looked at her boss, then shook her head. "No, it is not a temporary matter. The border is closed indefinitely. It is completely closed by order of the military. You cannot travel south to Sudan. Impossible."

I heard Barbie breathing heavily beside me. "I don't understand..."

"It is the construction of the Aswan High Dam by the Russians," the man said. "You did not know? The border is most definitely closed, it is controlled by the army and foreigners are absolutely prohibited. It has been this way for some months." He shrugged. "I'm sorry."

I was floundering. "But, my letters." I gestured at them. "And our visas from your own embassy in London... It was only in May that everything was in order. I knew that the dam was building, but I thought that it could not stop traffic on the Nile. Surely there is some temporary road around the dam site? We are going to East Africa, not just local tourism. What can we do?" I stared at them. "Why did your Embassy issue us visas if our application specified that we were travelling to the Sudan?" The world had contracted to the two sympathetic but obdurate faces in front of me.

The man shrugged again and, plainly embarrassed, returned to his office. His departure convinced me that there was no way

145

round; the unpleasant matter was settled as far as he was concerned. The papers were pushed back at me and the woman tried a smile.

"It is not the Sudanese who control travel in our country," she said. "Information from the Sudan Embassy in London about travelling in their country is not advice on movement south of Aswan within Egypt." She smiled sympathetically again. "Maybe our embassy did not read your application carefully; it was just processed with many others." She shrugged. "There are many things to do in Egypt. When you have rearranged your itinerary, come back and I can help you...."

I stumbled out into the baking sun and heat and stink of the street.

"What are we going to do, Den?" Barbie said.

"Shit! I've not the least idea right now. Shit! Shit! Shit! I just don't know. Go by sea to Mombasa, I suppose. What else?" I stood there looking blindly at men shuffling past in pyjama suits and a traffic snarl of elderly cars belching smoke.

*   *

Walking slowly along the street, not heading anywhere, my thoughts in a whirl, Barbie spied a Cook's travel office and aimed me into it. Very quickly the advice from the state office was confirmed. The southern border area was closed to foreigners. I now understood the hesitation and detailed questioning that we had been subjected to at the Soloum border post.

I tentatively mentioned going by sea to East Africa almost expecting to be told that was also impossible, but there was a ray of light. If I had definitely to go on to East Africa, Thomas Cook's would try to solve my problem. The woman cheerfully suggested that we take ship from Port Said to Mombasa. She thought there were passenger liners and cargo ships with accommodation which would suit us. She would contact their office in Port Said who would help me when I got there. When would we be ready?

"Have you no schedules?" I asked. "I would like to fix everything up so that we know where we are and can tour down the Nile. I would pay for the tickets here in your office."

She shook her head. "I'm sorry. That is not possible. Everything about ships is done at Port Said."

"What about your office in Cairo?"

"Port Said," she repeated, shaking her head.

146

We bought postcards and found the Ramses Restaurant where we ate steaks and salads and drank a good quality Egyptian wine. We talked around and around the problem. We could drive down the Nile and back before going to Port Said. My biggest worry was cost and money. I had no idea how much it would be to ship Landie and for our passages. I could not risk driving up and down the Nile, undoubtedly having to stay in hotels, and then having insufficient funds to complete our journeying. It was the uncertainty of it all and the disappointment that lay heavily on us.

I even talked of the gloomiest possibilities: we could abort and take a ship to Greece or Italy. We could even go back through Libya and Algeria. This talk angered Barbie and we sank into gloom and pointless argument.

I became furious and shaken by the failure of my plans. And yet at the back of my mind I knew that I had a premonition in Tobruk and wondered why I had not taken greater heed. Confident about the letters and the visas, I had intellectually overridden intuition and dismissed the warnings as travellers' gossip that did not have relevance to our special case. I thought that problems about steamers were temporary or could be overcome when we got there. I also realised that I did not want to believe that it was not possible to follow the planned route, which had been my dream for years.

It had all started back in 1958, eight years previously, when my wife and I put up a couple in Nigeria who had driven across the Sahara in a pre-war London taxi. We had talked about doing a trans-African journey often in the years since then, usually as a fantasy, but the germ had lain in my mind ready to bud, waiting for an opportune time. That was the most hurtful thing about it all for me and I could not shake off my disappointment and anger. I had taken a mighty plunge away from my career and my young family to indulge in this extraordinary adventure. And now it seemed doomed. I was assailed by homesickness as an additional intellectual burden.

I went over the planning and checking I had done in London, in a loop in my mind, wondering what else I could have done. There seemed to be nothing.

Back in the apartment, I even suggested that Barbie might want to fly back to London, and I would understand if she felt that her trip was now ruined. Guilt for disrupting her life was yet another black cloud in my thoughts. This made her furious at me for thinking she had no loyalty or guts and we had a stupid and fruitless row,

147

shouting at each other and ended up more miserable and depressed than ever.

In the morning we were cold with each other. The day before had been a disaster in every way ending with an unresolved personal clash of fierce intensity. We went to the museum and looked around somewhat aimlessly at Roman statuary, mummies of minor ancient officials of the great dynasties, and Ptolemaic relics. We changed more money and posted postcards. I told the young man at the apartment that we had problems and would leave for Cairo the next day. We ate again at the Ramses restaurant and it was a gloomy meal.

I went to the Cook's office as soon as it was open and confirmed that I wished to book passage from Port Said and the woman clerk told me that she would send a telex to their shipping office. I should go to Port Said as soon as possible, within the next few days. When I told Barbie about this, we talked uneasily again about alternative plans and possibilities and all our disappointment and frustration was stirred up.

We were mentally drained after the long journey we had already undertaken and were now facing a series of uncertainties none of which were under our control. Everything was a 'what if'.

*   *

I decided to take the desert road to Cairo and stopped for an early lunch at a seafood restaurant in an old building on the seashore which must have been an elegant tearoom in its heyday. We sat at a table within an airy belvedere with the sea washing on rocks below the wide windows. We had excellent grilled fish served by a smiling informal waiter. Suddenly, I relaxed. Whatever happened, we had already had a most extraordinary experience; there was nothing to feel guilty about. I had done everything I should have done.

In that friendly atmosphere, we talked again about our immediate plans. We would see the pyramids and a bit of Cairo then go across to Port Said and make our arrangements. It was not that far off, only something over a hundred miles, and when we knew exactly what was happening, we could explore the Nile and its wonders as much as money and time allowed, keeping out of the big cities which were upsetting us so badly. Somehow things would work out: we had setbacks, but luck would surely return to us and as long as we stood by each other, there was no need to panic.

I drove off the road up a small stony knoll to take photographs of the great Sahara before leaving it, and we saw a complex of buildings with high fences and the lattices of big radar scanners slowly rotating. There had been much publicity in England about Egypt turning to the Soviet Union for military assistance after the Suez debacle and I felt a cold hand on me. The shock of the closing of the southern borders for military reasons was reinforced by the sight of this installation in the desert. If we were seen with cameras we would be in serious trouble and I hastily went back to the road.

It was late when we approached Cairo and getting dark, so we thought that we would try for a simple hotel on the outskirts or camp in the desert. We should have driven off the road immediately and not attempt to penetrate the huge sprawl of Cairo in the dark, but we left it too late, stopping at a tourist restaurant within sight of the pyramids for a coffee.

There was a side road heading out into the desert with the pyramids looming in the dusk on a hill above us. A track went off that road to the right along the foot of the hill and on impulse I took it, assuming that it went off into the wilderness to the west of the pyramids. It did, but we were in for a harrowing ordeal.

Passing some cement block buildings sheltered by old eucalyptus trees, I saw a uniformed man running and brandishing a rifle out of the corner of my eye. "There is some little man looking angry and waving a gun at us," Barbie said urgently, and I stopped. He came up to us panting and shouting and he was soon joined by another. They were both agitated and using Arabic explosively. When they had calmed and caught their breaths, they walked round Landie inspecting us and came back to try an impossible mixture of Arabic and a few words of French and English.

I got out our passports and the vehicle Carnet and showed them to them and they both poured over them, turning pages back and forth and chattering to one another. I realised that they could not read European script when I saw that they had Barbie's passport upside down. They wanted to see inside the back and I opened up for them and waited anxiously while one crawled in and pushed our gear around. I realised that we had strayed into some restricted area, maybe a military camp, although there had been no gate or fence that I could notice. I tried several different ways of explaining that we were sorry and had only been looking for a place to sleep. It seemed to make no difference to their castigation of us so I started to use words like 'embassy', 'British', and so on, but that only seemed to make them more angry.

I gestured back the way we had come and made driving motions but that made them bang on Landie with their rifle butts. In despair I talked of police and how could we report to them. They shook their heads, they did not want the police. We had reached an impasse and they sat down on the sand, talking to each other.

"Are we going to be here all night?" Barbie groaned.

"It's possible. Do you have any suggestions?"

"It beats me. What have we done, what authority have they? They're only young soldiers."

"I suppose if we wait long enough they've got to go off duty and an officer must come around sometime."

It had grown pitch dark and when we lit cigarettes our lighters flared up in the cab. The flashes brought our tormentors back to us and one of them was smiling. He wanted a cigarette so I gave him my packet, and then they wanted lights which I gave them. They talked quietly, grinning to each and one of them suddenly shone his torch on Barbie's face. "Cut that out!" she complained but they continued to study her until she put up her hands to shield herself. One of the men then pointed at Barbie, then at himself and his companion, then gestured towards the darkness, smiling at me. I was horrified, because there seemed no mistaking their idea.

"Oh no!" I burst at them. "Not a chance!" I shouted.

"They want me to go and fuck with them, is that it?" Barbie said. "Jesus, what dirty rats! Maybe that's what they thought we were trying to do ourselves and they think they can get their share. Jesus, what a turn-up!"

I became really frightened then and my fear and desperation made me put on a great show of fury. This took them aback and a rifle muzzle was poked threateningly in the window at me. I pushed it away and closed the window with a slam and locked the door.

"I guess they may try and arrest us now," I said. "I wish they would, it would solve the problem. But maybe they haven't the nerve."

We sat in miserable silence for another quarter of an hour until there was a gentle knocking on the door. The soldier's face had lost its aggressiveness and he gave me a crooked smile. He held up the packet of cigarettes and waved it at me and I saw it as an olive branch. Barbie saw it just as quickly and we rummaged around and found several more which I handed over. The man waved along the

150

track in the direction from which we had come. I started the engine, wondering if I had misinterpreted him, but he was standing back with his rifle pointed to the ground. We drove away.

"I hid one packet of cigs," Barbie said, plucking two out and lighting them shakily. She stuck one in my mouth.

I felt quite dazed and my hands were shaking on the wheel. Somehow, we found ourselves on the straight road from Giza to the Nile, travelling between dimly lit tenements and shacks. Lights shone from open-air bars or restaurants. Dust seemed suspended in the yellow murk of dim street lights. It was after eight o'clock, and the traffic had eased so that we were able to concentrate our minds sufficiently for Barbie to follow the street map she had picked up in the Alexandria tourist office and for me to follow her directions without having an accident. Our most recent ordeal was temporarily buried beneath the imperative of finding our way in this huge city. It is wonderful how the mind can respond to crisis after crisis when pushed: that is how people survive the seeming impossible repeated stresses of battles in wars. The toll is paid later.

Almost without knowing that it had happened, we were suddenly crossing a long bridge. Looking sideways in quick glances I saw lights reflected on moving water. It was the Nile.

"Turn half right at the end into a main drag and then watch for 23rd July Street," Barbie directed. "There's a couple of hotels marked there. Look for the Ambassador."

The normality of stopping in front of a hotel with a neon sign and going into the lobby to ask for accommodation seemed dreamlike. The hotel was modern and anonymous if a little seedy and did not look expensive. It could have been anywhere in a hot country with a terrazzo floor and a fan turning above the reception counter littered with grubby airline and tourist brochures.

A quiet receptionist spoke good English and recognising my exhausted state and sweaty face attended to me with the minimum of fuss. There was a room with private bath and I could park Landie in the basement. A young porter fetched our bags and conducted me around the corner where a watchman raised the steel grill into the underground parking garage. There was farce when Landie got jammed against the low entrance and the watchman and I had to climb on the roof and struggle with the spare tire lashed to the roofrack to free us, both of us cursing in our own language and streaming sweat in the confined space up against the concrete ceiling.

151

When I told Barbie about the latest ordeal, in our brightly lit room with two simple beds and economical modern furniture, a telephone and a turning fan, all the hazards we had been experiencing seemed to be part of some other world. We stared at each other and laughed, hysterics were not far away.

There was a German restaurant next door to the hotel and we went there for a meal after a quick shower. I was starving and enjoyed the food.

I awoke with the sun streaming in and the noise of the great city rumbling away outside. We ordered breakfast in the room and I was filled with extraordinary lassitude. Safe in the capsule of the hotel, Landie locked away, nobody to bother us, I felt cocooned in a secure haven and did not want go out. Barbie curled up with letters to write and her diary. The morning melted away.

Eventually we rallied. I showered and washed my filthy clothes from yesterday's ordeals and we went for a long walk along the Nile in the bright sunlight of early afternoon. The great river slipped easily past the stone walls constraining it. Feluccas with their tall lateen sails drifted with the current in the calm air.

Opposite, palms and tropical green foliage graced Gezira Island and we walked to the next bridge up-river, taking photographs. A new skyscraper with a television transmitting aerial on the top reflected in the waters of the river, a symbol of the extraordinary march of history in 5,000 years in that place. Trams rattled past and traffic surged, directed by white-clad policemen with batons and whistles. There were people pushing handcarts laden with fresh bread or household goods, men in dark business suits mingled with the striped pyjamas of working men. Women in bright western clothes mixed with others wearing veils. We did not see other Europeans, they were cosseted away in the grand Shepherd's Hotel or in the walled embassy compounds.

Across the river, we walked along the waterfront of Gezira and found a floating restaurant where we thankfully stopped for a cold Coke, then decided to have a late snack lunch, watching the ancient waters of the Nile slip by and the bustle of movement on the opposite bank. Afterwards, crossing back to the eastern bank on the bridge we had driven over in the dark, a policeman stopped us and we were lectured about taking photographs on the bridge. From the end of the bridge, we were back into a section of the city that reminded us of the degradation of Alexandria while we found our way to the Ambassador Hotel.

152

I was still bemused by these two great Egyptian cities which had streets and streets of modern apartments and office buildings in disrepair. I had not realised that the great new curse of Africa was the exploding of populations. In South Africa in those years there was real per capita economic expansion and investment occurring in advance of population growth. Development was leading the way forward and people were forced to follow: much of the social engineering which was part of the morally indefensible apartheid dogma was the result of this. I understood that dilemma.

I had not until then seen the reciprocal effect: in Egypt populations were growing exponentially faster than the physical infrastructure which was stagnant. People were beginning to move into the cities in an expanding tidal wave causing shortages of everything and overloading every facility. Today this is the endemic condition of Africa, then it was only beginning and Egypt was the trail-blazer.

The next morning after a sound sleep, I felt refreshed and optimistic and was up early, ordering breakfast in the room again. But Barbie was not well, tummy upset and bearing a headache. We discussed staying on and decided against it, so I checked out - the hotel bill was surprisingly reasonable - retrieved Landie from the underground lair and we set off to explore Cairo in a mad whirl before moving on to Port Said.

In daylight the road out to Giza was chock-full of small shops and eating places, buses and battered cars crawled along until we left most of the suburbs behind. Palm trees stood beside the road and there was some green vegetation with leaves laden with dust. I noticed the entrance to a grand hotel with a tourist coach standing in the driveway and Europeans waiting about it.

And suddenly there were the pyramids before us rising so solidly and powerfully against the clear blue sky of a windless morning. Rusty barbed wire fenced off the area around them, but I hardly noticed that. There was a parking place and from there I wandered towards the stone giants resting on the rocky plateau, so serene and unmoved by the thousands of years that had passed them by. I saw them as personified even though their shape totally negated that idea. It was the enormous size and obvious age from the wind-eroded face of the great blocks of stone that was overpowering; but there was also a kind of all-knowing superiority that enfolded them. They were so patently artificial with their hard edges, flat planes and immaculate dimensions but it seemed impossible to ignore their seeming animation. They throbbed with brooding, infinitely slow-moving, giant life, incomprehensible but detectable: somnolent in an unknowable timescale but alive. Staring up at the nearest, that of Cheops, I somehow knew that it was watching my puny ant-figure with an other world detachment, just as it had noted the passing by of a million other visitors over all those centuries.

Peddlers of souvenirs came to tell us of their delights and camel-men brought their snuffling animals to us, hung with coloured tassels, little bells and gay saddles. I waved them away, saying that we wanted to have a good look first and they respected this. They had dealt with many tourists before and knew we were captive. A line of camels appeared around a corner, each carrying a tourist. They were fat, white-skinned, middle-aged people mostly but there was a young woman dressed in fashionable blue mini-skirt and high-heels perched awkwardly on her saddle, trying to ignore the embarrassment of exposing her thighs and a glimpse of white panties to the amused looks of the dragomen and the boys carrying trays of souvenirs. Barbie saw the direction of my eyes and said that she was not going on any camel.

"Why, you're wearing respectable Bermuda shorts," I teased. "You've got to go on a camel."

"I'm feeling lousy and I don't want to look a fool," she said. But after we had walked all about and the brooding piles of rock had begun losing the power of their immediate impression, the camel-men approached again.

"How can you go back to Aussie without a picture of yourself on a camel, Barbie?" I said. "I know you're not feeling well, but it's something you have to do."

"I don't see you jumping on one," she complained.

"Who's going to take the picture of you to show your grandchildren?"

But she had wanted to go on a camel all along and allowed me and the camel-man to persuade her. Once she was up, the camel was given a little flick and it shambled off in a trot with Barbie clinging to the saddle and calling out. It was all part of the show, however, and the camel-man quickly caught them up and led his animal around for a while as I took her picture.

The Sphinx stood below the three pyramids brooding on their plateau and was diminished by them. I wondered why the architect had placed this unique image in a subordinate position so that its own marvellous size and strength was lessened. Later I learned that it was part of a complex of temples, carefully oriented streets and vistas leading to the Nile, but walking about on the rough sand and gravel of the hillside below the pyramids there was no sign of that. Excavations were going on at the time and more barbed wire kept us away from them. Workmen's equipment was scattered about.

We drank the inevitable Fantas and Cokes and took more photographs. From the elevation of the base of the pyramids, looking southeastward, the view was over a sea of date palms stretching five or ten miles across the Nile valley. The ribbon of villages following the course of the river was invisible beneath that sea of trees and I told myself that what I was seeing was probably unchanged in five thousand years. It was a dry still day and over the desert the air was sharp and clear. Looking over the valley there was a mist from the moisture breathed out by all those palms and other vegetation. I had read somewhere that there was more water flowing through the sands beneath the Nile than in the upper streams. Seeing the grey mist above the valley, pumped up by vegetation I could understand that.

We moved off. If we had been staying in Cairo longer we would have come back, maybe several times. It was not possible either to absorb all the nuances of the meaning of it all, or to enjoy a range of aesthetic pleasures from the light and atmosphere without many visits. I would have loved to come back at night, when the full moon was shining and the sands were cool. I would have liked to have watched the sun rising and setting, causing the colours to change.

*   *

It took some time to get from one end of Cairo to the other because we got repeatedly lost. From Giza we went directly east, crossing by an upstream bridge. We could see the minarets and dome of a great mosque near the Turkish citadel and it was not difficult to arrive in its vicinity, threading a maze of streets filled with all kinds of human activity.

I enjoyed that part of Cairo, the older part, because the hundreds of small shops, peddlers, street stalls, donkeys, people carrying all sorts of goods on their backs or on handcarts, was how I expected a venerable Arab city to be. There were no decrepit modern tenements falling steadily into ruin; this part was really old and worn with a different kind of patina. Beneath the bulk of the great mosque, there was space and we could have parked and wandered about, but time was passing and Barbie was still feeling lousy. Briefly, I saw a wall and an ornamental gate as fine as in any European medieval city.

Following my nose in a northeasterly direction, we aimed for the main road to Ismailia in the centre of the Canal and at one busy junction I saw a road sign for that town and another for Heliopolis which I knew was in the right direction, but shortly thereafter we moved off the street map that Barbie was using. We drove endlessly and seemed to be going in circles. I stopped several times to ask the way but neither my questions nor the replies were properly understood. Eventually I found someone who spoke some English in a garage and he turned me about. He told us that he was a Jew, which is why he understood English.

Shortly afterwards, a traffic cop appeared alongside on a motor-bike and with enormous relief, I was able to explain my problem. With a grin, he rode ahead purposefully and guided us a couple of miles though outer suburbs until he was sure we were on the right road.

Suddenly we were in the desert again, passing through low hills leading away in yellow and pink distance. I stopped to take photographs and persuaded Barbie to take a couple of strong codeine pills from the emergency medicine supplies. She perked up after a while.

Ismailia had been a British military base for many years and when we reached it, lying amidst palms and the shade of tall mature eucalyptus trees, the evidence was there: colonial buildings, barracks lurking behind barbed wire fences or rough hedges and an atmosphere of calm. The map showed that there was a road that parallelled the Suez Canal all the way to Port Said and I headed in what seemed the right direction and found myself in a cul-de-sac facing a guard post. As I was trying to back round, a group of Egyptian Air Force officers came through the gate, dressed in uniform and very smart. They gathered round and we had a delightful conversation in 'proper' English. If it had not been for their handsome, swarthy faces I might have been twenty years back in time. They put us on the right road, of course, with good wishes and felicitations.

The road along the Canal was a pleasure. The road was sheltered by an avenue of ancient eucalyptus trees and there was no other traffic. We stopped in the shade and watched a convoy of

156

freighters move slowly and majestically past and took photographs. As each ship came abreast, we waved to the white-uniformed figures on the end of the bridge and got a wave back. They were mostly flying the red ensign and I recognised a couple of the funnel markings; they belonged to famous lines that sailed regularly to the Far East.

We came to a boom and a watchman came out to question us. It seemed that we were travelling on the private road of what had been the Canal Company in the good old days and we should not be on it. The watchman was middle-aged and spoke English, he had worked all his life for the Canal Co. I explained that Air Force officers had directed us to this route and he waggled his head.

"It is because you are English, you see. In those days, English always take this road. Now everyone must take desert road."

"What must I do? Go back to Ismailia?" I tried to look sadly desperate.

"I have a wife and children," he said. "My children are having birthdays soon." It was an agreeable solicitation and I fished out some crumpled notes which disappeared rapidly. "You can spare me a cigarette?" he asked, grinning. I gave him my packet. The boom was raised and we were waved through.

"Did you have to pay a toll, or something?" Barbie asked. She had been resting her head, half asleep.

"Something like that," I replied, smiling to myself and feeling high good humour. If only the awful, obnoxious soldiers by the side of the pyramids had been like that, our whole visit to Cairo would have taken on a different flavour. As it was, everything that day was different: the patient dragomen at the Pyramids, the Jewish garage man glad to use his English, the helpful traffic cop, the Air Force officers, the amiable guard at the boom. Spinning along beside the famous Canal with the dappled light of the avenue flashing across Landie I suddenly felt liberated again and happy. I patted Barbie's suntanned thigh beside me and whooped. I began singing discordantly.

Port Said appeared as a line of white buildings on the horizon beyond salt flats which soon moved towards us. Ships lay in the harbour, awaiting passage on the Canal. Work-boats and tugs dragging lighters moved purposefully about. It was a scene with which I felt familiar. Here was a famous crossroad of the whole world. There was the fresh tang of the sea in the air again.

Landie trundled down the straight main street and stopped outside the Hotel de la Poste. They had a room, up on the third floor, for about a pound a night. There was spirited argument over our passports because we were not married, the only time this happened in any hotel on the whole journey. It was against Egyptian law for unmarried people to cohabit. I said it had not been a problem in Cairo. More loud voices on both sides followed and I cheerfully signed a piece of paper absolving the hotel of responsibility. A day or two ago this would have led to gloom and depression, but I passed it off as a joke.

Things were going well now, there was a change in our fortunes and nothing could worry me. Two of the cheerful young men at the reception promptly suggested that Barbie go with them to a jazz club that night while I 'rested' after the arduous journey from Cairo. We laughed together.

There were European tourists from one of the liners in port around that evening when we ate dinner with a bottle of strong red wine from the Nile delta.

PART THREE : EAST AFRICA

CHAPTER ELEVEN : *SS 'LA BOURDONNAISE'*

In the morning Barbie was feeling fit and I was in good spirits. After breakfast we strolled to the post office for mail and then on to where we had been told Thos. Cook's office was, in the next block towards the docks. The streets were straight and relatively clean, the buildings white and in relatively good order. The people about were busy attending to their affairs, there were no hordes and no beggars, this was a prosperous working town, fuelled by the rich artery of the Canal which dominated it. Cook's stood on a corner beside other shipping offices, insurance firms and warehousing companies. This was familiar ground to me and my good feeling continued.

The office itself was somewhat old fashioned with a counter and desks behind, piled with documents in trays. Calenders and old posters advertising famous shipping lines hung on the walls. I asked the clerk if there had been a message from the Alexandria office about us and gave my name. He returned with a short swarthy man with tinted spectacles who introduced himself as the manager.

"Yes, we received a telex two days ago," he said. "I understand what you need and we will arrange everything in due course. You can rely on us. I need some details in the meantime."

"Well, we want to go to Mombasa with my Landrover which is full of camping equipment. We need economical accommodation. It doesn't matter what it is like, we have been travelling all the way from England, sleeping in the desert."

"Yes, yes. I understand all that," he interrupted. He was a bright and intelligent man and spoke rapidly and fluently. I was so used to battling with French and various varieties of pidgin that I was surprised to find my mind had difficulty keeping up with him. Later

I learned that he was Maltese. "I need your names and passport numbers, the dimensions of your Landrover, the number of the Carnet de Passage. All those things."

I told him our names but said that the documents were at the hotel.

"You are not married? That's a pity. It means berths in separate cabins." He frowned and shook his head. "It makes it a little more difficult." He smiled as if relishing the challenge. "Don't worry, I will start working on it. Come back immediately after lunch with your documents and I may have some news."

"When do you think there may be something?" I asked. "We want to make some plans. Two weeks, three weeks?"

"Come back at two o'clock. We shall see." He patted me on the arm.

Outside in the sun, I turned to Barbie. "He seemed a nice little man," she said. "He knows what he's doing anyway. Which is more than we seem to have had recently."

"I like this town," I said. "I just feel good here, it's something about a big port, I suppose, and I can understand everything that's going on for a change."

"Let's have a look in the souvenir shops," she said. "I want to change some money and buy something. Do you realise we've not bought anything in Egypt yet." She was right. Egypt so far had been too fraught for all of the ordinary tourist activities.

We spent an hour in a tourist shop, looking at the usual brass wares, cloths, carved ivory, pottery and leather goods. Port Said had been a transit port for European tourists for nearly a hundred years and, though insistent, the salesmen knew how to stop before giving offence. There were many things that attracted me and I admired the ivories and carved soapstone and alabaster from India. But they were not Egyptian and I wanted local souvenirs. In the end we both decided on big leather pouffes, well sewn with different dyed panels printed in gold with pharaohs' heads and other Egyptian motifs. There were also postcards to buy and Barbie went for some trinkets.

After a snack lunch at the hotel, we strolled back to Cook's to be met by the manager, smiling and gesturing at me. "All is arranged," he said. "You leave this afternoon. Now there is much to be done. You have your documents and travellers' cheques? Where is your vehicle? It has to be measured at the shipping office then go to customs before transport to the vessel. Come, sit down please. Do you want coffee?"

Dear oh dear! Barbie and I sat, bemused. It was happening too fast. What about our exploration down the Nile?

"Please," I gestured. "Please explain. What is the ship, how much is it all to cost? It is so quick. Is there nothing later on....?"

It was explained. We were very lucky as he did not have anything for some weeks that he could firmly book for us. There were always cargo vessels who could take us at the whim of the captain, but we should have to stay in town and check in every day if we were serious about passage. To go on a liner was the best bet and we should take it. It was a French ship, a big ship and the voyage was quick, only ten days. He had problems because we were not married. There was a berth for me but nothing was fixed yet for Barbie. The ship was full and he had told the purser a tale that we were important writers and photographers and about how we had been let down and had to get to Mombasa.

"I worked on their pity," he said, grinning. "They are French and like a little romance, but there is no time to waste. Once you are on board, something will be arranged."

I looked at Barbie and she smiled, shrugging her shoulders. "We'd better go for it," I said and she nodded. "What about the cost?" I asked the manager.

Time went into slow motion as we raced about, checking out of the hotel, posting cards to our families telling them our new movements, taking Landie to the shipping office and then the customs shed. Back to Cook's to collect the tickets and the shipping documents for Landie and then back to the wharf in the Manager's old Citroën. All the cars in North Africa seemed to be Citroëns. Barbie and I were both booked in as Economy-Third class, whatever that meant, at about £70 each and Landie with all the various charges cost 135.91 Egyptian pounds, about £110. I reckoned that the total cost was about what it would have been to travel overland to Uganda according to my original plans. But we were speeding up our traverse considerably, covering in ten days what would have taken two months. It could not be helped, and somehow there was a god on our side now.

We could have been just one day late, one extra day sightseeing or languishing in Alexandria or Cairo and we would have missed the ship. Fate works in strange ways, but it surely does seem to take a hand.

Petrol could not be carried and I had about eight gallons in cans in the back. It was low-octane Egyptian petrol which had not

161

suited Landie, causing her to knock, overheat and blow out blue exhaust smoke so I was not sorry to see it go, but it was an investment. The Cook's manager vaguely suggested that I could have sold it to a garage but it was too late now. He then looked meaningfully at his car. It was a work of minutes to pour it into his tank and a couple of old oil cans that were quickly found. He asked if I had any spares that I did not need as it was almost impossible to get such things in Egypt then because of strict currency control. I thought quickly because I felt obliged to him and a 'tip' seemed inappropriate. He was not a servant. I fished about in the back and came up with a packet of unused spark plugs still in their wrappings and a couple of spare shiny spanners. It seemed a small gift but he was as delighted as if they were gold. If they did not fit his car, he could sell them on the black market.

A battered old lighter was moored alongside a wharf and planks had been set as a bridge. A bunch of stevedores watched as I lined up Landie's wheels and awkwardly drove onto the deck of the lighter, jamming the brakes on fiercely as it rocked in the water.

"Keep the keys but don't lock the doors," the manager told me. "Your baggage will be safe." I looked at the disturbed pile of dusty gear in the back and wondered if it would be there at Mombasa, but there was nothing to be done. A small motor tug came alongside and the lighter's crew cast off. Landie looked quite bizarre heading off into the harbour perched on top of the rusty vessel.

I still did not know which ship we were travelling on and asked the manager as we got into his car again. "It's in that line of moorings," he said, gesturing vaguely.

Back at customs, we had to clear our own baggage and have our passports stamped by an immigration officer. Then we were at the passenger jetty and shaking the manager's hand. "You have looked after us so well...."

"Always remember Thomas Cook at Port Said," he said with a smile. How could I ever forget.

A launch with some other passengers carried us out into the busy harbour. Two lines of ships lay to the mooring buoys; freighters and tankers and a naval destroyer in what looked like a Russian design. We stopped at a British India Line ship to let off some people going to Bombay then went around its stern towards the second line.

A big black-hulled cargo-passenger vessel of about 17,000 tons with white upperworks and a squat black funnel lay straight ahead. It was the *La Bourdonnaise*, a French liner of Messageries Maritimes, trading between Marseilles and Mauritius via Djibouti, Mombasa, Madagascan ports and Reunion. Its hull was freshly painted and a sailor in well-pressed uniform waited at the head of the ladder to help us on board. I smelled the familiar odours of a steam ship: sulphurous furnace smoke, boiler steam, fresh paint, a whiff of cooking.

A petty officer directed us to the purser's office and a brisk youngish man greeted us in impeccable English.

"Mr. Montgomery. A very famous name, of course." He smiled. "And Miss Ellis. Welcome on board! I hope your problems are now solved, please relax and enjoy the voyage." I mumbled something agreeable and wondered what story the little Cook's manager had told. "I have a berth for you, Mr. Montgomery, in the second class with some very nice priests going to Reunion. Miss Ellis, I'm afraid I still have to make arrangements for you, but it will be in a simple cabin in what used to be called steerage class." He spread his hands apologetically. "I have had to move one or two people and they have been ashore until now. I hope you can be patient with us."

"Please," I protested. "We very much appreciate that you have taken us at the last minute and we don't mind any inconvenience. We have been travelling very roughly and your ship is a holiday for us."

"You are very accommodating. We shall arrange everything as quickly as possible. Meantime, here are details of the ship and our services. You are booked by third class but I have given instructions that you can use the second class lounge. You may find more congenial company there. But you will eat in the third class diningroom. The food is good even if it is simple." He chatted away and I kept nodding and smiling.

I had quite forgotten, over the last weeks, how great was the gulf between the standards Europeans expected from hotels, air lines and passenger ships and those which we had come to accept as normality. I suppose this pleasant officer may have expected a couple of snooty Brits ready to complain about any slight, whereas I would have accepted the deck of a dhow.

"Well, he was O.K.," said Barbie as a steward took us down corridors to a small saloon up towards the bow where our bags had been left. Barbie had to wait there while I was taken to my cabin in second class. It was a four-berth cabin, cramped but well fitted out with neat cupboards, two wash basins and room for empty suitcases. Three large middle-aged men were sitting on the lower bunks and a small armchair talking quietly, dressed in white clerical frocks. They were my companions, the priests, and very pleasant gentlemen they were. I usually saw them at night and morning, they were second class, and they always greeted me with grave courtesy. If I went to the cabin during the day to pick up a book or to shower and change, one or another might be there quietly reading his Bible or other holy book and fingering his rosary. One spoke some English and was prepared to make a joke and laugh. He invariably enquired if I was well and if I was enjoying the voyage. I remember those big, quiet men with affection and wondered at their devotion to a long missionary life of celibacy in the colonies.

There was a small open deck area available to third class, just forward of the main superstructure off which opened a lounge with simple furniture like a café, and that opened into a dining saloon with long communal tables and metal chairs. Those were our public areas. The cabins occupied a warren of alleyways on three decks which we explored in the next couple of days. There was a laundry, drying and ironing room which reminded me of a naval ship with coloured pipes and electrical conduits running overhead and along the bulkheads.

I don't remember exactly how many third class passengers there were, but it must have been about thirty. I suppose there was about the same number in the other two classes, but their accommodation was appropriately larger in ascending order. Second class had a portion of the promenade deck and all of the boat deck for their use, while first class occupied the after half of the upper-deck with a fixed swimming pool, outdoor dancing and games area.

Dragomen and salesmen had come aboard and the deck was a bazaar with much of the same kind of tourist goods displayed as we had seen in the shops that morning. Somehow I would have liked to have bought from these traditional men on the ship; it was exactly as described by many travellers on their way to India, Australia and the Far East throughout the great imperial age. My father described similar hawkers coming aboard his hospital ship in Port Said during the aftermath of the horrendous Gallipoli campaign in 1915, nearly fifty years before, and I thought I may have some old faded photographs of the scene at home.

Eventually, a steward fetched Barbie as our fellow third class passengers began filling the saloon. She came back a bit disconcerted but nevertheless relieved.

"I'm sharing a funny old cabin right down there somewhere with a young French dolly with a young kid. It's hot as hell and I'm not sure about the kid. It'll probably keep me awake at night. But the dolly is pleasant enough. Her husband is there with her now and he was sharing with her." She shrugged. "They were O.K., but they're probably mad about having him move out for me. I explained that *mon homme*, that's you, fat Den, was sleeping somewhere with some priests and that seemed to cheer them up a bit."

"It's only ten days," I said, "and we are lucky."

"Don't worry, Den. Anything to be away from those cungy cities and all that shitty business... Pity about not going down the Nile, though."

"I know," I sighed.

We tried the second class saloon bar and lounge, but it was not at all congenial, although I did appreciate the concession which had been made. That first evening, after showering and changing in our respective quarters, we went up chattering happily and full of good humour.

The lounge was seedy with furniture and decor somewhat like a 1930s seaside hotel. The people there were mostly middle-aged and sitting about rather stiffly, sipping aperitifs. *Petite bourgeois*, I supposed to myself, how interesting. I had not had much social contact with numbers of French people of different classes. The few that I had known well had worked for trading companies in West Africa and they had always been bright, full of fun and with a different style to the British. I wondered if we would get to know any of these people.

At the bar we ordered drinks and the barman served us with surly bad humour. We were laughing and joking and happy and he showed patronising condescension. I wondered if it was because we were British or whether it offended some personal snobbery to have been ordered to serve us.

"Sour bastard, isn't he?" Barbie commented. But when his regular customers came up to order he fawned over them, engaging them in elaborate conversation, enquiring solicitously about their trips ashore. He smiled readily but his eyes remained cool. We ordered another round and watched the darkness settle and the lights come on in Port Said. After a while we had enough. "We won't come back here, unless our own crowd is worse," Barbie commented and I agreed. We never went back.

We slipped away from our mooring and went down the Canal in darkness. From the small open deck area in our humble third class quarters we watched the dark loom of land slip by, punctuated by lights on beacons at regular intervals.

Suddenly, the feeling of this latest great change stole up on us and the reaction of the last days was heavy. We went early to our beds without bothering about dinner.

In the morning we were off Suez, at the southern outlet of the Canal. From the sea, it was a small town of white buildings dotted about the curve of the bay. Behind, bare brown hills rose gently to the low skyline. The desert was king there, not a scrap of vegetation showed. I watched for a while as we drew away: it was the last sight of the Sahara and I felt a powerful twinge of regret that we were not driving south, along the green ribbon of the Nile dividing that humming desolation. For the desert was alive, in its own way.

Already memories were beginning to coagulate into pools of nostalgia: pictures of the sun setting while the solitary shepherd walked across the blasted gravel plain for a cigarette, the sun rising from the pale dunes on Djerba, the rows of gravestones at Tobruk, the dull waves of sand and stone at El Alamein...

The days telescoped into monotony. There was no attempt to entertain the third class passengers. There was no swimming pool or library, no music, only the three public areas, and the dining room was open only for meals: so it was one's cabin, the saloon or the open deck, which was partly shaded by an awning. Barbie and I luxuriated in the pleasant ennui for most of the time, certainly in the beginning. We had hours to laze about and chat about inconsequential matters, mull over our journey so far, bury some of the unpleasant events and renew our comradely ideals.

It was incredibly humid going down the Red Sea. We were used to heat, much higher temperatures in fact, but the humidity was extraordinary. The sky was a pale blue and the sea reflected it, heaving gently with hardly any breeze to disturb it. The silver horizon merged sea and sky. My sleeping cabin had forced ventilation, but there was no air-conditioning in those days. In third class, whether the public rooms or the cabins, there was no forced draft either, which surprised me. Even Spartan naval vessels would have had fan-driven air circulating throughout the ship. The portholes were fitted with long metal wind-scoops to harvest a breeze, but as there was no wind, they harvested little more than a gentle draft from the ship's passage.

166

Barbie had worked out some sort of communication system with the French girl in her cabin so she and her husband could have some privacy every day.

"They like to be alone with their baby. They're rather sweet and not long married. I wish I could talk properly with them. I think he works for the government like most of them."

Occasionally, I would go down with Barbie to her cabin to do my laundry or keep her company while she did her chores. I did not like to intrude even though Barbie said that the other girl wanted to reciprocate with 'private time' for us, since Barbie was not allowed to come to my cabin, even if she had wanted.

We never spent long in her cabin because of the heat and humidity. It was the worst I have ever known: temperature in the high nineties Fahrenheit and humidity around 100%. On one occasion, Barbie had been ironing our clothes and I went down to sort and collect. I stripped off my shirt and she was down to her shorts and bra. We sat quietly on her bunk talking, opposite a wind-scoop, and the sweat was running down our chests in little rivers. We smoked a cigarette and watched the sweat streaming on our bodies. "We have not moved for maybe twenty minutes," I said in awe. "And it just keeps pouring out. I think I can actually see it pumping out of my skin! No wonder we are always thirsty and put the Cokes and Fantas away so easily."

A great advantage of our humble status was the cheapness of everything. There was a pantry with a hatch into our saloon which was open whenever there was a steward on duty. It sold cold Coca Cola and Fanta, beers, cigarettes, wine, Pernod and a few sundry toiletries like soap, tooth paste, Ambre Solair sun oil, razor blades, baby lotions, aspirin and tampons. The beers and Coke were the equivalent of sixpence (2½p) and a big shot of Pernod and ice was threepence (1¼p). There always seemed to be someone at the hatch buying cold drinks.

At meal times we all sat at the long tables together. Breakfast was croissants, long bread-sticks, butter and preserves. Lunch was cold meats and salads and there were two courses only at dinner. The meat, chicken or fish dishes, roast or casserole, were served out separately by our two hardworking stewards and then great bowls of rice, vegetables and salads were placed at intervals along the tables. We never had exactly the same dish twice in ten days. There were always baskets of fresh bread rolls and jugs of iced water and red wine at lunch and dinner. When any of these receptacles became empty, they were refilled if needed. The desserts were creme caramel, different cakes with a sweet sauce and fresh fruits and the coffee was dark and strong. You could eat and drink as much as you pleased and the evening meal was always a merry one as the wine jugs emptied and were topped up for the second and third time. The wine was Algerian or Provencal and was brought from the cold rooms in big 20 litre plastic containers with a tap, streaming with condensation.

The quality of food and wine, as simple as it was, was unvaryingly good. After all, this was a French ship and we were getting the same rations as the crew. What it was like in the 'upper classes' I do not know; no doubt it was rather more varied and fancy with several small courses served with elaborate style, but I doubt if it could have been bettered in quality. I never heard a serious complaint from the other passengers, who were all on intimate terms with the two stewards and there was much badinage and calling back and forward during meal times. I wished that I had been fluent in French and could have followed all the conversations and shouted jokes at meals. They were always jolly and comradely, like a giant family reunion, sitting together at those long tables. We were treated with a certain reserved friendly politeness, but only because we were British and could not fit in properly. We were the only foreigners.

Most of our fellows were young technicians or junior administrative assistants, clerks I suppose, going out to Madagascar or Reunion in the French colonial service. They were married and some had young children who had to be urged to eat in the stifling heat at mealtimes. There was always a murmur from the mothers and the occasional exasperated command: *"Mange, mange! Vite, Vite, Claudine!"*

There was also a section of regular soldiers in their late twenties and thirties who came to dinner in immaculate tropical uniforms and polished shoes. They must have washed and ironed daily as if they were in barracks and I was impressed by them. Some drank a lot but there was never any bad behaviour. They were supervised by a senior sergeant with fine black moustache and two rows of medal ribbons, accompanied by his flamboyant wife. They were going to Antananarivo. The sergeant reminded Barbie and I of our good friend, 'Le Gros', at Bouchera. I wondered if they had been both companions-in-arms and antagonists and I would have liked to have questioned him about the Algerian War to have got an opposing slant to the story.

168

There were three others who spoke English and we spent time with them, because by chance we were compatible. Notably, they were private passengers going to Mauritius. There was a quiet, scholarly middle-aged man with glasses, who read a lot and said little about himself even though he was prepared to discuss any subject. The other two were delightful: a poet with a slim, almost emaciated body who had lived eight years in Australia, and his lovely half-Chinese girlfriend from Indo-China, Cambodia I think. The poet had a chequered career. I guessed that he had gone to Australia to escape the army draft. The French had been engaged in several colonial wars and civil disorder since 1945 in Indo-China, West Africa and Algeria, while we British had been concerned about war and strife in Palestine, Cyprus, Malaya, Aden and the Kenya Mau Mau. All of those conflicts were still close in time then.

We talked about those things as well as any number of literary subjects and I thoroughly enjoyed our little poet and his shy girl. Barbie was delighted to find someone who understood her and could respond to particular Aussie witticisms and reminisce about Australian places and events.

We usually gathered before lunch and dinner. Barbie and the Indo-Chinese girl would have a couple of beers while the poet and I had a few Pernods and ice. He had already been to Mauritius, maybe he had family there, and he regaled Barbie and I with stories about how pleasant life was; the informality and lack of racial consciousness, the light hand of the British colonial regime, lack of pretentious tourism, the mix of cultures and the amazing tropical climate. I have never been to Mauritius, except for an airline stopover, and I should have gone in those days as our friend described it, before packaged tourism began in the 1970s.

We passed through the narrow Straits of Bab el Mendeb at the end of the Red Sea in the night and tied up in the port of Djibouti one morning. Djibouti was the French enclave opposite to Aden and looking out at the town from our deck space there was nothing much to see. There was a flat, dusty town sitting on a flat dusty land. Cranes moaned as cargo was discharged and lethargic dockworkers shifted it about and a forklift truck moved pallets into warehouses.

Parties from the 'upper classes' went ashore to be taken away in buses on some excursion and a notice had been put up on our board inviting us to join. I do not think any of our class went ashore and Barbie and I decided against it. "What is there to see?" the poet asked raising his hands in dismay. "Arabs, Arabs, and some Arab

169

houses? Camels and many, many flies! French officials walking proudly and beggars whining. Pouf!"

But there was a dry breeze off the land and the sweat on our bodies cooled and left a fine powdering of salt rather than running in streams.

* *

The next day we were off Cape Guardafui, the easternmost point of Africa; rounding the ancient Horn where civilised sailors had been active for three thousand years. The thought made me realise how pretentious was the fuss we Europeans made about Christopher Columbus.

I had now completed a circumnavigation of all four compass points around my own continent of Africa in just less than six months. I spent several hours of that day standing at the rail, thinking, and marvelling at my great adventure. And there was so much still to do. I told myself that if I had gone up the Nile, I would not have seen the sight before me. How many people have seen the easternmost point of Africa? There is always a balance to everything.

Cape Guardafui was a bare yellow rock cliff rising from the blue sea and as we rounded it the weather abruptly changed. A fierce gale blew down the coast, churning the sea to a dark blue laced with spume and tumbled by white horses. Over the land, sand and dust streamed out in orange plumes from the gaunt cliffs. The sky directly above was a deep blue and the air, whilst still at furnace heat, was dry. It was too windy for the usual deck activities and we were all crowded into the saloon that day. The beer flowed and it was rowdy. I kept going out on deck to watch the coastline passing, forcing my way through the door which was kept closed for the first time in days. In the late afternoon, we were out of sight of land and the wind moderated.

One evening Barbie and I were on the deck, watching the bow-wave crashing below us. "You know, I'm getting fed up with being with people all the time, every bloody minute," she said. "Going down to my cabin is not much fun and there's no chance of being alone. I think about the good old Sahara a lot."

I agreed. On big passenger liners on which we had both travelled before, there was always plenty of deck space and several public rooms where one could promenade or sit quietly away from the mob.

"We could always sneak up onto the fo'c'sle," I suggested.
"Where is that? Don't give me your navy-type bullshit."

"There's a door that connects our laundry area with the crew's quarters and just beyond there's a ladder going up to a hatch which opens onto the fo'c'sle by the anchor cable winches," I explained. "There's no sign actually prohibiting passengers from going through that door although I suppose there's a notice somewhere. But naturally, we can't read French can we?"

"Been doing some exploring, have you?" she said. "Come on, it's quite late, let's go."

We sneaked through and up onto the steel fo'c'sle deck, right up near the bows and spent sublime time there alone in the warm night air, the ship swinging against the stars, our passage silent except for the faint swish of our wash below and out of sight. The constant murmur and distant rumble of motors and engines was stilled. There was no moon at that time of the night, but that made it more magical in a way. The stars shone brightly and we both picked out the southern cross for the first time, a nostalgic moment for us citizens of the Southern Hemisphere. If anybody saw us from the bridge, nothing was ever said about it.

On the 11th August, we crossed the Equator, almost in line with the port of Kisimayo in southern Somalia and Mount Kenya 600 kilometres inland. Our voyage was coming to an end.

A notice was put up saying that all passengers were invited to a *gala soirée* in the First Class from 8 o'clock. Rules for *le smoking* dress would be relaxed for the occasion. We decided to go and had to delve into our suitcases to find 'proper' clothes. I dragged out dark slacks, shoes, my only tie and a white shirt for Barbie to iron along with her silk blouse and a fancy mini-skirt. She even found some stockings and high-heels. The poet's girlfriend wanted to join us I think, but he would have none of it.

"I'm not going to pander to those *bourgeois* ideas," he declaimed. "It would be degrading for such nobility as us." Before Barbie could retort, he smiled. "But you go and enjoy yourselves, my children. Drink a toast for me! Frankly, I have nothing to wear and would disgrace you by becoming disgustingly drunk." We were the only ones from Third Class who braved the social divide.

Our dinner was as usual although the army platoon was in good form, quaffing a lot of beer and teasing those of their number who had not crossed the line before. We showered and changed afterwards.

The chains separating the classes on the deck two levels above our humble section had been taken down and we felt strange walking

171

along the length of scrubbed promenade deck to where we heard music and laughter. The First Class lounge was spread across the full width of the ship at the after end of the superstructure with sliding doors opening onto a small games area with a swimming pool.

"How the mighty live in comfort," Barbie remarked. "I could have lived in that pool coming down the Red Sea."

The 'upper classes' were mostly in evening dress and some distinguished looking gentlemen had put on miniature medals and decorations. There was one party grouped together who seemed to be very important people, maybe an ambassador, governor or army general with his aides and their wives. Coloured streamers had been strung about and the others all wore paper hats from their dinner parties. A small band was playing dance music.

We found a table near the dance floor and staked our claim to it. We received some smiles from those about us and a pleasant woman leaned over to make some welcoming and enquiring remarks. I could not be bothered to use my pidgin French so excused myself. *"Excusez-moi, nous sommes Anglais,"* I said and the lady turned to explain to her companions. They all beamed at us and nodded and we smiled and nodded back.

"You see, Barbie," I said. "The old Frogs really like us Brits underneath it all. Now, let's do it in style."

I ordered a bottle of non-vintage champagne and we had a jolly time, dancing to the staid foxtrot and waltz music, and laughing and joking. The purser came over to ask us how the voyage had been and I assured him that we had been quite comfortable and the food had been excellent. He was pleased about that and chatted for a while.

Later there was a prize-giving for sports and other competitions in First Class during that section of the voyage and the Captain made a bit of a speech. It was good fun and reminded us of the other world. Naturally, I thought about crossing the line in the *Klostertor* about four months previously, and told Barbie all about the crew singing in the steel box awash with Beck's beer bottles and the full moon shining on the Atlantic. Barbie reminisced about parties on the P & O liner crossing over from Australia to Europe. It was a good evening.

*   *

Two days later we approached the coast of Kenya and Mombasa was lying in rich greenery on top of grey coral cliffs. Coconut palms waved amidst a riot of big leafy trees and casuarina pines. I fancied I could smell perfume mixed with the distinct smell of wet earth and woodsmoke coming off the land. We were coming into tropical East Africa, far from the deserts of the north.

CHAPTER TWELVE : *ASHORE IN THE LAND OF ZENJ*

Arabs, Persians, Indians, Greeks, Jews, Phoenicians, Indonesians and Roman citizens travelled to East Africa by sea across the ocean before the birth of Christ. Ptolemy, the great Egyptian geographer, used the name Azania to describe the coast of Somalia and northern Kenya but the Arabs always called East Africa the lands of the Zenj or Zanj, the Black People. That is how Zanzibar got its name: 'the coast of Black People'.

Most of British eastern and southern Africa had become politically independent by 1965, the dates being: Sudan 1956, Kenya 1963, Tanganyika 1961, Uganda 1962, Malawi 1964, Zambia 1964 and Zanzibar in 1963. Zanzibar suffered instant revolution when thousands of Arab-descended Swahilis were massacred with Tanganyikan government connivance and forced union with Tanganyika followed. The new state was called Tanzania. Botswana, Lesotho and Swaziland were still colonies but would have their independence a year later.

Southern Rhodesia, which had internal self-government long before World War II, had been unable to negotiate a constitution with Britain. It was in November 1965 when UDI was declared followed by nearly fifteen years of growing civil disorders escalating into widespread, increasingly vicious guerilla warfare. The Union of South Africa, of course, had become an independent British Dominion in 1910 and a Republic in 1961. Namibia was a pawn of South African politicians in their disputes with the United Nations and although it had more than one internal self-governing constitution, it did not become politically independent for many years.

None of the newly-independent states were economically self-sufficient and later became clients to Britain, the Western banking system or South Africa. Resentment at this economic dependency and an inability to improve the average income or quality of life of their exponentially exploding populations led to many years of blaming European colonialism and 'neo-colonialism' for their problems, until the distance in time became so great that those excuses and accusations became increasingly farcical and counter-productive. Soviet and Chinese propaganda infused the continent and perpetuated the belief that European colonialism was the source of Africa's failures and Marxism was the panacea.

The South African government's aggressive and obdurate racism, evidenced by its *apartheid* policies, fuelled the fire of anti-European and anti-capitalist sentiment and concentrated the distorted vision of leftwing intellectual liberalism in the West.

In 1965, South African *apartheid*, though universally condemned , had not yet become such a powerful rallying point and propaganda tool for Soviet agencies who later took the Cold War to Africa and precipitated the terrible wars in Angola and Mozambique and finally defeated the illegal Rhodesian regime.

Whatever everyday changes had occurred by 1965 were trivial and cosmetic compared to those which were going to follow. 'Independence' was still very close to all those countries when we travelled through them. Politicians were excited by their new power and still at the stage of trumpeting success, establishing their own style and striving for ideals. The bureaucracy still operated efficiently with British systems.

We arrived in East Africa at a time when tension between aspirations for independence and the departing British administrations was safely over and yet the countries still operated in the old ways in every practical way for two overland travellers. It was to travel in Africa at this particular time that inspired me to carry out the grand expedition which had been that vague dream for several years. I was disappointed that Sudan had to be left out of our journeys and I was determined to experience something of all the others.

Perhaps the most notable attribute of sub-Sahara Africa at that time was the emptiness of the countries and the compactness of the towns and cities. The population of Kenya, for example, in 1950 was 5,500,000 and Nairobi 125,000, only about half of whom were native Africans. By 1990, population explosion had increased numbers to approaching 30,000,000 and greater Nairobi was a sprawl of at least 1,500,000 people, 70% living in shantytowns. Mombasa, when we were there, had a population of no more than 200,000 living mostly on the island, today greater Mombasa is difficult to define and the population is maybe a million, but who knows? A proper census has not taken place in most African countries since independence.

It is difficult to remember how empty Africa was and how orderly and neat the towns were in 1965.

[Some statistics have been added in the Appendix at the end of this book.]

*   *

Standing at the rail as we entered Mombasa's Kilindini harbour we looked down from our eminence. Sliding quietly and swiftly by, impressions were picked up. It was the lushness of the vegetation which immediately impressed of course. Great baobabs clustered at the edge of the grey coral cliffs together with coconut palms, varieties of giant tropical figs, flame trees and spathodeas with their brilliant red blooms. Casuarina pines mingled with broad-leafed indigenous trees. Pawpaw and mango trees grew in backyards and the grass was a brilliant green. The red corrugated-iron roofed bungalows of the residential areas were mostly hidden behind all that foliage and there were no high-rises poking above the tree line. The streets of double-storied shops, offices and small apartment buildings in the commercial centre showed themselves in shifting glimpses. Mombasa, from the sea, seemed to have been placed haphazardly within a giant park. The off-white and yellow desert colours of North Africa, to which we had become deeply accustomed, were gone.

The customs and immigration formalities were confusing for us because none of our Third Class passengers were landing and we had to find our way about the unfamiliar First Class section to find out what to do. Of course, we were at the end of all the queues so by the time we had been processed and got ourselves on shore with our bags it was after 4 o'clock. It was not possible to clear Landie through customs that day although I was able to be sure that she had been landed. The ship was leaving early the next morning.

We shared a cab with another passenger up town and asked for a cheap hotel and the driver dropped us off at the Metropole Hotel. It was owned by an Indian family and was a bit rough and ready but had everything we needed including big baths and hot water. The room heaved gently to the motion of the ship and the noise of cars and people in the street was strange. The street sounds were different to those of North Africa. There were musical African voices instead of the guttural intonation of Arabic. But it was more than that, there was the unmistakable swish of the breeze in a coconut palm outside and the timbre of the noises was different. We were in the tropics and on the coast and the air itself was different, moist and rich with new odours and smells. Gone was the pervasion of dry sourness of Alexandria and Cairo, in Mombasa there was a pungency of wet earth and thriving green vegetation with a whiff of vegetable decay and mould. Indian curry smells wafted to the bedroom from the kitchen below.

Being an Indian hotel, the food was always a variety of curries and some of them were very hot, but we did not mind and the people were kind and helpful to us. The first evening we were early to bed.

In the morning, the priority was to get Landie and we walked down the streets until we found a cab to take us to the docks. A Sikh customs officer was on duty wearing a navy-blue turban together with his neatly pressed British-style white shirt and long shorts.

Again, I found myself confused by language and amused at myself. Because he was an official and a dark-skinned man I instinctively began talking in a sort of West African pidgin only to have him replying in educated English. It was some days before I lost this impulse. Barbie and I had begun to invent 'private' words for various of our possessions and everyday routines, a sort of shorthand and comfortable cocooning of ourselves against the strangeness of the human world we were travelling through. Until the end of the journey, we kept it up without second thoughts and years later I still used some of the words especially when camping or travelling in the bush. Some became implanted in my own family and we use them today.

There was some formality with Landie and I had to declare that we would be travelling on within six months. I ascertained that Kenya, Uganda and Tanzania still operated a customs union except for some goods like liquor and cigarettes which had different excise duties. Those particular differences were already beginning to expand and in a few years caused the breakdown of the customs union and eventually the failure of joint East African cooperative administrations which had been set up by the British. Political independence in East Africa led to bureaucratic retrogression and conflict, not progress.

A drizzle began falling out of a leaden sky and the inside of Landie smelled of a mixture of desert dust and gathering tropical mould. Everything was filthy and covered with a film of pale dust.

177

Everything felt sticky or greasy in the damp air whereas we had been used to the feel of dry powder. It was strange driving on the left again along the streets of Mombasa, the first time since embarking at Newhaven thousands of miles before.

We had a rough street map and we drove about, locating the Post Office and the banks. The business centre of Mombasa was quite small and I quickly mastered the few main streets. Away from the centre there were tracts of open grassland studded with dark African figs with scattered buildings along embryo streets. There were some marvellous old baobabs. At the bank we picked up our mail and changed money, I filled up with petrol and drove north across the clanking old toll-bridge to the suburb of Nyali, to the Nyali Beach Hotel which I had heard about often enough. On the way we passed through some suburbia. Iron-roofed, verandahed colonial bungalows rested in large gardens filled with brightly coloured shrubs and flowering plants, poinsettia, crotons, hibiscus, golden shower creepers, brilliant flame trees, shady spathodeas and a few jacarandas.

The sun came out and the greens of vegetation and the brilliance of the flowers changed to a bright glare. It was amazingly different to what we had been accustomed. I kept exclaiming at it all and I felt a kind of liberation to be within a world that was more familiar to me, the Africa that was my home, and yet in its own way was different. This was tropical East Africa, neither the forests of Nigeria nor the temperate coast of Natal. The adventure was continuing and it was all exciting. I was not sure what was going through Barbie's mind, but she was also full of good spirits.

The Nyali Beach was a colonial hotel, two wings of bedrooms angled off from the central reception hall, public lounge and dining room. There was a terrace in front with steps leading down to an open-air sitting area and a polished cement dance floor. A path led away between stone pergolas with bougainvillaea trained over them. There were beds of canna lilies, hibiscus and variegated crotons. Flowering trees made some shade and the path went on through some bushes to the brilliant white coral sand of the beach.

Barbie and I wandered down to the beach and gazed at the perfection of fine white sand, the maze of green and blue tinted water over the reef before us and the splash of white water where the ocean swells were breaking on the outer bastion of coral. The sun lay heavy on our heads and the little beach was deserted at midday. A swimming platform bobbed at anchor offshore. Looking north along the line of the shore the shapes of a few beach cottages loomed within the foliage of trees and the feathery heads of coconut palms towered over them. The shining beach was deserted at first sight and then I picked out the dark figure of a solitary fisherman sitting beside his beached dug-out canoe tending his net or lines. Further along, the sweep of sea was fringed by wilderness scrub, casuarinas and palms.

"This coast is a paradise," I said. "It's almost empty and just look at this beach and sea." I waved my arms about. "It's just fantastic!"

"Come, Den, we have to paddle in the Indian Ocean. It's my first time!" Barbie kicked off her sandals and I followed her. The water was cool to our feet which had been in contact with the hot sand, but it was a balmy cool, perhaps a little warmer than the water at Djerba Island. We splashed about for a while. "It's paradise," I called to Barbie and she called back enthusiastically.

*   *

On the verandah we read our mail, each absorbed in that other world for a while as always. Which was the real world? It was difficult to tell sometimes. I called for a Tusker beer and we talked quietly of our situation and then I suggested that to-day had to be the first 'civilised' holiday since leaving England.

"Let's do it all properly," I said. "We can start with lunch here."

The lunch was very civilised, proper table linen and several pieces of shining cutlery. The beer was ice-cold and the food stodgy English-colonial. The others in the dining room were vacationing settler families from up-country. I looked about with interest at the men with neatly cut hair, longish shorts and long stockings with shiny shoes or sensible leather sandals. Their wives wore printed cotton frocks and their children were scrubbed and well-behaved. Cheerful talk and laughter filled the room with its open windows looking over the gardens to the ocean, but it was genteel. Me with my scuffed North African sandals and broken toe nails and Barbie in her crumpled mini-skirt were out of place, but we spoke English and knew which knives and forks to use so we were O.K. The waiters in their immaculate white uniforms, sashes and red fezzes served slowly and with dignity; their rough, very black Swahili faces smiling gently at us.

The heavy meal sent us to our beds back at the Metropole for a siesta and we emerged in the cool of the evening to bath and dress. We unpacked and I wore slacks, shirt and tie for the second time and Barbie found a smart evening outfit which she had brought over from Australia a couple of years before. There was a decent restaurant attached to the 'Supercorte' petrol service station with its sign of a fire-breathing black gargoyle on a yellow background and we ate there for the first of several times. It was formal enough to dress up to, but had a relaxed atmosphere. The menu was pretty standard: steaks, fish and chicken dishes with salads and the wine was ordinary French and Italian which had not travelled well, but it was exactly what we wanted. The holiday was continuing.

Afterwards we found our way to the Casablanca Nightclub. Tables were set out in two levels around a dance floor and a small space for the band. It was well-lit and the decor was simple. When we went in, the band was taking a break and eyes switched to watch us come in. All of the people already seated were black and to my surprise and embarrassment there was a low hiss from one corner. I felt Barbie stiffen at my side and I wondered for a moment if there was some kind of colour-bar which we had infringed. But the people at the hotel had recommended the place, so I ignored the hostility and led the way to an empty table at one side. A waiter came to take our order as if nothing was amiss and shortly afterwards the band began playing. Apart from that disconcerting hiss which created a feeling of affront and inferiority, there was no problem and some young whites and Indians came in a noisy group later and the 'nightclub' atmosphere grew with the passing of the evening. The lights were dimmed and the band's singer was quite good with a range of ballads from a year or two ago.

"This band's not bad," Barbie told me. "In fact it's terrific!"

We danced and had several beers. Near midnight a good-looking blonde stripper came on and performed with fair enthusiasm, dancing for several minutes with perfectly shaped bare breasts bouncing about before removing the last garment and scampering away. There was a limbo dancer and then a group did a kind of 'African' war dance dressed in loin cloths and feathers. The place was full with cheerful partying people by the time the cabaret started and there was a good racial mixture, so the hissing when we went in remained unexplained. 'Nairobi' was a pop song at the time in England and the film, *Born Free*, had long runs in the West End in London that year. 'Nairobi' always seemed to be playing in Kenya

180

bars or nightclubs when we were there. 'Wimowe', a Xhosa click-song, and 'Skokiaan' from South Africa, were also popular.

We fell into bed happily in the early hours of the morning.

The next few days were spent in exploring Mombasa, doing a bit of shopping and getting Landie serviced properly for the first time since Tunis. I was a bit anxious about the result of the servicing because of the hundreds of miles of potholed tarmac we had travelled through Libya and the low-octane petrol I had been forced to use. But the bolt tightening I had done at the campsite in Spain had done the trick. A new set of plugs and points, carburettor clean and tune-up, new filters and the usual lubrication and oil-change had her running sweetly. It had not been expensive.

There was a Mombasa municipal information office and branch of the AA of East Africa in Kilindini Road. In both there were bright and efficient white settler women in charge who were a great help. The AA office provided several maps, including a detailed set of all the game reserves, and a guide to hotels and petrol stations. In the information office we got street maps, list of hotels, restaurants, shops, the cinema and so on.

"We were hoping to stay on the coast for a while," I said to the young blonde woman. "We were planning to travel overland from Egypt but had to go by sea instead because the border was closed, so we are a couple of months ahead of schedule."

"Well, that shouldn't be much of a problem. The school holidays are over now so there are a number of private cottages up the coast which could be for rent. You've got your own vehicle, of course. Do you mind how far out of town you are?"

"Not at all," I said. "We prefer the 'bush', we've been camping in Algeria and Tunisia and across the Sahara."

She grinned at us. "Lucky you. Anyway, I'll write the name of a good estate agent who specialises in holiday cottages and so on. He's an Indian but very honest and reliable."

The 'honest and reliable' Indian estate agent understood exactly what we wanted with the minimum of explanations.

"If you will take a short lease by the month, this cottage I am thinking about will be perfect for you. It will be cheap, it has most essentials except bed linen and you can't see any neighbour it is so secluded. It is right beside the sea and it's a bit rough, but that's what you want isn't it? You don't have to worry about looking after the garden and so on. Just keep the house clean, that's all."

"It sounds perfect," I said. Barbie was nodding.

"Of course you have no references." He paused. "I will have to telephone the owners in Nairobi to explain that you are from England and are travelling. I'm sure it will be alright if you pay monthly in advance. But it takes sometimes hours to get through, so I'll phone this evening and you can come back in the morning."

"It's the sixteenth of August now," I said. "We want to tour around, so maybe we should do that first and take the cottage for the months of September and October."

"Good idea. And if you want to leave any of your things with me while you go on safari, I will look after them."

"Better and better," I said.

The next morning all was well. He told us how to find the beach cottage so we could inspect it before signing a simple agreement. It was at Bamburi Beach, about five miles or so further north than Nyali. The road went past a new cement factory which sent a thin stream of white dust and steam into the sky day-in-day-out. We did not notice it except when driving past and it made a good landmark at first. Beyond, there was an Aga Khan community settlement and the second turn after led to the cottage. Two wheel tracks led the way along an overgrown path which passed through a screen of bushes into the backyard of the cottage.

It was square, painted green, with the universal corrugated iron roof. It was built of wood with louvred windows, standing on low brick piles because of the termites. Tall trees shaded it on the landward side and in front there was an open area of coarse grass growing in the coral sand. A few ornamental bushes and bougainvillaea had been planted but were stunted and straggly because of the sandy soil and there was a rough coral stone outline of a flower bed.

A tall coconut palm tree, a beautiful old palm with a long straight bole, stood at the end of the 'lawn' where a faint path led directly to the fine white beach. A clump of young coconut palms clustered at the foot of the grandfather tree and formed a natural barrier or fence. Through the palms, there were glimpses of the blue of the ocean and the flash of white foam on the reef. We did not have a key but looked in through glass windows facing the sea.

There seemed to be a huge living room with a couple of divans, wicker work settees and battered old chairs with stained cushions scattered about. A dining table stood beyond and a door led off to what had to be a quite large bedroom.

182

"There's only one bedroom, I think he said," I commented, my nose pressed against the window. "I suppose the children or guests sleep on those divans in the living room."

I turned and breathed deeply of the moist salt air drifting from the sea just fifty yards away. There was a gentle roar from the waves on the distant reef. On either side of the property there were no signs of any neighbour, the next cottage must have been some distance away behind trees and bushes. Two pied crows alighted on the tall sentinel palm and called loudly at us - "*Gwaak-gwaak! Gwaak-gwaak!*"

"It's going to be good, Barbie?"

"Too right!"

CHAPTER THIRTEEN : *ON SAFARI*

The next day we got ready for our safari. We repacked our suitcases and roughly sorted our equipment and drove to the estate agent's office where he showed us a store room at the back. There we deposited most of the petrol and water cans, a suitcase of spare clothes and bits and pieces and some other bulky gear we did not think we would need. There were no long distances between towns in Kenya or Uganda and the 'long-haul' equipment would not be needed until we set off through Tanzania and Zambia.

We shopped for a fresh range of basics; cooking oil, salt, sugar, rice, coffee, dried milk, reserve tinned food, washing powder, toiletries, paraffin and so on. We warned our friends at the Metropole Hotel that we were leaving and had a last hot curry dinner.

"I'm not sure that I'm not glad to be having a break from all this curry," I said. "We've more-or-less gone through their menu a couple of times."

"Yes, I've been getting indigestion these last couple of meals," Barbie agreed. "That chicken Madras is bloody fierce."

It was exciting. We were heading into the Africa of legend and Barbie had been reading about white-hunters and the man-eaters of Tsavo. She had enjoyed the film, *Born Free* and remembered *Where no Vultures Fly* and other 'safari' films of the late 1950s and 60s. I told her that we had a friend who was the stand-in for Ava Gardner in *The Snows of Kilimanjaro*.

After breakfast on the 19th August we packed up and I organised the back of Landie while Barbie washed her hair and then we were off, heading westward into Africa.

After crossing the causeway connecting Mombasa Island to the mainland there were a few warehouses which were depots for wholesale firms and a straggle of trading stores and native huts and then we were away from town. The tarred road lasted for about thirty miles after we had climbed up the low coastal escarpment. There had been a big British military depot at Mackinnon Road rail station and the tarred surface lasted until we reached it. Thereafter the surface became rough red and orange laterite. Immediately, dust was circulating within Landie and I thought of the uselessness of the perfunctory cleaning I had done. Mentally, I shrugged: the white dust of North Africa was now being thoroughly overlaid by the red dust of Kenya. Once one accepts that everything is suffused with dust which penetrates everywhere, then there is no point in bothering about it. It is natural.

Away from the coast, the air became noticeably drier, as if we had passed through an invisible barrier, and we may have felt we were back in Algeria but for the absolute difference in the vegetation. Thick acacia thornbush encroached closely on the road, painted red by the dust from passing vehicles.

There was no mistaking that we were in a different part of Africa. Five-ton Bedford and Ford lorries laboured, lurching in the ruts and wash-aways from the last rainy season, and we met them at intervals of five miles or so. There were occasional Landrovers and pick-up trucks. These other vehicles churned up great clouds of dust so that it was impossible sometimes to pass the slow-moving trucks until we came to a stretch where a breeze blew the cloud off to one side and the way ahead could be seen clearly. Because of the heaving of the road surface, the lorries hugged the best track and were reluctant to move to the side. I had to use my horn repeatedly whilst crawling on the flank of a toiling monster and peering through the swirling dust.

Sometimes we came across two or three trucks travelling in convoy when a slower or more heavily-laden vehicle was holding up faster ones and then we would have to wait, in the cloud, while they overtook each other, travelling side by side and lurching dangerously close, engines roaring, for maybe five minutes until we could sneak by. But there were long clear stretches as well, and where the land levelled out onto a plain for many miles, the road paralleled the railway. Every so often there was a railway halt with a metal water tower for the wood-fired steam locomotives, a few small cottages for the railway workers and an Indian 'duka' or trading store. The dukas often had a petrol pump outside them and some locals selling produce. The names of the stations were ordinary enough I suppose, but they seemed romantic to me, producing images of the great enterprise of building the railway at the turn of the century. Between Mombasa and Nairobi there were Mazeras, Samburu, Mackinnon

Road, Voi, Tsavo, Mtito Andei, Kibwezi, Makindu, Kiboko, Simba, Sultan Hamud, Konza and Athi River. Apart from these few rail stations with a duka and a straggle of a few houses there was no town or village. That part of Kenya, mostly acacia bush and, further on, grassy plains with bush along the course of the few rivers, was empty of humanity.

When I was at school in the late 1940s, I read all of the biographical and autobiographical books of African adventure that could be found in our school library. Several which were still circulating in South Africa in those days were written by East African pioneers: hunters, colonial administrators and part-time soldiers, many of whom were South Africans who ranged widely. When the construction of the Uganda Railway was halted by lions at the railhead on the Tsavo River, Colonel J.H.Patterson of the Indian Army, who had prowess as a tiger hunter, was called in to settle the matter. His book, *The Man-Eaters of Tsavo* was a 'Boys' Own' adventure story, but others have described the actuality as a farce as the bewildered Patterson sought ways of killing the devious and clever pride of lions. I though of those times, only two generations away, while driving through the fog of dust thrown up by the straining lorries, or coasting along on empty stretches beside the railway.

Late that morning, approaching Voi nestling beneath the dominating Taita Hills rising to 7200 feet, we turned a corner and suddenly confronted a great bull elephant lazily pulling at the branches of a thorn tree close to the roadside. I skidded to a stop and scrabbled for my camera which lived inside the carefully padded, custom-built case made for me by my friend who saw me off at Durban. In that dust and on rough roads my camera and its lenses always lived inside the case because in those days my cameras were precious possessions. The fine old bull waited patiently and I was rewarded with an excellent picture. Barbie and I were both quite breathless with the close encounter with the elephant: it was the first large wild animal, potentially dangerous, that we had met since we set off from London. And it was gentle-looking there by the side of the road, apparently oblivious to the occasional vehicle with its noise, fumes and dust cloud.

There seemed to be nowhere to stop on the road from Mombasa to Nairobi apart from driving off into the veld as we had done in North Africa and although we soon became accustomed to this practice, I was still a little wary of conditions in Kenya. In any

186

case, the best solution to overnight accommodation was obviously to use the camp-sites within Tsavo Park which straddled the road about halfway. So, at Voi we drove into Tsavo East, paying the entrance fee of ten shillings for the vehicle and the same amount for two of us to camp in the site near the gate. It seemed reasonable enough although we were used to camping for nothing. We inspected the site which was an open space with a neat but rough block of showers and toilet.

There was a road that wound alongside the stream of the Voi River which watered a stretch of riverine forest and we drove out along it, around rocky hills. It was an exciting introduction for Barbie of some of the commoner mammals of the African savannah. We were rewarded by some close sightings: more elephants, giraffe, hartebeest, Thomson's gazelles, waterbuck, duiker, klipspringer, zebra, a clan of baboons and out on the plain beyond the hills, a huge herd of Cape buffalo. I had seen all those animals before except the Thomson's gazelles, but I had never seen such a great herd of buffaloes.

On the way back, close to the camp, a uniformed game-guard was herding a black rhino and two baby elephants along and I stopped with amazement. The guard grinned at our surprise and told us that there was a small colony of orphans being looked after by the warden and his wife at the nearby headquarters.

"Are they tame?" Barbie asked, eyeing the rhino which was coming close to Landie.

"Not really, memsahib," the guard replied still grinning, but relented at Barbie's expression. "But, of course they will not harm you. They are quite used to people."

I got out with my camera and got an extraordinary close-up of the young black rhino, the image of his head filling the frame. Barbie had been nibbling some custard-cream biscuits and she impulsively held one out to the great bulky animal and he moved up close and took it gently from her hand and munched it. "Jesus, Den! Did you see that?" she called quietly. I was still busy with my camera. The rhino made soft mewing noises and edged closer, his round bulk rocking Landie on its springs and the guard slapped him on the haunches shooing him on as if he were cattle.

"It will damage your Landrover by mistake," he explained, and then turned to point to the two young female elephants which had been waiting shyly about twenty yards away. "The older one is called Eleanor," he said. "She is still not so used to people, but very quiet."

"What about that?" I asked Barbie when I was back behind the wheel.

"The rhino was so sweet," she said. "And did you hear it calling when it wanted more biccies, just like a baby. I had no idea that they made a noise like that."

"Nor did I," I said, driving slowly to our camp.

It was our first night in the sub-Saharan bushveld and it was magical. There was a broken overcast sky so we did not see many stars, but the air was balmy after the sun set and we sat about in the dead still of the tropical night, eating steak bought fresh in Mombasa that morning and drinking a bottle of red wine. The water in the 44-gallon drum on top of the shower room had been warmed during the day and it was luxury washing the sweat and layers of red dust off afterwards. Before going to bed, I shone our torch around and there were the bright blue sparkles of eyes watching us.

"What are they?" Barbie breathed. "It's so quiet, I had no idea anything was there."

"They will be antelope," I said. "Maybe impala."

On the ground where we had dropped grains of rice when cleaning up our dinner there was a trail of safari ants carrying their spoil away into the darkness. "What about them, Den? Don't they attack and leave us just skeletons in the morning?"

"I hope not," I said. "I'm sure we will feel them biting before they get too serious."

*   *

Our excellent Shell map of the park systems showed that a road traversed the western edge of the park to a lookout and then came out at another gate at Manyani, so after a breakfast of good local tinned pineapple juice we set out.

Not far away we rounded a corner and there was a small herd of elephants in our way, browsing from some tall umbrella thorn trees. I was able to get another excellent photograph with the morning light on the Taita hills behind. The map showed where Mudanda Rock stood and there was a rough sign to a parking place in its lee. It was a huge whale-back of granite dome, long and narrow and rising to maybe fifty feet over the plain. I teased Barbie that there were Ayers rocks in Africa too and she snorted at the idea. We felt strangely naked climbing the rock, unprotected by Landie and looked down upon by that vast silver sky. It was another overcast day with not a touch of breeze.

We breasted the crest and looked out over a plain leading to the smudge of an escarpment maybe twenty miles away marking the course of the Galana River. Immediately below, there was a waterhole surrounded by a stretch of thornscrub which merged into grassland. Elephants were there, snorting and blowing water about, bathing and drinking. Big birds stood at the edge and there were a few gazelles. The gazelles immediately looked up at us as we quietly lowered ourselves onto a ledge to watch but the elephants did not bother, although I was certain that they had monitored our arrival.

"Everything is so tame," Barbie whispered. "It's just fantastic."

It was, and proved how untroubled the animals in the park were in those years. We stayed on, watching until the elephants had taken their fill and finished their toilet before moving off in a slow promenade, the young ones trotting beside the females.

I had read in the Mombasa papers that the U.S.Navy had recently helped the Park authorities with helicopters for an elephant count and some zoologists were claiming that there were too many of them for the health of the trees and wanted to cull off some thousands. This started a public argument and there had been furious letters to the editor. The tree cover we saw on that brief visit seemed adequate and healthy to me, but I was no expert.

I was sorry to get back onto the dust and pounding ruts and holes of the main road. It became a bone-jarring grind as almost all African travel was then, away from the few towns. At Mtito Andei, we stopped for life-saving Cokes and biscuits at the Tsavo Inn Service Station and I filled up with petrol because it got more expensive the further we travelled from the coast. Dust gave way to a gravel surface and deeper ruts and washaways as the country became more undulating. There were giraffe and 'Tommies' on the grassy Athi Plains.

Suddenly we were on a good tarred road and the singing of Landie's lugged tires on the smooth surface was a joy. A sign told us it was 17 miles to Nairobi and I began thinking about how to spend that night and where we might get accommodation, or a camping site. The pounding of the road for the second successive day after a break of a month since Libya was bringing on a headache which I recognised as a migraine. I used to get migraines fairly frequently when younger but had not had one for many months. I was thinking about why I should be starting one when two police motor cyclists came roaring at us, waving frantically for us to get off the road. A pick-up truck ahead of us swerved abruptly well off the verge and I followed it. The driver, a big black man, got out and wiped at his face with a cloth and I went over to him.

"What is it, do you know?" I asked.

"Jambo!" he greeted me. "It is our Prime Minister, the Mzee, he is travelling to Mombasa today."

"To Mombasa, on this road?" I asked, my surprise unconcealed.

"The Mzee always travels by road, he does not like the aeroplanes," he replied seriously. "Because of the narrow roads and for respect, the police warn everybody to park until he passes. You should come out of your car and stand to salute him when he passes."

I thanked him and returned to Barbie. "It's Jomo Kenyatta, going down to Mombasa. We are supposed to wait by Landie and stand when he passes."

We waited more than an hour in the noon sun which had broken through the cloud cover and my incipient migraine got to grips with my head. "What a bloody joke," Barbie said with Aussie disgust. "The whole traffic held up all this time."

"I don't envy those poor policemen on the motor-bikes," I said. "Just think of that road and the dust."

"I suppose they feel proud at what they are doing. I hope all the drivers know what they are supposed to do."

Eventually, a police Landrover appeared, followed shortly afterwards by a convoy of black limousines, Chevrolets or Buicks by the look of them, trailed by another Landrover. A small crowd had gathered from seeming nowhere and children waved tentatively. I wondered at the Prime Minister choosing to drive that distance on those roads when he could have gone by plane or train. I learned later that Kenyatta suffered from high blood pressure and never flew.

The migraine was taking its course, but it had not gone beyond the steady throbbing stage and we had agreed to go through the Nairobi National Park, so entered it at its Embakasi Gate about five miles from Nairobi. I followed the Shell map and we did a good circuit around to return to the same gate. We saw zebras, wildebeest, hartebeest, warthog, giraffe with strong red markings, hartebeest, hippos immersed in a pool of the Athi River, vervet monkeys, Thomson's gazelle, waterbuck and kudu. We both hoped for lions, but saw none. Barbie had by then seen most of the large African mammals available apart from the big cats. I suppose we had been lucky with our viewing, but there was plenty of wildlife in Tsavo and the small Nairobi park. We were the only vehicle there that afternoon except for a couple of local cars.

I explained about my migraine to Barbie and said that I did not want to be bothered with Nairobi that afternoon; we could have a look around on our return trip. So we drove quickly through the centre which did not make much of an impression on me. There was a blur of two and three storied colonial-style buildings, some with verandahs to shade the pavement, lining the rectangular grid of half-a-dozen streets in the centre and then we were suddenly through, driving in a leafy suburb.

"It's smaller than Mombasa," Barbie commented. "Something like a medium town in the outback of New South Wales. I expected something more interesting." So did I.

We mounted a rise on Government Road beyond the Nairobi River, watching for directions and saw a sign to Thika and Fort Hall. In Parklands there was a small, bright shopping complex and we parked outside a modern grocery store. Next to it was a chemist and I tried there for something stronger than the codeine-aspirin tablets I had with me, but there was nothing they could recommend. In the grocery store we bought some fresh food and moved on and out of Nairobi on Forest Road.

We were soon into farmland and lush plantations. Mango trees and pawpaws stood around shamba homesteads and there was coffee, tea, sugarcane, sisal and maize in well-cultivated fields spreading over rolling hills. I looked for the famous bulk of Mount Kenya and the loom of the Aberdares but low cloud obscured the heights as evening drew in.

My migraine became fierce and I began driving with one eye closed, my worry about where to stop the night increasing the tension.

"How about over there?" Barbie suggested, pointing to a disturbed area of red earth which seemed to lead naturally away into a depression away from the tarred road. I swung into it and found that we could settle on excavated ground shielded from the sight of passersby. It was a small quarry for gravel used to maintain the road and I learned in that way that gravel pits are a haven for overland travellers all over Africa. Gratefully, I allowed Barbie to organise me and the camp as I sat watching night climb over the sky. It was cool, cooler than anything we had experienced since the night in the

Kabyle Mountains of Algeria which seemed a lifetime away. I could not eat, feeling nauseated.

In the morning my head was clear of pain but I felt foggy from the painkillers I had been taking. We sat for some time quietly over coffee after eating a hearty breakfast of sausages, fried eggs and potato crisps bought in the Nairobi grocery.

"Let's have a lazy day," I suggested. "I would like to see Mount Kenya and it's still a bit cloudy. We could drive along slowly, watching the map, and find a really proper place to camp within range of the mountain and see if the clouds lift."

"Yes, sure," agreed Barbie. "Poor old Den. That was a bad head you had last night and I know what they can be like. Anyway, I'd like to see the famous snow on the equator too."

We packed up lethargically and moved on along the twisting narrow tarred road, climbing gradually out of the lush cultivated valleys around Thika. Beyond Fort Hall, a small town with dukas in the centre, the tarred road stopped and we were on good gravel. We must have climbed quite high because the land became grassy with clumps of exotic eucalyptus around the homesteads and the few scattered African shambas. We saw herds of cattle and goats being tended by boys wearing tattered shirts over bare legs. They looked cold and we felt the chill despite the warmth of Landie's engine seeping through into the cab.

Somewhere beyond the turn-off to Nyeri, I spied a farm track leading off to the right and on a whim took it. There was an open farm gate dividing two fenced fields about half a mile from the road and I took that to be an invitation, although we stopped to close the gate behind us. Driving now over rough grass we passed through a line of scrubby bush and sisal gone wild and found ourselves out of sight of the road and in possession of a vast camp site of maybe fifty acres. At the far end of the field, bushes spread widely over the slope leading upwards into misty overcast some five miles away.

I parked and we set up camp in Landie's shelter from a cool breeze coming down the mountain. We got out books and caught up with diaries and did a bit of tidying in the back where our gear had been thrown around by the rough passage of the Mombasa road. The sun showed a silver disk from time to time but the cover did not break all afternoon although it got warmer and felt quite humid. From time to time we both snoozed in the back of Landie in between keeping an eye on the direction where the mountain had to be.

Next morning I felt bright and cheerful and full of energy although Barbie complained that after snoozing in the day she had not slept well and the cold had frequently awakened her. The ground was wet with dew and the air misty. I was reconciling myself to not seeing the mysterious heights when there was a clear patch in the sky after breakfast. We hastily took photographs of the jagged peak rising from the gradual slope of the great volcano's massif and we both swore we could see the glint of snow and glacier.

I was disappointed. I had expected a more abruptly sloping giant of a mountain towering over us and had underestimated the effect of the altitude we had already reached, possibly nearly 8,000 feet above sea level, nearly half way to the top of Mount Kenya. Studying my map, I calculated roughly that we were camped about 17 miles from the peak which was about 9,000 feet above us, so it was quite a long way away.

But, we had seen snows on the equator. That was something which had eluded European explorers for two thousand years since first being reported by a Greek trader called Diogenes before the time of Christ, which produced the legend of the Mountains of the Moon.

CHAPTER FOURTEEN : *THE GREAT NYANZA*

Shortly before entering Nanyuki we met an 'Equator' signpost for the first time: a yellow road sign with a black Africa with a red line painted across it. We stopped and photographed each other.

Nanyuki reminded me of a typical country town in Natal and I realised there quite clearly why so many Kenya settlers had felt at home with places like Lion's River, Nottingham Road or Rosetta which I knew so well from my boyhood. At that altitude of 7,000 feet not far from Mount Kenya to the east and the Aberdare Range to the west, the countryside itself was also very similar to the Midlands of Natal. There was the same tussocky veld grass and coarse scrub in the shelter of folds in the ground and there were plantations of gum trees, pines and firs, but not so much of them. Cattle were being driven along the road to Nanyuki from a farm nearby and in the short main street of the town with its Indian dukas there were battered Chevrolet and Ford pick-ups and a tractor or two with a trailer behind. We stopped for Cokes at a filling station. The local blacks wore worn cast-off trousers and jackets against the cold and the same old greasy felt hats pulled down over their faces that I might have seen at home.

The sun appeared when we moved away from the shadow of the Mount Kenya massif which generated its own weather, and it warmed up. The sky was a bright clear blue of high altitude, again reminding me of my boyhood home. The road west to Thomson's Falls was good gravel though corrugated so we rattled along at speed. On the way, we passed a fine herd of giraffe which I would not have seen in Natal. The road was empty, I don't think we passed another vehicle, and there were no people.

Thomson's Falls was entered through an archway with a faded handpainted sign framed by tall gum and pine trees. "Welcome to the Healthiest Climate in the World", the sign proclaimed. The perfume of resin was in the air. I remembered my Aunt Inez talking about parties at the pub in Thomson's Falls, Barry's Hotel, when she had lived nearby in the 1950s. I was thoroughly enjoying the day's travels.

Thomson had been one of the great colonial explorers, who travelled and mapped the interior on his own and recorded the wild life. The ubiquitous Thomson's gazelle was named after him. Outside of East Africa he never had the stature that Livingstone and the others had, but he may have contributed as much in detailing the geography.

The road directly southwards towards Gilgil traversed the edge of the escarpment above the Rift Valley and along it were the hamlets of Ol' Joro Orok and Ol' Kalou which I remembered as being the postal addresses of my aunt when writing Christmas cards or 'thank you' letters. Her husband, Nick Craven, had managed farms in the district and one of them led down to the marshes and open water of Ol' Bolossat where he told me they went shooting wild ducks and snipe for sport and the pot. It was only about twenty miles off our way, but there was nothing I could have used as a landmark to identify where they had lived and I did not remember the names of the farms they had lived on. So we continued instead westward down the road over the escarpment to Nakuru at the bottom of the Rift Valley.

The scene was enormous from the edge of the escarpment and it was a beautiful clear day with tufty fair weather cumulus clouds riding high against the blue sky. We stopped in the shade of a gum tree avenue for a smoke and to admire the view. We could pick out Lake Nakuru with its faintly pink colouring from the hundreds of thousands of flamingoes who lived there and wheeled about low over the water. Nearer was the town of Nakuru. Nearer still, just below us, there was a village where some kind of family ceremony was going on with singing and clapping and the beat of a drum. Perhaps it was a wedding or the welcome home for someone who had travelled far. People were dancing and the sound of their merrymaking came up to us with a nostalgic feel to it.

Nakuru was a pleasant town, larger and more prosperous than the others we had passed through. The main street was lined with a variety of dukas and small office buildings, clean and fresh with bright advertising posters. Beyond, it was easy to follow signs to the 'Nakuru Bird Sanctuary' and we stopped on the shores of the Lake to admire the wheeling clouds of flamingoes and the many other water birds wading in the shallows. I walked out to get a photograph and found myself getting bogged in dark mud, smelly with the droppings of all those birds. Behind the ever-shifting pink clouds, the pale walls of the Mau Escarpment reared up and the sun blazed down almost vertically above.

Back through the town the road went through cultivated lands then began climbing out of the Rift Valley again. It was an excellent road, newly tarred, winding in easy curves through pine plantations and we came to another 'Equator' sign: we were crisscrossing the line back and forth that day. As we photographed it, a local pick-up with tanned young white people in the back came racing down and they waved gaily to us.

Landie began labouring and the air became sharp and dry with a deep blue dome of sky above. The reason was obvious when we met another sign proclaiming, 'Timboroa Summit - 9320 feet'. It was the highest altitude either of us had ever reached by road at that time and I felt cheated because there we were driving along a fine tar road which allowed Landie to move along without rattling and clattering and throwing up dust; it was a pleasant drive and nothing was out of the ordinary. The grass on the stretch from Nanyuki to Thomson's Falls had been dry and sere in the shadow of Mount Kenya, but up on the Timboroa it was a rich green again from recent rain. I realised that the great mountains and the Rift Valley had an immediate effect on climate in that region.

Evening was approaching and we found a place where we could drive off the road and find a level patch on the slope of a hill and there we stopped the night. It was very cold and in the morning there was a fine dusting of frost on the grass until the powerful sun touched it when it disappeared. We were used to the cold nights by then, and the rarefied atmosphere made us sleep well.

In Eldoret we bought fresh produce and decided we would press on fast that day and see if we could reach Lake Victoria where our AA guide-book said there was a good camping site. The road was dirt and rough to the Uganda border and the countryside was somewhat empty. Off to the north, the land was flat and green though lacking in cultivation or apparent population. The distant bulk of Mount Elgon (14,100 feet) loomed; another great volcano. It's shape was similar to Mount Kenya, rising from the plain in a gentle slope from both extremities to the lump at its peak. I now understood the structure of these East African volcanoes and did not expect the jagged majesty of great folded mountains like the Alps. I knew it was an equivalent of the Alps I had been expecting which had been my first disappointment. One had to see the volcanoes with different eyes

196

and if one wished to be awed, it was the thought of great belching clouds of smoke and ash that had to be visualised and the rain of blistering clinker and rivers of smoking lavas that built their gentle shapes.

The Uganda border was marked and there was a control post but we were waved casually through. On the other side there was an excellent tarred road and it could be sensed that Uganda had a greater wealth than Kenya. It was Uganda that had always been seen as the Eldorado of East Africa and the railway from Mombasa which had been constructed sixty odd years before was aimed at exploiting the agricultural riches of the land around the great lakes. Kenya had been empty of people apart from wandering cattle herders and a scattering of simple farmers where there was perennial water in the Highlands. Uganda was where there were concentrations of people in powerful, well-organised native kingdoms. But it was those kingdoms which frustrated the British exploitation, because they would not easily give way for settlers. It was Kenya that had room for settlers who came out and carved out vast farms encompassing the native hamlets which were useful for providing labour.

Nevertheless as time passed, great cotton, sugar-cane, coffee and tea estates had been established in Uganda with the processing plants to go with them, and the country thrived. The value of exports from Uganda in the 1950s was almost double that of imports and considerably exceeded the value from Kenya, a much larger country. We could see the tangible results of that favourable balance of trade over many years. The first town after the border was Tororo and it had a greater range of more sophisticated goods in the smart dukas than we had seen in Nanyuki or Eldoret.

The road being so good we made good time. We stopped a few times to admire and photograph. The tea estates were richly prosperous, the bushes immaculately trimmed of their shining leaves and shaded by mature flatcrown acacia trees from the drying effect of the tropical sun and planted carefully to give a good spread. But it was Jinja that forced us to pause longer.

I remembered a photograph of my cousin, Deon, standing beside a plaque with a surging cataract behind him with a caption stating that it was the Ripon Falls, "the source of the Nile". That cataract had since been tamed by a great curved dam wall downstream on the site of the Owen Falls at Jinja and its top served as the road. The dam had submerged the river and the Ripon Falls and shifted the old native town where Speke and Grant had found that source of the Nile on 28th July 1862, just about four weeks and 103 years before. We stopped on the dam and got out to enjoy the majesty of the scene.

On the one side, Lake Victoria spread away from us, a great sheet of silver meeting the sky. On the other, below the curve of concrete, clear water flecked with froth burst from the sluices and surged away in swirls and eddies downstream. This was the main source of the Nile which we had crossed over, back and forth, at Cairo just a few weeks before. Standing there beside Barbie, both of us quiet as we thought about it, I sensed my feelings when we were at the pyramids and I had looked away from the burning yellows of the Sahara over the green of date palms, hazed with their expelled humidity, which filled the Nile valley. Here at its source, there was rich green tumbling over all the land in sight in the grand mix of virgin tropical vegetation.

Immediately below on one bank of the surging torrent, women were washing clothes and spreading colourful cloths on the ground and draping them over bushes to dry. I could see them gesticulating as they talked and called to each other, but any sound they made was drowned by the thunder of the water. There were molecules of that water which would reach the Mediterranean sometime, maybe a year or more into the future.

Beside the road there was a hotel and well-tended ornamental parks and gardens filled with flowering plants and shrubs. Bougainvillaea, poinsettia and flame trees flared with brilliant orange and red bloom in the sunshine.

The rich green of plantations interspersed with long stretches of virgin rainforest was explained shortly after we left Jinja. Quite suddenly, the sun disappeared as heavy clouds appeared above the canyon of the road. It was quite dark and gloomy and the temperature seemed to plummet making us shiver even though the temperature itself did not fall. The rain began soon after. It was not a gentle splattering growing to a steady fall; it began with an immediate hissing downpour as if we had entered a waterfall. Rain drenched us instantly, the road was awash and spray bounced two and three feet from the surface. I was thankful that it was a tarred road and well drained, but even so we were soon driving through an inch of water. The windscreen wipers had difficulty coping and I pulled off the road where I saw a picnic place.

"I've not seen anything quite like this since I was in Nigeria three years ago," I told Barbie.

198

"We have terrific storms in New South Wales, but not like this. They start with thunder and wind, but this just came out of nowhere, and there's no wind at all. It just comes straight down. I suppose it's like this in Queensland, but I've not been there yet."

"Landie is getting the first proper bath ever," I said, wiping at the condensation forming on the inside of the windows.

We had made sandwiches with fresh bread bought in Tororo and ate them as the rain continued to thunder on the roof. Afterwards Barbie wanted a pee. "I needed to go earlier, but all this water is making it urgent," she said, laughing. "What can I do?"

"It's just rain," I said. "And it's actually warm enough so you'll dry quickly."

She hesitated, then threw the door open and ducked out. When she was back in again she was soaked, wet hair hanging over her face. I had a towel ready and she rubbed at her face and arms. "It may be all right in here, but the rain is not that bloody warm," she complained, making blowing noises. Of course, the rain ceased as abruptly as it started five minutes later and we moved off into wan sunshine, the road steaming.

We took the road down to Entebbe before entering Kampala and found a sign to the Entebbe Sailing Club which we followed. They had a camping area beside the club house and I paid for a few days. It was an excellent site, surrounded by fine old trees, about half an acre in extent, and we could use the members' toilet and showers. A mown lawn sloped gently to the heaving waters of Lake Victoria where small waves washed onto a narrow sandy beach.

Reeds grew luxuriantly to one side and we were warned not to swim because of the risk of infection with bilharzia and because there might be crocodiles and hippos. We never saw any sign of the animals, but the idea that they might be there gave a good feeling that we were in Africa on the shore of romantic Lake Victoria.

That afternoon, children of the sailing club members were paddling about in canoes and rowing boats. There was nobody else camping and we arranged our table and chairs with a view across the water to establish our presence before cooking a meal in a more civilised fashion than we had since arriving in East Africa. There was a stand pipe with clean water and the neatly cropped lawn was an incentive to do things properly and keep our own gear and surroundings neat and tidy too.

The air was warm and soft after the rain and the sun set with a rich range of colours in the clouds reflected on the placid waters.

The sky was always changing over Lake Victoria and with the frequent showers the visibility was always sharp. After the cold nights in the Highlands around the Great Rift Valley in Kenya the temperature was always equable there at the lower altitude of 3,700 feet above sea level. The inland sea made its own humidity and the air was always balmy. We spent many hours in the next few days sitting in our chairs on our 'private' lawn, chatting idly, reading or just watching the changing scene with nature's paintbrush grandly washing fresh colours and contrasts over that huge sky and the reflections below.

White tufty clouds would grow until their bases became blue and purple; high cirrus streamed over and the next time you looked up from your book there would be a rumble of thunder and the horizon would be filled by a towering storm trailing a dark fringe of descending rain. Maybe once or twice each day, there would be that strange quiet that seemed to still the birds and insects as a storm shower moved closer and there would be a cool gust of air before the rain dropped on us out of a suddenly purple sky above. Usually the vertical shower lasted not more than half an hour and we would scramble into Landie and watch it, but one day it went on for a couple of hours off-and-on while we waited, getting impatient. Always afterwards the sun would be out with tropical power and steam would rise from the lawn and the trees around. Table and chairs would soon be dry.

The sunsets were particularly glorious and different every evening. Our site faced south so we could not see the ball of fire itself disappearing behind the horizon, but it did not matter. If there were clouds, it was an absorbing entertainment to watch the colours change on them as the sun descended. If there were no clouds, the sky itself became an immaculate golden curtain merging to crimson when the shadow of the earth rose up from the eastern horizon behind the silhouetted branches of tropical trees. Sometimes, the ancient shape of a dugout canoe slipped by with a fisherman casting his net. We would sit, sipping a sundowner like old colonials, watching it all every evening.

Barbie carried out a regime of washing everything that could be washed making use of the endless supply of water; the first time we had camped with that facility since Spain. We showered morning and night and Barbie used up a lot of hair shampoo. It really was very civilised there at the Entebbe Sailing Club. Every evening the nightwatchman came over to chat briefly when he came on duty,

200

greeting us gravely and asking if all was in order. We would give him cigarettes.

The first morning we did a tour around Entebbe which was a decent sized town with a variety of good shops and dukas providing anything we could need. We saw where the Imperial Airways flying boats used to dock before the War and where BOAC kept up the service until the new long-range airliners came into general use in the early 1950s and an airport had to be built which then served as Uganda's international entry-port. The Botanical Gardens at the edge of town were internationally famous and we passed them by to my later regret, because we should have taken the opportunity to visit them then.

There were plenty of fresh fish from the lake and good cuts of meat available and we ate well. I got into the habit of driving the short distance into town each morning for fresh milk, bread and vegetables. I even bought the local daily paper. We had not camped so well since setting off from England. Indeed, in retrospect, we never camped with our own resources so well during the whole of our safari. Barbie preferred to stay behind after the first day's exploration and potter about and read. She was catching up on books that we had both bought to read in North Africa but had somehow never got around to.

Travelling across the Sahara there never seemed to be a proper time or place to relax after we left Djerba Island and our books had been packed away in Landie during the ocean voyage. The Entebbe Sailing Club was a good place to catch up on various things, to let our souls become easy as well as spend physically lazy days.

One day we went into Kampala to see what it was like. It seemed to be mostly a new town although I knew it had been established for many years. There had been a lot of construction since the war and the centre was served by well-made roads and traffic roundabouts. Two and three story buildings flanked the streets and there was bustle and movement everywhere. The shops were filled with consumer goods and there was a variety of cars which were not expected in Africa: Morris Minors and new Austin Minis mingled with giant finned Pontiacs and Chevrolets as well as the usual Landrovers and Ford pick-ups. Buses paused to pick up passengers at orderly queues.

The Indian shopkeepers were well-dressed and friendly and there were many Indian businessmen about in grey tropical-weight suits and shining shoes striding the pavements. Some wore the distinctive Sikh turbans above their grave bearded faces. Expatriate Englishwomen were shopping trailed by their pale children in brief shorts and shirts. The local Africans looked prosperous and cheerful, the men invariably wearing well-pressed slacks, white shirts and ties as they went about their business and the handsome women either in frocks or embroidered blouses over multicoloured cotton wrappers decorated with bright prints in bold designs.

I thought of my Nigerian days, but Kampala was much smarter than any Nigerian town even though it was no larger than Benin City. The commanding *gopuram* of the modern Hindu temple and the minaret of the central mosque dominated the skyline. The difference between Kampala and any Nigerian city was the dominance of the Asiatic-origin population.

After one of my shopping excursions into Entebbe, Barbie told me that she had been observing a secret love affair. At about morning tea-time every day, a well-polished Wolseley car would be driven into the camping area by a European in a tropical suit and tie. His passenger was a pretty blonde woman, also conventionally dressed in urban style. They might get out and stroll for a while hand-in-hand or sit talking animatedly in the car. She had seen them locked in passionate kisses, but they did not seem to come there with only that in mind. They were probably in their forties. Being feminine, Barbie enjoyed this intrigue acted out before her and tried to make herself unobtrusive, buried in her book or domestic activity so as not to disturb them.

One morning they were still there when I returned from town. The man was plumpish and his slicked-down dark hair was balding. The woman had curly fair hair and wore a floral frock. I found their clandestine trysts saddening. It was obvious that he was an expatriate official and no doubt she was the wife of another, maybe a colleague and friend. Their regular escapades seemed rather innocent, although maybe their passion was more thoroughly spent when they had the place to themselves. But it would have to have been hurried and unsatisfactory. Sooner or later it would all have to end as these affairs always did in those circumstances in those days. I hoped they would not have too much pain or regrets.

We were beginning to feel inertia building up during the pleasant lazy days. We talked about going on to Fort Portal and the Ruwenzoris but the local paper was carrying reports of roads badly bogged by heavy rains. I toyed with the idea of driving up to the Sudanese border in the north, but it seemed a little pointless. It was easy to let the days slip by in the comfort of our camp by the beautiful great lake with its luxuriant vegetation, balmy air and ever-changing skies. We were jogged out of this complacency when our privacy was invaded by another party. They were German and younger than us, two good-looking fellows and a pretty girl. They had a Volkswagen Beetle and put up one small tent into which all three squeezed quite early after cooking a simple meal from tins.

"They can't be having satisfactory nights cramped in like that," said Barbie "Do you think they're all screwing or is it just two while the other turns the other way."

"What a thought, Barbie," I replied, laughing. But it seemed to be a signal that it was time for us to move on.

There had been some fuss in the local papers about Kenya imposing customs checks on the borders because Uganda was manufacturing local liquors which were being sold much cheaper than imported whisky or gin which had high tariffs on them. Kenya did not manufacture any alcoholic drinks except beer, so it was said that a flourishing smuggling trade had begun. Editorials in the paper warned that this would be the thin end of the wedge as more goods were manufactured locally in go-ahead Uganda which would be much cheaper than imports. Cigarettes would be the next problem it was forecast. Sure enough, the East African Customs Union broke down later. I was intrigued by this development and questioned the owner of a general dealer in Entebbe who sold liquor.

"Oh yes," he told me, "Before independence we used to import all our popular brands of spirits, like gin and brandy, from South Africa and there was a low tariff for them. After independence all the East African countries are trying to boycott South Africa because of that *apartheid*, you know? So some businessmen here decided to take advantage and we have set up a modern distillery. We started marketing our own brand, Warigi, this year but will try other products like gin and vodka."

"What is Warigi?"

"The name is the local one for a traditional strong drink made from fermented bananas. It is really something like vodka, but the government encourages it because the illegal Warigi is distilled very badly and makes people blind after some time. Like methylated spirits."

I bought a bottle for ten shillings (50 pence) and we tried it. It was as the shopkeeper told me; a pure sugarcane-based alcohol with a nauseating artificial banana flavour. It was potent enough though and could be disguised by Coca-Cola.

*   *

We left Uganda on a hot sunny day. It had been warm all the days we were camping beside the lake and the rain storms merely cooled the air for their duration. We stopped to take photographs here and there and enjoyed the magnificence of the Owen Falls dam and the source of the Nile again. Barbie particularly commented on the hotel which overlooked the dam, she thought it more closely resembled a country pub back home in Australia than others we had seen so far.

At Tororo, a police check stopped us and I was directed to a kiosk. I thought at first it was something to do with the Warigi furore and felt guilty about the bottle packed in the back and whether I would have to pay duty, but it was to do with my vehicle papers. We had been waved through into Uganda and I had been ignorant of the need to register with the licensing authority. I had an instant recall of the problems of Algeria, but the police inspector was amiable enough. He gave me a mild lecture but accepted my plea of ignorance.

"People forget that it is no longer the colonial times," he said. "Uganda is an independent country you know. We are not connected to Kenya these days." I apologised and assured him that I was well aware of Uganda's sovereignty and he took out the appropriate page of Landie's Carnet without further fuss.

After the border we were back on gravel roads through open country and kept going until I felt tired and began looking for a place to stop. Somewhere after Broderick Falls, another country village and local railway centre, there was a river running through a rocky valley hung with thorn trees and we found a track to follow down to a clearing by the waterside. I suspect that it was a ford for cattle and a place where local village women came to do their laundry. It was an attractive place, with clear water running through pools and between worn rocks and boulders strewn about. A low cliff made shelter for our campsite. We wandered about for a while until it quickly clouded over and rain came down.

As dusk approached the rain stopped and we got out the cooking equipment and our chairs as usual for a simple supper. We had not bought meat that day and were having boiled eggs, bread and fruit. The eggs were boiling when two young men joined us and stayed to chat. We had met hardly any local people since arriving in

East Africa who were ready to socialise and this was a change. I supposed that colonial times were too close for there to be relaxed relationships between white and black and I am sure that this assumption was correct. These two lads were bright and intelligent and had recognised that Landie did not have local registration so no doubt decided to approach us and risk a snub.

They wanted to know where we were form and what we were doing. They were delighted that we were travelling their country to see what it was like.

"We do not see people from England just driving in Kenya to see everything like that," one explained. "I hear that there are tourists who come from all over to Nairobi and go on safari to see the wild animals, but we are far from Nairobi here."

They told us that they were students and hoped to study further and make a good career. They were pleasant and eager and naive. Barbie put on the rest of our eggs to boil and we shared our supper with them, talking into the night by the light of Landie's inspection lamp and with the rushing noise of the water in the river close by. When we wearied of their chatter we had to tell them that we wanted to go to sleep because we had a long journey and they immediately stood up to go, thanking us for sharing food with them.

"They were nice boys, but I was beginning to wonder if they were going to stay the night," Barbie said, yawning. "And if more of them were suddenly going to turn up and mob us."

"I realised that we were a new experience for them," I said. "I suppose it was very important to them; chatting over a meal with two white strangers."

"Yeah... It's you white slave-drivers that have kept all these Affies down," she said. "No wonder everybody is so shy and we never have conversations. It's a lot different to North Africa and all those Arabs."

Barbie was quite right. Wherever we had been, we were met either by blank-faced reserve or, in the case of the occasional contact with young men such as petrol attendants, by noticeably assertive attitudes proclaiming equality. In dukas where I had been shopping the Indian proprietor automatically came to serve me even if there were several black assistants serving at the counter and he had to get up from his desk. I thought about this and recognised that the same kind of behaviour prevailed in South Africa in those days, but it was not so self-conscious there, as if it was more deeply entrenched. Thinking further away to Nigeria, I knew that it would have been more natural there, but the colonial colour-bar and social reserve was still very powerful all over sub-Sahara Africa in the 1960s.

In the morning we were up early and stopped in Eldoret again to stock up with fresh food. After the rain shower the evening before it was clear air and bright sunshine as we climbed up into the Timboroa heights: a lovely sparkling day and the aroma of pine resin was strong driving through the plantations. We stopped at the highest Equator sign at the edge of the escarpment looming over the Rift Valley above Nakuru and had a late breakfast.

We had an argument about what the rest of our Kenya Highlands excursion should be. I was increasingly aware of our agreement to take up the lease of the cottage on the beach on the 1st September and Barbie, rightly, felt we were not going to see as much of Kenya as we should. I realised that I had misjudged the distances involved in my enthusiasm to shack up at Bamburi and lead a beachcombing life. I wanted to get back to the coral reef and coconut palms and be a romantic beachcomber but Barbie wanted to see more before succumbing to my plans.

We had agreed to stop over in Nairobi on the way back after bypassing it because of my migraine on the way up. Although she did not say as much, I guessed that Barbie wanted to haunt the Nairobi of legend, stay where Earnest Hemingway stayed before going off on hunting-safaris, see where the Prince of Wales attended wild parties in the 1920s and where the aristocratic 'Happy Valley' set painted the town red in the 1940s. Barbie wanted to get a feel for the romantic Kenya of the popular novels of the day. Robert Ruark's descriptions in fat blockbuster books were close in time then. But, suddenly, I had no desire to do any of that.

In retrospect it is quite obvious that the amount of travelling we had done since leaving England and the vast amount of experiences we had hastily absorbed whilst skimming through new countries was having an effect on me. I had been doing all the driving, and continued to do so. This was on my own insistence because Landie was not insured and Barbie did not have an international driving license. I did not want her to carry the responsibility if anything went wrong. No doubt, this was having an accumulating effect on me and stress was building up. My lassitude at the Lake Victoria campsite was a symptom.

We went on through Nakuru in strained silence whilst I tried to work these worries out in my mind. I did not have the objectivity of distance in time, of course, and was not coherent enough about my

206

thoughts or subconscious feelings to begin to describe them. I am sure Barbie was also harbouring annoyance at my stubbornness in wanting to stick to a timetable and was not aware of my problem. She was right, of course, what were a couple of weeks this way or that when we were traversing a continent? But I could not see it that way then.

I made what I thought was a compromise with bad grace, and suggested a diversion around Lake Naivasha. Before Gilgil, however, we pulled off the road at Kariandusi with a view of Lake Elementeita with flamingoes on it. The countryside down in the Rift was dry and sere again and muggy. I had another migraine hovering. Kariandusi was the site of excavations of Early Stone-age people and there was a small museum where a collection of shiny obsidian stone tools were found and showing how the original layout of the primitive camp had been. The date of the site was not well-established then but it was known to be several hundred thousand years old. I was still unhappy with our awkward programme and so did not get as much out if it as I should have.

After Gilgil, I took the circular road around Lake Naivasha. It was particularly bad and potholed, but was spectacular. This lake was freshwater unlike most Rift Valley alkali lakes so there were no flamingoes, but the vegetation was much richer. Fine yellow-boled fever trees and other less-spectacular acacias crowded the water's edge. Reeds stretched out in the shallows and we stopped to study a rough construction over the water. It must have been a fishing platform of some kind I thought, but I could not imagine the local Africans setting out for a day's sport with rod and line: catching fish for them was a serious business of getting food. There were thatched shelters on them which showed that they were used for lengths of time. I felt something special about that platform over the water, as if we were in touch with truly old Africa. Maybe it was a lingering feeling from the Stone-age hand-axes at Kariandusi.

The AA guide book had described a camping park on the south shore of the lake and we found it near a boating club. It was called Marineland and had good facilities and a large cleared area under giant fever trees where camp sites were laid out. There were others camping, local settler families, and there were sailing dinghies and fishing boats moored in the water or hauled out on trailers. We had a good dinner and hot showers and enjoyed our companionship.

My incipient migraine was dissolved but we were bothered by mosquitoes in the night.

CHAPTER FIFTEEN : *MZIMA SPRINGS AND MALINDI*

As often happened, we had lost a day or two and realised over breakfast that it was Sunday. The only reason why it was a different day was that two or three camping parties had arrived the evening before and a number of day-outing and boating parties started coming in. Boats were being launched from trailers, children were rushing about and women were unpacking folding chairs and the food and equipment for barbecues and lavish picnic-lunches from cool-boxes and wicker hampers.

We used very little money in the way we were travelling, camping and buying our food economically and fresh from local dukas and markets. When on the move we only had one really proper meal a day, in the evening, and that was usually an economical chunk of local beef or goat sliced up, or piece of chicken fried in whatever oil was locally available (olive oil along the Mediterranean, groundnut oil in East Africa and sunflower in the south). A mound of chopped onion and garlic and pieces of tomato were then cooked in the juice with more oil. Quite often there would be fried eggs or eggs scrambled in with the onions.

Boiled rice was used to soak up the juices left from the frying and all of this was eaten hungrily, always with fresh tomatoes but there would be bananas, paw-paw, pineapple or any other local fruit to go with it. Sometimes we would have a green vegetable if we could find it. At breakfast we usually had bread, toasted on the end of a fork over the Primus because it would be stale, and fruit with two cups of very sweet coffee and dried milk.

For lunch we would have fresh bread if we could buy it with cheese and tomatoes, or whatever snack was available in the market or a café. Samousas were always good value in East Africa and along the Mediterranean there had been those magnificent and succulent 'sandwiches' made by slicing open a round loaf of unleavened bread and stuffing it with an oily mix of salads flavoured with anchovies or cheese.

Cigarettes were cheap all the way across Africa and so was wine in the North. Wine and spirits (apart from the Warigi) were expensive in the East, but beer and soda drinks were cheap. Petrol was much cheaper when we got to Kenya, especially on the coast. So we lived simply.

*   *

I suppose I was selfishly pleased that morning beside Lake Naivasha to discover that it was a Sunday because it gave me a rationalised excuse to myself for not 'doing' Nairobi. Everything would be closed up and the city would have been dead. We would have checked into a relatively expensive hotel and mooned around or sat in a bar drinking. We knew nobody and had no contacts.

As if reading my thoughts, Barbie admitted over our coffee: "Not much point in stopping in Nairobi, being a Sunday."

I smiled gratefully at her and waved at the increasing domestic clamour about us. "We don't want to stay here do we?"

She made a face. "I don't really go for all these jolly colonial Pommies having their family holiday. It's a bit different to Entebbe."

I laughed with relief. "Nor do I," I said. "To be honest with you, Barbie, I'm truly happiest with just you and me in the bush. I'm not interested in these Kenya towns and cities and all. ..."

She held up her hand. "We know all about that, Den. We've had discussion about that. Secretly, I agree with you... I admit that I'm disappointed. I expected something much more sophisticated about East Africa. You know, Hemingway and romantic White Hunters and all. We've both seen the movies, but I suppose you had a better idea that they were not really real, being an Affie yourself in a way.

"I've seen that the local whities are all stuck-up settler-colonial types looking down at us as if we were some kind of tramps and the local blackies are scared of us because they think we are the same as the stuck-up local whities. And we don't begin to have the kind of money to go on one of those marvellous safaris we read about."

"It's a Catch 22," I said. "We are neither fish nor fowl. Maybe in future when there are more budget tourists and travellers like us it will change. We've not seen one other European-registered vehicle

209

and no campers except for the young Germans at Entebbe, and these people coming out for the weekend from Nairobi. The hotels are all 'proper', with dressing up for dinner and quite expensive. We don't even have the right clothes to stay in a city hotel! We left ours in Mombasa."

Barbie was nodding. "Yeah. It's like on the ship and the difference between us and those nice Froggies we travelled with and those who were in the first class. If you're a whitie in Kenya, you're expected to be going first class whether you like it or not."

"I'm afraid so," I explained what I had often felt from my own experiences. "When we are in our own countries, we can choose what style we want to experience. We're both accustomed to 'first class' as well as roughing it. That's the great advantage I've always seen in being an 'old colonial' from Australia, South Africa or wherever. Our families went to the colonies in the hard times of the nineteenth century. Class mostly got rubbed out. Europeans are so conscious of class, and these Brits brought that whole bag of tricks with them to Kenya."

Barbie agreed. "Too right. To begin with, I could never understand why some of the boys I went out with in London would never go to a really posh place, and others would go nowhere else. That's one of the reasons I stopped going out with them. There was also the sex thing. Because I was from Aussie, they thought I was fair game and it was the upper-class boys who were worst at that. They thought they were doing me a great bloody favour by taking me to some West End bar or restaurant. I could have taught them a thing or two."

We sat there for a while in that tranquil place by the great African lake, in the dappled shade of the giant fever trees, sipping our coffee and watching the settler parties and expat families getting on with their Sunday outing. I felt quite alienated from them and sudden irritation made me restless.

"Shall we make a move?" I asked.

Barbie got up. "So where are we heading today?"

*   *

The main road up the escarpment and then on to Nairobi was surprisingly busy with local Sunday traffic. There were a few beat-up old pick-ups crowded with blacks going to visit family and there was a stream of cars containing whites and Indians out for the day to

210

picnic or lunch with friends. Around Lake Naivasha there were famous residences where the 'Happy Valley' set had created the notorious legend with their riotous living. But apart from the decadent aristocrats culled from different parts of Europe, there was a rich spectrum of colonial society farming in the district. Some had left with the coming of independence but many hung on for a number of years before the pressures of black population growth, the unreliability of labour and political uncertainty made them take up government offers or sold out to new organisations employing modern agro-technology. This was the well-established settler society into which we had no entree, had we wanted it, and who made their own pleasures in their private clubs and estates.

At the bottom of the Rift Valley escarpment there was a pretty little chapel with tiled roof that Italian P.O.W.s had built during the war while they were constructing the road which cut its way into the steep flanks. There was a similar chapel, somewhat larger, which had been built in a huge P.O.W. camp on the Oribi Flats outside Pietermaritzburg and I was intrigued. At the top there was a place to park and gaze at the view and we did that. We both wondered if we would ever come back and supposed that we probably would not. Of course I have been back several times since then, but Barbie has not.

I felt a sudden hint of sadness there, that we were definitely more than halfway through our great odyssey in distance and variety of geographical experiences. My feeling of sadness was probably enhanced by the rumblings of the strained discussions over the last day or two. We were both feeling the same kind of emotions although we did not share them openly or understand them properly. We had suddenly moved into the second half of our adventures without noticing and without dramatic fanfare. It was beginning to go too fast.

We drove about the Sunday-dead centre of Nairobi easily with little traffic. We entered on the Limuru Road which met Forest Road near the smart little shopping centre in Parklands and were able to buy some provisions at an Indian duka which was open. Government Road led us into the heart of town and we admired Delamere Avenue shaded by an avenue of trees. There was a branch of Woolworths. Barclays DCO and Standard Bank had solid stone head-office buildings, there was a branch of a South African building society, the Colonial Mutual, and we saw the famous New Stanley Hotel which did not impress us much. It and the nearby Ambassadeur Hotel were both new concrete blocks and could have been in any city anywhere.

"Robert Ruark's characters stayed at the Norfolk Hotel, in bungalows at the back where there was lots of drinking and happy fornicating. I wonder where it is?" I said. We did not find it, not realising that it was on the edge of the city centre. We saw the central market and would like to have shopped in it, but it was closed.

"Well that's about it," I sighed as we drove over the railway bridge and out on the Athi Road, passing the police lines and the prison. We filled up with petrol and checked Landie then were on our way southeast to the Indian Ocean.

After Athi River, we were back on that long haul of dust and rattling and crashing.

*   *

At Mtito Andei, we had cold Cokes at the Tsavo Inn and I topped up with petrol. It was getting late so we set up camp at the official site near the entrance gate to Tsavo Park West. We had it to ourselves and parked Landie amongst thorn trees and Barbie had a luke warm shower. It was very dry in the Tsavo Park and warm with balmy air. I was glad to get away from the cool of the Highlands and although the rainforest and agricultural plantations in Uganda had been rich with green lushness, I really preferred the dry thornbush and semi-desert conditions of Tsavo.

There was an old baobab tree at the camp and I told Barbie a story about camping in the Kalahari with an old school pal three years before when we had enjoyed several idyllic days in a bush camp in the midst of giant baobabs and had seen much game including a moonlight stampede of wildebeest. The sun, conveniently, lowered itself behind the baobab there and added truth to my rambling story.

In the morning when we looked out of the back of Landie, a small herd of waterbuck were startled by our sudden appearance. Some scuttled away but most melted quietly into the surrounding bush. Barbie exclaimed at waking up to see the antelope all around us, so gentle and at ease.

Following our trusty Shell map of the Park we made our way across a wide plain between the Chyulu mountains to the north and volcanic hills to the south. We followed directions to Mzima Springs which we had been reading about. It was an oasis of pure water fed by underground geological systems from the Chyulu mountains and filtered by the volcanic structures. Some water maybe even came

212

from the glaciers on Mount Kilimanjaro which was not that far away; maybe forty miles as the crow flies.

Mzima Springs was quite well organised. There was a parking place and paths down to the water. Guides were available and although I do not usually like to be herded about, we seemed obliged to use one as there was a sign warning against the dangers of elephants, hippos and crocodiles. He was a pleasant fellow and did not intrude on us. Barbie was glad to have a guide I think when we came in sight of the pools and there was a fine old solitary bull elephant not thirty yards away on the opposite bank, pulling at some cherished fresh leaves on a tall fever tree. I felt marvellous standing there in the open and watching the elephant so close and at ease. I photographed him and we watched until he had finished stuffing the leaves into his mouth and sauntered off.

The guide took us to the observation platform where we could watch the hippos in the crystal-clear water. They had a particularly pink tinge to their skin and were resting in the shade of a clump of reeds on the opposite bank so we could only take pictures when they surfaced for air every now and then, blowing and snorting, before going down again. The pools were surrounded by green vegetation. Fever trees were the backdrop and in the foreground there were many indigenous palms with shining fronds. Smaller bushes filled the gaps and reeds grew in the shallows. The sandy bottom of the pools was easy to see in the gently swirling water but because of refraction I could not make out the bulks of the hippos until they surfaced and whooshed or grunted at us.

Further along, we went down into a cylindrical underwater viewing point which was like a miniature submarine conning-tower with thick glass windows. Fish swam close to the windows, swimming round and around and, beyond, we could see into the water as far as the shadows of the opposite bank. The sunlight flickered constantly from the rippling and swirling of the surface and we were disappointed not to see hippos swimming by. I asked the guide about that and he said that sometimes you could see them but not often.

Gently rushing rapids separated the upper pools from a lower stretch where there were crocodiles but we did not see any. Vervet monkeys swung by in the branches of the fever trees, chattering when they saw us watching them. A large group of English tourists came then, talking and laughing, so we left. There was no sign of the elephant and the hippos had put their heads down so the place looked quite deserted and I hoped the tourists were not going to be disappointed. As always, you see so much more in the African wilds if you are in a small group or alone, move slowly without aggression, and keep quiet.

Nearby there was a simple 'Safari Lodge' at Kitani and we were hoping to stay one or two nights there. The brochure had told us that there were simple *bandas* (cottages) with their own toilets where you did your own catering and it had seemed to be ideal for us. There were outdoor fireplaces and firewood so you sat around your private fire in the wilds, grilling meat or merely savouring the delights of the starlit night. Maybe there would be the thrilling grunt of a lion or the whooping of hyenas. It would have rounded off our touring safari perfectly.

But the lodge was fully booked. We felt desolated and somehow insulted. We had no problems with accommodation anywhere and had travelled so far without any constriction. Even in those huge North African cities, we had always been lucky with places to stay. So we stood nonplussed outside the lodge office staring at each other.

We had a snack lunch and discussed our next move. "Let's go to the smart lodge at Kilaguni and see what it's like. If it's not too terribly expensive, we might stay the night?" I suggested.

From Kitani we missed a turning which must have been important because we drove for what seemed a long distance in circles in an area of volcanic hills. It was not serious but it was hot and we were getting weary.

The Kilaguni Lodge was a proper tourist hotel. From the gravelled car park a path went through well-kept gardens with flowers and decorative bushes scattered about a lawn. There seemed to be nobody staying there and I mentally counted my money remaining, then thought that they would surely cash a travellers' cheque. A pleasant young black man at reception shook his head. The place was fully booked with a tour group.

"Well, we can have a drink at least. Can we have a drink on the verandah?" The lobby led directly onto a shaded terrace.

"I'm sorry, Sir. If you are not resident we can't serve you."

I stared at him. I was hot, dirty and tired. "Not even a Coca-Cola?"

He grinned uncomfortably and shrugged. "The bar is closed, Sir."

We walked out onto the verandah and sat there for a while in resentful silence.

"Shit!", Barbie said after a while and we smoked cigarettes. Kilimanjaro should have been visible, but although the sun was shining strongly there was haze and cloud in the direction of the highest mountain in Africa. We were not having much luck. And then a small herd of elephants came out of the surrounding bush to drink in the artificial pool which had been created in front of the building. We watched them for a while, grateful that the animals were not letting us down.

"How much is it to stay here?" I asked the receptionist on the way out.

"A hundred and thirty five shillings a day for a double, Sir," he said. "That includes a private bathroom. But, all meals and drinks are extra."

"We could camp for two weeks for the same money," I said as we climbed into Landie which was as hot as an oven from standing in the vertical sun. "I'm glad they were full up, because I was so mad I might have checked in out of spite and bad temper." Barbie laughed at my childish anger.

There was a signpost to the Roaring Rocks lookout and we parked Landie and climbed up to see a breathtaking view over hundreds of square miles of bush country: the real Africa. I took a photograph which I treasured for years thereafter. Whenever I showed it, it generally produced indrawn breath. Twenty years later I took another photograph from the exact same place with the exact same lens although the camera body was different.

We drove all the way back to the campsite at the Mtito Andei entrance gate because we had no alternative. Barbie complained that she was feeling filthy and went off to the shower. We had no fresh food and while I was warming up a mediocre meal from tins a party arrived in locally registered cars and pitched camp cheerfully, all jolly and full of good spirits, hauling out a case of beers. They barbecued steaks and chops over the coals of their fire later.

*   *

Barbie was feeling "a bit off" the next morning and I was feeling jaded too. I was beginning to long for the cottage by the ocean and to be able to stop moving and driving on endless dirt roads. The malaise I had been infected with after leaving Uganda was not going away despite all the efforts I was making to keep cheerful and level-headed. Instead of being a pleasure, the safari was becoming a trial.

Nevertheless, in the spirit of 'doing' it properly because we would not be back again, we decided to drive through the Park to the Tsavo Gate. We stopped again at the Roaring Rocks and savoured the view over the escarpment. To descend into the country of the view, we traversed the broken lava flow off the Chiemu Crater and I got out to take a picture of the broken mass of eroded black rock. I was so used to going everywhere with my hardened bare feet that I did not put on my sandals and immediately suffered, cutting myself on the razor-sharp clinkered lava.

"You can be a bloody idiot, Den," Barbie told me.

The road was particularly bad, twisting all the way along the course of the Tsavo River with many washaways and stretches with large stones and deep potholes. It was another clear sunny day and the heat built up as noon approached. We travelled over two hundred miles within the Park and I was grateful to reach the main road although I would have been amazed at that feeling two or three weeks previously.

The red dust boiled about us and we bumped and crashed along, but it was possible to go faster, hitting 45 miles an hour for long stretches. At Mackinnon Road the tar started again and we seemed to reach the outskirts of Mombasa in a flash.

The Metropole Hotel had a room for us and we checked in with relief.

*   *

On Wednesday, 1st September, we moved into the beach cottage. It was a day of rush, rush; bank to change money, post office to pick up mail, to the estate agent to collect our gear deposited with them, get the keys and pay a month's rent in advance, then shopping to top up basic foods and domestic needs as well as fresh food.

The cottage was lying quiet in the sun with the wind sighing in the tall casuarinas and clattering in the coconut palms. There was the gentle roar of the waves on the reef. The scent of the sea was strong and the air was damp and salty. I loved it. I felt so excited about being a beachcomber in the battered old cottage which was what I had been dreaming about. It could not have been more perfect. I walked about with bare feet on the coarse grass and had an almost ecstatic liberation of mind and spirit. We were not moving on anywhere!

But, there were real matters to attend to and Barbie was quickly into the building and going through it. Her feminine instincts were to the fore; to see to the home before being romantic.

"Hey, Den," she called. "It's all pretty cungy. The kitchen is a mess and everything is kind of stale and mouldy."

We set to, getting the first level of order established. I unpacked everything from Landie, either taking the obvious things inside and roughly deciding which should go where, kitchen, living-room or bedroom, and then leaving the rest outside the back door for the moment. Barbie did the finer sorting, deciding which particular box or case should be unpacked in what area. There was reasonable cupboard space and there were basic cooking and domestic equipments, so we did not have to use our own pots and pans. But she wanted to wash all our things thoroughly before putting them away.

Everything that came out of Landie was covered in layers of dust and the evidence of hours and hours of rattling and crashing about on the long roads of Africa was there. The oil and grease protecting tools and spare parts had turned into a dirty sludge. Boxes and containers were worn and abraded, anything metal had scars of rubbing and scratching, cloth was worn through in places. I went up onto Landie's roof and heaved down the great green canvas awning with its poles and the extra spare wheel which had been lashed to the roof rack. The awning had been rubbed through into several holes.

I left all the petrol and water cans, awning and so on outside and we concentrated on the interior of the cottage. The refrigerator stank with that particular odour that old fridges get when they are shut up after not being properly cleaned. I had switched on the power at the primitive fuse-box as a priority and the fridge was humming and the water was getting hot, so Barbie used detergent powder liberally, washing and soaking. I got out the broom and swept the floors which had accumulated trails of dust and scattered leaves which had blown in through the louvred windows. Ants had made little pathways and mounds of dust and there were dead insects and the wings of their flying types everywhere. With all the windows open and the late afternoon breeze blowing fresh sea air through, it all began to come right.

By sundown, Barbie reckoned that she had broken the back of the cleaning, fresh food was in the cooling fridge and I could cook while she tackled the unpacking and organising of the bedroom. There was a giant old bed in there and two single beds. Musty sleeping-nets which had not been washed in ages hung from square frames. We had to use our own linen and Barbie brought out clean sleeping sheets. A mountain of personal and general washing was growing ready for the next day.

Eventually, we were sitting at a dining table, eating dinner off china plates and grinning at each other. Afterwards, I wandered out on the front lawn and down to the edge of the untended garden. The tide was in and white flashes showed where small waves were washing over coral outcrops and splashing on the beach. The breeze ruffled my hair and the warm salt air filled my lungs. Above, in gaps between clouds, the stars were shining clearly.

We had long hot showers and slept like the dead.

In the morning after mentally luxuriating in the peace and stability of our situation, there was the pleasure of a more leisured cleansing. Barbie set to with the mountain of laundry and I tackled Landie. There was an old garden hose and I soused everything. The outside, the back, the cab, the engine. Hosing out all the white dust from the Sahara and the red dust of Kenya, I watched it rush away in orange rivers. In the back, hosing was not enough and I had to get in with a broom and sweep out fine mud and layers of grit and gravel. The effect of the hosing and washing with an endless stream of clear water captivated me and I went over and over this or that part.

For months now, water had been so precious, carried about with us in our own containers and filled at irregular intervals and with some effort. Spraying and splashing with a hose was miraculous.

Barbie called to me once or twice: "Careful you don't wash Landie away," or: "Come on, Den, I need some help here!"

I had to give it up in the end and left Landie to dry out with everything open and the bonnet lifted. Steam rose from the metal and little piles of drying red mud showed a pattern where Landie was parked.

After that orgy of cleansing, there was time to re-read mail, write letters and postcards to friends and family. And to realise that there was nothing imperative to do next, or some place we had to reach by that evening.

One of the serious projects I had set myself was to see if I could write a novel on our grand safari, especially while we were beachcombing. When we first met, back in England, I had explained to Barbie that whilst I was going to meet all the joint expenditure for the whole safari and obviously expected fellowship and help through all the exigencies of the journey, I wanted her to keep our diaries and type up any writing that I did. Barbie's work in England had been various jobs as a temporary secretary or pool typist and she was obviously competent to help me in this way. Now, at Bamburi, with all our gear out in a stable place, my old portable typewriter and the stationery I had brought with me was sorted and laid out, ready for the literary activity. Barbie looked at it and gave me a rueful grin.

"Now begins the slavery of the typewriter, I suppose," she said.

"I've got to produce the raw material first," I replied. "That's always supposed to be agony far surpassing any mundane activity like typing."

She snorted. "Why can't you type your bloody great novel straight off, anyway?"

"I can of course, and I've done it before more than once. I wrote an adventure story on that very typewriter when I was in the Navy twelve years ago. That was the first big purchase with my own wages. But, it would take twice as long if I did that. I thought if I wrote the first draft by hand and did all the crossing out and messing around and you could roughly keep up with me, then what you typed would be more-or-less the clean second draft. In the same time, we would be doing two jobs."

"It makes sense, I suppose. Of course I will. When are you going to start?"

I looked around the living room which we had begun to make comfortable and homely. Barbie had put some bougainvillaea blossoms in a vase, there were our books and maps and my portable radio, my writing equipment and even our precious souvenirs scattered about. To make it a real beachcombers' creative base, I should get going, make the vibes start, have a psychic feeling of purpose.

"No time like the present, I suppose," I said.

The writing actually got going easily. I had done some scribbling earlier on: a bit on Djerba Island and at Tobruk when we were staying in the hotel before the attack on Barbie, but I had torn up the results. Bamburi was the right place and time. I suppose one reason for determining to write a book there was to 'prove' that I could do it, and that we were not just languishing unproductively.

Related to that was the puritan ethic. I should be justifying this adventure in some tangible way.

But there was also the genuine creative urge. I had written immature and romantic adventure stories since the age of fifteen at boarding school, writing in an exercise book during evening prep because it looked as if I was writing history or English essays. I had written the next while in the Navy, one in London, and two more while in Nigeria and after we moved to Natal. Writing was my natural hobby, I did not feel right unless there was a book in the making. One day I would publish, maybe.

In the next weeks, unless there was a serious reason not to, I always got up early with the dawn and wrote for maybe two hours until I took Barbie tea and she came out to start the day. In the afternoon, I would write some more, although that was more irregular even if I often produced much volume. It was the morning stint that got the core of the pages covered. It is a writing routine that first became ingrained in me during those beachcombing weeks at Bamburi. Nearly thirty years later, after writing seven more books and after seeing three of them published, I still work in exactly the same way, except that I work on a computer now.

*   *

We only did one other exploring expedition before leaving Kenya. I was interested in the history of the Indian Ocean, which became a passion in later years, and the East African coast was a rich lode to mine.

I was, in fact, quite ignorant of the role the East African coast had played, not having studied African history north of the Limpopo River or outside of Nigeria, and in those days there were no popular books to read. My knowledge of the Indian Ocean did not go further than British naval history which did not really begin until the colonial wars with France, or a sketchy outline of the pioneering Portuguese explorers. But I did know that Vasco da Gama, the greatest, had stopped at Mombasa and then, crucially, had anchored for some days at Malindi where he negotiated with a sophisticated Swahili Sultan, met Indian ships and hired an Indian navigator from Gujerat who took him directly across to Calicut on the Malabar Coast of India. So I knew that there were competent sailors traversing the Indian Ocean long before Columbus crossed the Atlantic, but that is about all.

Barbie and I explored Mombasa thoroughly in the weeks to come, but I wanted to visit Malindi and the Arab city of Gedi which had been made into an open air museum not long before.

We set off immediately after breakfast on a bright sunny day. At Mtwapa there was a toll-bridge and the road to Kilifi passed through fields of sisal. At Kilifi there was a ferry and after that the road was red dust and corrugations barrelling through high forest. The forest was virgin, I was sure, and filled with a rich variety of trees in a spectrum of green colours.

I could imagine how it might have been for early Arab colonists and the native people living there a thousand years ago. They would not have communicated much with each other because there would have been no easy way of moving through that tangled forest and to keep footpaths open would have been an unending chore which would have been profitless unless there was a good reason to do so. The trade which Arabs would have been interested in was up-country, for ivory and slaves, so they would have made tracks along rivers or directly through to the open thornveld beyond the coastal strip in the easiest way. The guide book showed that there were Arab settlements at the mouths of rivers where the Arab dhows could come in to anchor through gaps in the coral reefs.

We reached Malindi about noon. It was a small town with a road parallelling the sea with some rough dukas on the landward side and several hotels with extensive grounds on the seaward side. Ernest Hemingway is said to have come to one of the hotels during his Africa safari days for the marlin and swordfish fishing and did a lot of drinking and hell-raising there. No doubt he wowed the local settler wives holidaying there and bedded a few whilst their husbands were still back at their shambas getting in the harvest.

We had a look at Lawford's Hotel which was pleasant in an old-colonial style and where I would been happy to stay awhile. It had rambling pre-war buildings with palm thatch roofs and the bar opened onto a terrace with a swimming pool. That is where Hemingway passed his days, I believe. There were old palms planted amongst poinsettia and cannas on the wide grassy lawn leading to what seemed to me to be a rather muddy beach with silt-stained water lapping it sullenly. There were not many people staying there, or they were all out for the day.

Nearby was the Sinbad Hotel with a high pseudo-Arab facade and colonnaded verandah with arches. It looked as though it had a recent face-lift and I did not find it as attractive as Lawford's. The tariff was seventy five shillings a day per head for full board with air-conditioning which could be considered reasonable, I supposed, but it was way beyond my meagre budget. I asked about Vasco da Gama's monument at the reception and was told it was further around the beach.

The main street was partly shaded by tall gum trees where there was a roadside café with tables outside, gay with advertising placards. We were getting hungry so we stopped and had cold Cokes and packets of freshly fried chips. It was like being at an English seaside resort, especially when young 'Engie-types', as Barbie called them, sat at adjacent tables. I drove to the end of the single main street and there seemed to be no way to the beach except through the grounds of the hotels. I was disappointed about not finding da Gama's monument and supposed that we would have to go through one of the hotels and then walk along until we found it. I had not liked what I saw of the beach and there seemed no sign of the clear water and coral reefs that we were expecting. Time was passing and we both wanted to visit Gedi, so I gave up.

[I visited Malindi twenty years later when I learned that we had not been properly directed. The old settler hotels faced north on the westward side of a point of land and it was on the eastward side where the original Arab town was sited, and there were the coral reefs and the small bay where the Portuguese fleet met other Indian Ocean trading ships in 1498. The replica of the Portuguese padrão stands on a coral promontory there, overlooking the clean blue ocean.]

Gedi was not a disappointment. The ruins were just off the main road, deep within the forest. Once parked and having paid our entrance fee at a gate in an old coral-stone wall, we were away from the 20th century. We wandered along a path amid the 14th century ruins in ancient peace. The sun was shining through gaps in the giant coastal rainforest as we studied the Great Mosque and the Sultan's Palace and took photographs. If the sun had not been shining I am sure it would have had a sombre and mysterious, even somewhat frightening, feel. There were old ghosts there and the sense of mystery was heightened because no one knew precisely why the city had been abandoned. There are no records of it in Portuguese journals of the time. We picked up an official descriptive brochure at the small museum which said:

222

It is possible, from the quantity of sherds of 15th century porcelain found in the surface levels, that Gedi ceased to exist as a town early in the 16th century. The cause of her downfall may have been the punitive expedition which was sent by Mombasa against Malindi after the sack of Mombasa by the Portuguese in 1528.

It all seemed obscure to me and more research has produced a better and more cohesive historiography since then. Nevertheless, both of us had our eyes opened and we were suitably awed by the visit.

This was not Egypt with pyramids and amazing temples thousands of years old, it was 'real' Africa of the sub-Sahara region and my whole concept of it was changed that day. Not that I suffered a blinding flash of inspiration, but it worked on me in the next few years and influenced my thinking and my interests, particularly when I worked on a large tourism project in Mozambique in the late 1960s. Barbie was also much intrigued and with eager interest we both read a book by James Kirkman, the doyen of East African history and archaeology, which was amongst the collection of books and magazines left on the bookshelves at Bamburi for visitors to read.

CHAPTER SIXTEEN : *BEACHCOMBERS AT BAMBURI*

We spent nearly two months in the cottage at Bamburi. In the end we had to move out a week early because the owners wanted to use it, but by then a week this way or that seemed to have no significance. Time had become flexible in the way it does when there are no pressures on it.

In the next years, those weeks at Bamburi achieved the aura of a brief glimpse of tropical Paradise. In the golden glow of memory, nothing seemed to go wrong, everything was a slow-moving experience of warmth and light and easy freedom of endless days by the tropical sea and its coral reefs. Even now, writing nearly thirty years later, Bamburi has a unique place in my memory: there is powerful nostalgia for a time which can never be repeated, when all life seemed to be simpler and we were young and fresh and that capsuled experience, separated from all other experiences, was a symbol of youth and freedom.

Today, when the world and Africa in particular is more complex and Africa has become a fearful continent of social degradation and turmoil, I look back on the Bamburi experience with gentle yearning. Within a lifetime, it is a long time ago and there are no sharp sentimental aches, but the fond memories are there and will always provoke a smile of pleasure in recalling.

Especially, there was the pleasure of total isolation. We had not particularly sought isolation and had no plan to 'cut ourselves off', but it happened. We did not appreciate it then because it seemed natural and had more-or-less crept up on us. After all, we were inhabiting a cottage in its own grounds, separated from neighbours by vacant land, tall trees and scrub bush. I was not sure who and where our nearest neighbours were. I don't think we bothered to find out although I have a memory of having to dump our garbage from time to time in a pit off to one side amongst some bushes, behind some sweetly perfumed frangipanis, and shovel soil onto it to keep the flies down; and from that place you could see the white flash of a lime-washed wall of another cottage through the trees.

Nobody came to the door in all those weeks, no human passed though 'our' property and the beach was almost always deserted. Only at week-ends did a few Indian families come near to us on the beach because there was the Aga Khan recreation centre some distance to the south, but they were respectable middle-class families and neither they nor their children presumed to intrude. There were two or three fishermen who kept dugout canoes somewhere along the beach and on most days the pencil shape of their simple boats could be seen out by the reef. They became a reassuring sight removing the possibility of absolute loneliness. The white triangles of open-decked sailing dhows passed up and down beyond the reef occasionally and these were evocative of ancient continuity and were specially treasured.

Barbie and I did not become hermits, we frequently went into Mombasa or to the duka at Nyali for shopping and recreation, but we did become introverted and self-contained physically and psychically. No doubt, 'experts' would say that this was not entirely healthy and from time to time we had a silly argument over a triviality, but we were not conscious of any need to change what we were doing or the way we managed our days. We established strong bonds of sincere and loyal friendship. We had already stood together during the trials and pleasures of hard travel amongst strange people. At Bamburi we had the leisure and the incentive to learn about each other. We had intellectual and cultural differences, but there was a solid base of a sense of discipline and honour which tied us together. In retrospect, I know it was a unique experience and it is treasured for its simple truth.

The ability of the mind to recall the good times and forget the bad, about which psychologists place great emphasis, is real. Reading our diaries, I know that the sun did not always shine, the breeze was not always mild, our happiness was not always untrammelled and we did not exist in a constant state of euphoria.

The monsoon blew and there were days when it rained constantly from a leaden sky and waves thrashed in the lagoon and pounded on the barrier reef in a sullen roar. Other days, after a spell of rain, it was very hot and the air was like a steamy fog creating unpleasant lassitude and one's clothes stuck to greasy, sweating skin when we went into Mombasa for some essential.

There were occasions when we were both somewhat depressed, probably for similar reasons. It was when we picked up mail from home or friends living in the 'real' world we had left for the duration of our journey that strains were felt, when that other alien world seemed to intrude on the strange delight of the Bamburi capsule. We both knew that there had to be an end to the idyll we were living and that we had to return to normality sometime in the months to come. As time passed, the reality of this impinged more often, I suppose. I did not know what I was going to do with my career when I got home.

I realised that I was not meeting enough people and 'characters' to enliven what could be a dull description of events in the travel book I wanted to write. I did not have the journalistic experience or know-how to go out and find the 'characters' to put in what I imagined might then be a successful popular story. I did not realise that a real-life story does not have to be contrived if it has sufficient interest to make it worthwhile for others to share. This made me feel inadequate at times and spurred me on to at least complete a simple adventure novel while I was there. I needed to justify my grand safari in some way. In retrospect, I know that it was unnecessary, the acquisition of experience itself was enough justification, but I was subject to the pressures of the ethics with which I had been brought up.

No doubt Barbie had enough of her own concerns to worry her, although we neither of us discussed our private lives in the world that lay outside our mutually committed months together. No doubt Barbie worried about what she was going to do when it was over. But we did not talk about these matters. Maybe we should have done. We both, unspoken, created an invisible intellectual barrier about that 'other' world. We told simple stories about our families or friends but never in greater depth than if we were gossiping with casual acquaintances. That may seem strange, but it was the mechanism we both unconsciously invented to cope with the strange friendship we had forged. It was something stronger than casual friendship of everyday; it was mutual dependance and complete trust.

It was accepted that we would have to bravely part no matter how close we had become during the tenure of our travelling. The occasional personal stresses were painful but they were not destructive. And for the great majority of the time we were very happy.

The invention of particular private words came to fruition at Bamburi. They were personal shorthand, either evolved naturally or adapted from books we were reading. If castaways are left together for many years, they must end up with a personal pidgin or creole and we saw the beginning of it in our own experience. This was another natural symptom of our isolation in the invisible bubble of our own introverted world. We had become increasingly self-contained and found that we had no need of other people to stimulate or entertain.

We did not consciously break away from ordinary life at all; indeed we seemed to spend a lot of time in Mombasa, but the important things happened when we were alone and I was happiest in our cottage and its environment. In any case it would have been rather surprising if our personal relationship and our attitudes to our mutual experience had not changed as time passed and the experience itself began shaping our attitudes. Positive feed-back was at work and our characters themselves were being moulded no matter how mature we might have thought we were.

*   *

The bug that had invaded me in Algeria made its presence felt again and I found out where I could attend a private clinic in Mombasa. A young British doctor took a lot of care with me asking a great number of questions about where I had been and our general lifestyle. I told him about the rough-and-ready treatment I had been given in Libya and he made a face.

"It could be that the penicillin prescribed merely suppressed the organism, or possibly, since you are travelling with a companion that you have been re-infecting each other."

"My friend did complain of something similar briefly in Egypt," I said. I described disturbing Barbie's rash in Egypt and the several times she had complained of tummy upsets when I had not been affected, which had seemed to be unconnected. I had also been afflicted by frequent migraines since arriving in East Africa.

"There you are. This is obviously one of those bacterial infections which we generally call non-specific, because we don't actually know anything about them. They can have apparently different effects in different people to a casual lay inspection, but are the same. If untreated, they either seem to go away but cause damage to an organ which only appears much later, or the symptoms reappear elsewhere with strange rashes or internal manifestations. I'm going to try one of the most recent drugs available. And your companion must take the same course, or you'll just be wasting your time and money. At the end, we'll take some tests and see if it has worked. If not, then there will be something else to try."

"Will this all be very expensive?" I asked, anxiously.

"It's not free! But maybe fifteen pounds will cover it all so you should manage it. But if that's a problem, don't go away; we'll see what can be done."

Barbie and I had to take six pills a day for a while which disgusted her. She hated taking pills. There was our normal Paludrine for malaria, a multivitamin, vitamin C, two fat green antibiotic capsules and some other pill the doctor prescribed, a diuretic I think he said it was. Ten days later, tests showed that the bug had been defeated and it did not raise its head again.

*   *

When we did not go into Mombasa we had a simple routine. I invariably got up with the dawn and wrote my novel on the dining table. When Barbie emerged, we had breakfast of toast and coffee. Sometimes we had a more elaborate breakfast with eggs and once or twice when the weather was particularly fine, we would carry an occasional table out onto the lawn and eat breakfast there. Breakfast was usually prolonged with idle chatter and talk about what to do, did we need provisions and so on. Sometimes, when we were lazy or I was involved with my writing we had a more elaborate brunch and once when I was feeling full of the Bamburi 'good life' I arranged a special lunch out on the lawn with wine cooling on ice and all the trimmings.

Unless the monsoon was blowing strongly that day, and it usually wasn't, I always wore nothing more than one of the soft cotton loincloths that I had bought in Tunisia. One was pink with blue woven patterns and the other was blue with pink patterns. Barbie was able to get out her cotton mini-dresses which had not been recommended wear in the Moslem countries. She dispensed with wearing bras so our clothing was kept to a minimum. She did a lot of sunbathing on one of the several lounging mattresses with which the cottage was furnished. Once we were sure that we were never disturbed, she took to sunbathing in the nude and soon had a dark golden tan all over. My fair skin did not allow that indulgence.

We both read a lot. The cottage had a wide selection of books left there by various tenants and guests over the years. I particularly valued several local publications of history and biography on East Africa and similar books, some published many years before. I 'stole' one of them, *In the Wake of da Gama* by Genesta Hamilton, which I still use as a reference sometimes. We left three or four of our own books behind when we left, which is the acceptable thing to do, so it does not rest on my conscience. Barbie was always happy with plenty of reading material and so was I. The range of books left there by any number of different people over the years which neither of us might ordinarily have read was stimulating and provided themes for conversation.

We both splashed about in the warm sea water when the mood took us but I spent more time down on the beach than she did. I must have spent many hours wandering on the fine white coral sand. I loved that sand which had the consistency of granulated sugar without any of its stickiness. During neap tides when there was a wide swath of dry sand at the edge of our 'garden' it had a special texture that demanded that you walk barefoot on it and loll about with bare skin. Where the sea flooded it, it changed instantly to a hard, compact floor on which it was easy to walk long distances. I used to sit beneath our coconut palm for long periods, especially when I wanted to clear my mind from wrangling over the plot of my novel, and watch the ever-changing colours of the water over the reef and the fair-weather clouds speeding up the coast out at sea in the south-east monsoon. When the monsoon turned wet, the great masses of grey and purple clouds surging and exploding over the ocean had fascination and one could wait to see if one could predict when the grey mass overhead was ready to drop its burden of evaporated sea with a white hiss. If one was caught in the rain it did not matter, for whatever skimpy clothes got wet soon dried and so did oneself.

Almost transparent pink crabs were a constant source of amusement. I watched them endlessly too. They were in every size up to about the breadth of a human hand and were not without cleverness and bright intelligence. They were shy and would come instantly to standstill if they were suddenly threatened. But if there was warning they scuttled fast towards the nearest hole in the sand. Sometimes two might head for the same hole and there was frantic scrabbling. I would tease them by waiting until two seemed equidistant from one hole with none other nearby and them toss a twig at them to see what would happen. Otherwise, it was pleasure to watch them digging holes, scuttling about; examining bits of weed, sea-fruit, dead sea animals or palm nuts for their suitability as food and then struggling to get the salvage to their holes.

They moved very fast in their sideways manner, stopping and starting almost instantly with great acceleration and braking. Their eyes were on stalks of course and they cleaned them by a rapid retraction. There was one crab I identified, it did not retract its eye-stalks together but did so in sequence, one then the other. They re-dug their holes fast too if one trod on one. The sand would fly in a continuous cascade out of the hole. There would be a break and a pink shape would appear to check the surroundings and then there would be another flurry. I took them bits of biscuit and bread to see if they liked them and after a week or two of suspicion they began dragging the strange food into their holes.

One morning when Barbie was sunbathing or busy with chores, I saw one of our local fishermen out by the reef in his canoe. I knew that the tide was ebbing so decided to walk out towards him. I did this, striding out in the lagoon whose water was about a foot deep, stepping from one little dead coral island raised maybe six inches closer to the surface to the next. The floor of the lagoon was level with a rash of worn old coral laid over it in a pattern and it was covered by green sea-grass in swathes and patches. Close to where the fisherman was busy with his throw-net, there was a deep blue channel and I waited there watching him until I thought I was getting too sunburnt and headed back. About halfway, I stopped on a whim to see what shellfish were hiding amongst the sea grass and squatted to look about me. The level of the water had dropped some inches as the tide neared the end of its ebb and it was shallower.

Suddenly I was filled with horror. Amongst the sea-grass, clear now, I discovered a mass of scattered dark purple sea-urchins. Some moved along infinitely slowly, others shifted their wicked spines suggestively in the quiet flow of the water. The gentle breeze ruffled the surface, so you had to look carefully but they were everywhere.

At first I could not believe my eyes and assumed that I had strayed into some unusual domicile of the poisonous creatures and had to get away from it quickly. Weighing each step carefully and suddenly feeling extraordinarily ungainly I stepped from one clear patch to the next. But they were everywhere and I spent a fearful half-hour inching my way back to the shore. I could not understand the strange phenomenon of my strolling out, a quarter of a mile or so,

230

nonchalantly moving along with my eyes on the reef and the fisherman, and not either noticing the sea-urchins nor standing on one. It was an extraordinary mystery and can only be explained by the not understood workings of one's subconscious mind taking care of semi-automatic activities like walking.

Two or three times, or maybe more, Barbie and I walked down the beach to the Whitesands Hotel, our nearest clearly visible neighbour, about a mile to the south. It was a pleasant walk of about twenty minutes and the hotel had much character. It was built of wood close to the sea and its façade was largely constructed of a continuous row of small-paned wooden windows. A verandah ran along the front on which stood cane furniture with faded chintz cushions. The verandah creaked when one walked on it and I imagined the whole building creaking and shaking when a monsoon storm blew. There was an old Swahili waiter with white coat and red fez who served quietly and slowly. At that time of year there were few people staying, mostly elderly settler couples, and certainly no foreign tourists. It was a delightful, old-fashioned colonial beach hotel and its atmosphere charmed me. We would stroll down the beach in the late afternoon when we felt we had to have a break, drink a couple of iced beers and then stroll back in the gathering dusk. From the verandah of the Whitesands you could not see where we lived except for our tall sentinel coconut palm.

In the heat of early afternoon we usually had a short and luxurious snooze on the settees of our living room with the windows and double door wide open. After that there was tea and I might get down to more writing and Barbie either typed or did domestic things. She enjoyed ironing her clothes immaculately after the previous months of not being able to.

After the sun set, I made the evening meal in the little kitchen at the back. I enjoyed cooking and invariably did it and Barbie washed up. Having easy access to fresh food we ate well and with much greater imagination than when we were on the move. Fish, potatoes and pumpkin, green vegetables and a range of spices and condiments entered our diet and we had a fine selection of local fruits.

In the evening we played the radio quite often. There was a western pop music session called the 'Sundown Hour' with an amateur European DJ who made predictable casual conversation and relayed messages between playing ballads and dance music of fairly recent vintage as well as regular favourites like Nat King Cole, Frank

Sinatra, Pat Boon and so on. We usually listened to that programme. Later in the evening there were English language programmes from Kenya Radio which at that time were often political harangues or long reports on the progress of *Harambee,* Jomo Kenyatta's philosophy of self-help to national greatness. Some of the politicians or local pundits commented with what I thought of as being a load of complete rubbish, building imaginary castles in the sky. That annoyed me, because there seemed to be no purpose in exhorting the ordinary mass of people towards some unexplained abstract concept of national togetherness, which would then miraculously produce a prosperity somehow denied them by the wickedness of colonial exploiters.

When I could get Radio Tanzania from Dar-es-Salaam without too many atmospherics, the rhetoric was worse. Julius Nyerere had launched his own, further to the left, programme of *N'jamaa* which seemed clearly Maoist in its inspiration and his people were being pushed into collectivisation of the land and a socialist national economy. There was much exhortation and discussion of four- or five-year plans, all of which eventually failed. Politicians were supposed to give up all their personal possessions before taking office and no doubt some of the idealistic ones, like Nyerere himself, did so. But I was certain that these dreams of utopia were fatally flawed and doomed.

It annoyed me at a time when I visualised all kinds of exciting new opportunities for carefully-encouraged entrepreneurial activity which could have been loosed on the people. I saw cooperative activity as being excellent, but that it should be driven by individual ambition, not commanded by an anonymous state government in the name of patriotism when most people had no traditional or tribal affiliations to each other. The states of East Africa were the relics of European colonial structures created in the 1880s and did not reflect tribal or cultural entities. Instead of resolving this basic problem in the first years of political freedom, politicians tried to hammer together national traditions which were still lacking many years later.

Barbie did not necessarily agree with me, she had gentle liberal-leftist views then and we argued sometimes about what was best for Africa. My experiences in West Africa working in commerce closely with local produce merchants and independent store-keepers had convinced me that Africans were great traders and were better at going for an objective on their own or in family groups than by becoming drones in a great bureaucratic hive. I acquired a pessimistic view of political objectives and the conduct of government in post-colonial black Africa in those days which was reinforced as the years passed.

*   *

We were able to buy wines and spirits at one or two good grocery stores in Mombasa but they were expensive so our budget could not stand a regular supply. So I tended to go for treats every now and again, when we would have sundowners on the lawn or in the easy chairs facing the open windows as the dusk grew, followed by wine with a special dinner. There was a cheap French cognac available, replacing the South African spirit previously popular, which we called Duval's Blood from the name of the shipper, but it was somewhat rough.

We went out on the town twice in the evening. Once was a disaster when I decided that we should do things in style. I began to grow a migraine as we got dressed but was determined on the plan so foolishly took no notice of it and Barbie was spending much time on her appearance. We went to the Oceanic, Mombasa's newest hotel overlooking the sea from a cliff-top eminence. It was a concrete tower of what nowadays would be a mediocre and featureless design but was very modern on the East African coast then. It was air-conditioned so the plate glass windows were sealed, but for whatever reason the air was warm, humid and stale and this put me off and my migraine gathered force. Clearly, the machinery had broken down.

The food from an elaborate and expensive printed menu was poor and badly cooked with tinned vegetables served in a country burgeoning with fresh produce. I assumed the menu was a pre-planned approximation of European haute cuisine which an inexperienced chef was trying to follow. It did not work and made me feel sour about the whole outing.

The white wine was even worse; it was Italian and served warm, the cork was suspicious and it fizzed lightly. I should have sent it back but I was determined by then to have a 'good time'. I felt quite ill afterwards, which had to be the bad wine on top of the incipient migraine, but by now my stubbornness had inflated beyond appeasement and I insisted we go on to the Flamingo night-club right on the seafront. It was noisy and crowded, I drank too much and the whole party was an expensive wash-out. Barbie was upset and I was remorseful.

I had only one more migraine on our safari after that doleful escapade. I later realised that the cessation coincided with the antibiotic treatment I was receiving from the clinic. The frequent migraines I had in East Africa must have been connected to the mystery bug that had invaded me in Algeria. Barbie's tummy upsets also ceased.

Another time we went to a dinner-dance at the Nyali Beach Hotel on a Saturday evening. That was a great success. I do not remember the meal because it was quite inoffensive, but I do remember sitting out on the highly polished cement terrace beside the dance-floor under the balmy tropical night. There was a competent live band which played the conventional dances, foxtrots and waltzes, as well as more popular music of the time and the inevitable 'Nairobi' and 'Wimowe'.

Barbie and I danced a lot, flirted and laughed. It was the only occasion we really spent time together behaving in an ordinary girl-boy way out on an old-fashioned date. During the evening a crowd of young U.S. Navy officers arrived with white girls from the local settler population of Mombasa complete with chaperons. The young officers were from an American aircraft-carrier task force which was in harbour and they were all immaculate in smart tropical uniform and behaving with gentlemanly good manners. I was somewhat amused by them, having been in similar shoes ten years before and appreciated the whole scene. Their arrival added to the jolly atmosphere and increased our enjoyment. The band reacted to them and played better and increased their range of dance-tunes. One of them asked Barbie for a dance, whether out of duty to the 'locals' or because he was showing off, but as I watched I thought Barbie was certainly one of the best looking girls on the floor.

Our usual evening recreation, when we wanted to go out was to the cinema. We went several times although what were showing were usually Hollywood 'B' movies. *Ryan's Express* and *My Fair Lady* (the second or third time for us) were probably the best films we saw. Once or twice we had a meal out in combination with the cinema at what we called the 'Supercort', the restaurant attached to a petrol service station which we had discovered when we first arrived. During the day when we were in for shopping we usually had a cool drink on the terrace of the Manor Hotel or in the courtyard of the Fontanella tea lounge.

234

I decided I would see if I could service Landie myself. In England before departure, I had bought spare oil filters, lubricating oil and a grease-gun and I had all the necessary spanners, so there should have been no problem. I changed the oil all right, lying on my back underneath to unscrew the drain plug and getting hot oil splashed all over my arms. I could reach some of the grease points and seemed to squirt grease in satisfactorily. Others I could not find or could not reach and I thought I would attend to them later. It was the filters that defeated me and I knew that they were particularly important because of the fog of dust in which we had travelled up and down the road to Nairobi. I scraped my hands and cut my fingers and got into a furious temper. Barbie was sympathetic but could not help laughing at me as I got filthier and more angry at my clumsiness and the intractability of machinery. If it had been a real emergency, I would have approached the problem with a different attitude and Barbie would have added necessary psychic support, but since I was more-or-less playing at being a mechanic, nothing went right.

So, Landie was taken to the local agents to be serviced properly for the second time. We spent the day being tourists in Mombasa. We 'did' Fort Jesus and the old town, taking pictures and lingering over curios and souvenirs. Fort Jesus was partly open to the public but was being renovated before being turned into a complete museum complex. It had been a prison for many years and the inside was a mass of red earth being filled and levelled to make a garden in front of the low building in which the various exhibits and archaeological finds were displayed. But we clambered on the great stone walls, streaked with tropical mould and were able to get a feeling for its three centuries of history.

One of the books at the cottage told of its horrendous siege of nearly three years at the end of the 17th century when the Portuguese and local Swahilis held off invaders from Oman with desperate courage under conditions of extraordinary hardship. Thousands died on both sides, mostly from disease. Each batch of reinforcements from India or Arabia brought the plague, it was recorded, which was probably cholera, but dysentery must have been just as serious.

The 'old town' of Mombasa was alive, still inhabited by Swahili people, many of whom displayed their Arabic heritage. There were some big sea-going dhows in the harbour adjacent to the narrow twisting streets of double-storied balconied houses with fine brass-studded carved doors. There was a particular old mosque with a distinctive East African-style minaret and a tiny surviving 17th century Portuguese chapel nearby.

We both bought some souvenirs after spending some hours looking at various carvings and imported ivory and brassware from India. Most of the local carvings, displayed in the main shopping street along from the Manor Hotel, were stylised animals: antelopes, elephants, rhinos and giraffes, but there were some fine heads and full-length sculptures. Carved ivory and genuine antiques were only seen in the Indian stores. I bought a couple of spoons and a print of an elephant by David Shepherd which I still have and occasionally hang it. There were often sailors in uniform from the U.S. Navy ships in port and 'bargains' were advertised with scribbled notices in chalk on blackboards.

*   *

We had no human visitors but there were animals. There were plenty of birds; bulbuls and doves were always about in the garden and weavers chattered high in the trees where they built their hanging nests in a communal group. Of the birds, the pied crows gave us the most delight.

One morning, while I was writing, I heard a crash from the back, outside the kitchen. It seemed very odd that we might be having a visitor at last, especially so early. I went to the kitchen which overlooked the back door but there was nobody there and there was no vehicle apart from Landie. I went outside and found the lid of the rubbish bin lying on the ground and some bits of trash lying beside it. A dog, I thought, and put the lid back on. Another day, I found the lid off and wondered about this dog which we never saw but which came to rummage in our rubbish. It happened again and at last the mystery was solved. Our two resident crows had learned how to get the lid off. They attacked it in unison, grabbing it and beating their wings until it was loose and then prized it off, little by little, until it fell with a crash. Then they disappeared inside to pick and choose. I was so entranced by these crows that I did not bother to weigh the lid down or tie it up.

We did have a dog visit us once. I had sauntered along the beach and was on my way back for tea or coffee when a shaggy dog bounded up to me. I did not see where it came from because it came out of the coastal scrub and had left no footprints. It was well-fed and friendly, licking my hand and submitting happily to my petting. It followed me into our 'garden' and would not be shooed away. "I've got a wolf," I called to Barbie and she made a fuss over it too. It stayed with us for more than a day although we refused to feed it.

Barbie was tormented by reptiles. One day I had gone to Nyali for fresh bread and milk and when I returned she was wrapped in a cloth and quite excited. "I was bathing in the nude out there and suddenly there was this great thing next to me. When I moved it shifted away fast, but it might have come right up to me if I hadn't."

"What was it?" I asked, laughing at the thought of a naked girl leaping up in fright after dozing in the sun.

"Don't bloody laugh! It was a huge goanna, and it could have been dangerous."

"What's a goanna?"

"A huge lizard thing, like a dragon. We have them in Aussie. I didn't know there were such big ones here."

I thought for a moment because I had not met monitor lizards at the seaside before then. "They're what we call a *likkewaan* in South Africa. African monitor lizard is the proper name. They would never harm you, they're too shy."

"Well, I didn't know about your lizard things..."

I saw it once, moving between some bushes in the early morning and it was a big one, maybe four feet or more to the end of its long tail.

Another time, Barbie shouted from the lavatory: "There's a snake in here, Den." That was no laughing matter and I rushed to her.

"What colour, how big, any markings?" I asked. My immediate fear was that it was a night adder which like to come inside buildings and could easily find its way though the wooden louvres. Night adders are dangerous and their venom is a haemotoxin which does serious harm and coagulates the blood. Even if you do not die, there can be bad complications damaging your health in the future.

"It was a thin green snake, I didn't it see while I was on the loo, only afterwards when I pulled the chain." There were tendrils of plants penetrating the shutters and it would have been easy to confuse one with a small snake. I felt relieved, it was probably harmless.

"Was it fat?" I asked. "With a big head?"

"No, it was thin like a twig, but quite long." So it was not a green mamba, but it could still be a boomslang which though back-fanged had a deadly poison and can fasten onto fingers or the side of a hand. I went into the lavatory and rattled things about which produced a head looking over the back of the cistern. It was a slim, streamlined head, quite pretty really. I was sure it was harmless, but there was no way we could live with a snake in the loo.

I fetched a long bamboo and tried to flick it, or persuade it to come out and return through the louvres. I left it for a while, but it was happy to stay there, or terrified of moving. Eventually, I got a piece of fencing wire and used it like a whip, and killed it. I was sorry about that, but there seemed no alternative.

The animals I did not like were the centipedes which came out some nights. We were periodically invaded by all sorts of flying insects at night, buzzing or fluttering around. They were irritating and a nuisance, and their corpses had to be swept up next morning from around the lamps, but there was nothing one could do about them and they did not harm us. There were spiders, too, but we left them alone because they were good at keeping the flying insects at bay. I liked millipedes and was able to convince Barbie that they were harmless, and they disappeared at night anyway. It was the big, fat red centipedes that set my skin crawling. I did not know where they lived, which was the problem. They would suddenly come into sight moving in an exact straight line across the living room floor; fast and utterly purposeful, not like ordinary insects at all which always seem to move about in a random pattern. I killed them without mercy, slapping them with a sandal and then gingerly taking the mangled mess out for the ants to devour. Barbie did not seem to mind them as much as the flying ants, the termites, which came out in swarms in response to some secret natural signal and then left their wings in drifts to be swept up in the morning.

There were some beautiful moths too, huge some of them, and when the atmosphere was right for them, there would be fire-flies dancing in the garden. Bats fluttered against the starry sky.

*   *

At the end of September, I went to the estate agent to pay the next month's rent in advance and he said we may have to leave early, so I should only pay half a month's rent and check with him in a fortnight. In the end we had to leave a week early, and our beachcombing days were suddenly over. We had not been there all that long, seven weeks only, but it seemed to have been forever. We had settled in and become used to the slow-moving days and the easy routine that had naturally evolved. We had not seemed to do much apart from write and type the book, but that had only taken three hours a day on average. What had happened to the rest of the time? We had not been bored, the time had floated away.

I felt awful packing up, and nothing seemed to fit together in the back of Landie. We had lost the art of arranging everything economically with space left over for us to sleep on our foam mattresses lying on top of everything else. We packed the really big and heavy things, like the water containers and the suitcases with clothes and gear not usually needed and then packed and repacked the cooking equipment, the food boxes and the bits and pieces. When we were finished it was not right, but we could not seem to return everything to the way we had arranged the packing so well before.

We had definitely passed a big milestone in time. We were heading south from Mombasa. There were still thousands of miles to travel, but we were long past halfway both in time and distance. Barbie had red eyes when we left Bamburi and I was also choked so that I did not wish to talk. I knew I had left a significant slice of myself there.

On the last morning, 21st October 1965, we rushed around in Mombasa delivering keys, cashing travellers' cheques, posting letters and cards, paying the bill at the clinic, shopping with a different regime in mind, checking Landie and filling all the petrol cans. We were on safari again.

PART FOUR : ON THE WAY DOWN

CHAPTER SEVENTEEN : *KILIMANJARO AND NGORONGORO*

There was all the sadness of leaving a place into which we had become integrated for a while, and been happy, which we knew we would never return to together. Mombasa is unique in any case. Other tropical coasts in the Pacific or elsewhere may seem similar to casual inspection, but the eastern African coral coast with its barrier reefs and atolls has the distinction of being African, and that makes it different. We had spent over eight weeks there, all told. So it was not just nostalgia for a pleasant episode, it was yearning for something particular which had now irrevocably passed by.

We stopped at a roadside stall on the low escarpment outside the mainland suburbs of Mombasa and drank Cokes. There were still coconut palms there amongst the dark green mango trees and bananas in the shambas beside the road. I knew we would not be seeing coconuts again and that touched me in a peculiar way, as if they had become a symbol of everything we had experienced there.

At Voi where the road south branched off we stopped for glasses of fresh milk and potato crisps. Barbie had got a craving for crisps while in Kenya and we had them wherever we could get them. She found them at Malindi for the first time after leaving England and in East and South Africa they were available in packets in most city cafes or petrol stations. After Voi we were on a road new to us, it was gravel and rough. We were gradually climbing and the railway line was winding its way upwards along the same route, crossing the road at frequent intervals. We drove through a section of Tsavo Park West and hoped for the last sighting of an elephant, but were disappointed. At Tavera we crossed into Tanzania after having Landie's papers briefly checked.

Although it was sunny and hot, there was a layer of cloud towering up high off to our right and that had to be where Kilimanjaro was hiding. We were keen to see it and kept on watching, but there was only that frustrating mass. The road was tarred after the border and we spun along. Sisal plantations suddenly replaced the endless scrub bush outside Moshi and we seemed to have arrived at that neat little colonial town quite suddenly.

I stopped for petrol and was harassed by a well-spoken and well-dressed young man who wanted to know how I reconciled my wealth with the state of the exploited masses of Africa. I compared my faded and worn shirt and shorts with his well-pressed trousers and neatly buttoned white shirt with flashy tie. I was not feeling wealthy although I understood what he meant well enough. What surprised me was this aggressive approach from a stranger out of the blue. Africans are traditionally polite and are private people with elaborate courtesy. He ostentatiously left the filler cap for me to replace and counted my money with elaborate care. "What can such as you do for Africa?" he asked me as I was getting into Landie.

"I'm helping to pay the wages of such as you. I wonder why?" I replied angrily.

It was the first personal evidence I had of the far-left politics of the Nyerere regime in Tanzania which were getting into their stride then. I had often thought it strange that socialists who endlessly promoted themselves as being so 'humanistic' and of the Common Man seemed to be capable of the same aggressive arrogance towards those not holding their faith as any racist or nationalist. I remember being particularly angry with that young black socialist in Moshi. His approach to me was clearly racist: he had no idea of my circumstances, wealth or anything else. I was merely judged on my white skin.

"What's the matter Den?" Barbie asked as I drove off. "What was he on about?"

"Nothing really," I said, still thinking about it and not ready to discuss it. "He was having a go at me for some reason. Because I'm a European. Let's find where this municipal camping place is."

There was a new hand-lettered sign to 'Jamhuri Park' and we found ourselves in a pleasant grassed area screened by trees from the road. There were showers and clean toilets. As we rather clumsily set up our 'camp', unpractised after the break at Bamburi, Barbie noticed a flash of white amongst the clouds looming above us. There was a

241

break in them and the setting sun was touching the snows of Kilimanjaro.

There was heavy dew when the sun had set and everything was damp and smelled of rich vegetation. This brought out mosquitoes in the heaviest swarms I think we ever experienced. We were early into bed in the back of Landie and for the first time closed all the windows to try and keep the mosquitoes out. Even so, there were some in with us which tantalised with their whining. Being in bed earlier than usual, the beds themselves being badly made on top of gear that had not been properly packed and with the sense of being closed into the metal box of Landie, we had a hell of a night. Every time one of us turned over the other would be woken and I kept banging my head on the metal roof close above me. In the morning I realised that we had used new and different shaped cardboard boxes in which to store our provisions and sundry gear while at Bamburi and that was why nothing fitted as it had in North Africa. I was stiff from lying on an awkward shape and we were both groggy and thick-headed from lack of fresh air. I did heave the boxes around a bit and our 'beds' did improve.

After breakfast of tinned fruit, Kilimanjaro appeared clearly. It was an incredible sight because there had been recent snow storms and the top 4-5,000 feet was capped by a smooth dome of sparkling white. We took photographs, of course, and marvelled at the great volcano's majesty. I have seen 'Kili' several times since, but never with so much snow on the top.

The road along the periphery of the mountain massif was lined by an avenue of mature trees and the slopes were intensely cultivated. There were sisal and coffee plantations and fruit orchards as well as fields of maize. Arusha impressed me. There was a long, tidy main street lined with prosperous-looking, cleanly white-washed, Indian dukas. The grey conical cone of Mount Meru (14,978 feet) stood immediately behind the town, but its summit was shrouded. 'Kili' had disappeared soon after it had kindly revealed itself to us.

An excellent newly-tarred road took us quickly to Makuyuni which was the junction for the way up to Ngorongoro where we were to do the last of our tourist sightseeing in East Africa.

After leaving Arusha, the landscape changed to open grassy plains with scattered acacias, but when we turned off onto the rough dirt secondary road we entered forest. We hammered along through ruts and over sections where quite big stones had been laid on the surface. There had been recent rain and there were muddy patches. Judging from the forest and the road, this was a wet region, affected no doubt by the great volcanic massifs which sprouted there out of the vast savannah plains. There were two or three small villages in the forest and then we were climbing a steep escarpment and Lake Manyara was spread out on our left. We stopped for a break and to admire the fine view.

My head had begun pounding in that familiar run-up to a migraine and I was disgusted with myself. It was the last migraine of our safari and did not last long, but I did not know it at the time.

Climbing higher we could not see the crater rim above us and shortly after entering the park gates we were into tall and dense rainforest with mist wreathing through the trees. It was suddenly quite cold and we shivered in our minimal clothing.

Barbie had been reading about the Grizmek family who had done so much to preserve the Serengeti Plains and the Ngorongoro crater and she spied the memorial to Michael Grizmek who had died nearby, killed in a plane crash. My head was bad, probably exacerbated by the high altitude, we were up to 8,000 feet, and I was not taking it all in. I dreaded the thought of another uncomfortable night in the back of Landie in the cold and penetrating damp, so suggested rather forlornly that we might find accommodation at the Lodge.

We were lucky. They had a room and it was in one of the cottages scattered about the grounds. A servant came to light a log fire in the fireplace and it was bliss. After taking codeine, I snoozed on my bed for a while and recovered somewhat. A hot bath cheered us both up. On the lawn between the bedroom cottages and the main building there were zebras grazing and beyond there was a grand panorama of the enormous crater. Before going into dinner we sat on benches and stared down into the immensity of it all, lying two or three thousand feet below us and spreading for ten miles to the opposite rim. There was at least one lake and swaths and patches of forest and scrub which looked like dark rashes against the golden brown of the grasses.

I was fascinated by the variation of the vegetation in this region, how there were wet patches with rich forest and almost immediately after crossing some invisible natural border there was dry grass or a landscape of leafless acacia thorns with dust blowing. It was clear that the monsoon rain clouds blew over the plains of East Africa until they reached mountains of a certain altitude which forced the release of their cargo of precious water. No wonder that people over the ages had fought for particular stretches of land while tens of thousand of square miles of adjacent plains were empty.

As the sun set we went into the main building of the Lodge. It was not large, a lounge and diningroom, but it was warm and cheerful with high thatched roof supported by dark wooden beams. Roaring pine log fires were going in stone fireplaces and friendly red-coated stewards were at hand to attend us. We had drinks by the fire and then enjoyed a simple but well-prepared and cooked meal with coffees and brandies afterwards. We were laughing and joking and very happy to be there. My headache suddenly left me as I ate and we slept well. A day that had seemed doomed to be a bad one had changed around dramatically. It was a memorable interlude.

In the morning, the sun was breaking through the overcast and the air was so fresh and clean up there at that altitude after heavy rain in the night. The herd of zebras was on the lawn and we tried to see how close we could get. They moved off when we got too close, watching us rather haughtily, but they did not run and as soon as we stopped tormenting them they went back to steady grazing. They kept the lawn in front of the Lodge immaculate.

There was a traditional English breakfast of porridge, fried bacon, eggs and sausages, toast with imported marmalade and all the trimmings, served by quiet and attentive waiters. I could not remember when we had last had that luxury. Had we sat down to such a breakfast since the pub in Newhaven? Those breakfasts and the newly-laid log fires sealed our pleasure at stopping at the Lodge. I felt particularly warm and happy about the experience there.

We had wanted to go down into the crater for what has always been reported as spectacular game-viewing, but the heavy rains over the last few days prevented us. Visitors were not allowed to use their own vehicles without a special permit issued by the Warden and the tours which were operated from the Lodge were being held off until the tracks down the side of the crater walls had dried off. There was an organised tour group staying (we had been lucky to get accommodation) and they had priority. I was told we could hang on for another couple of days and take our chances. We would both have been glad to do that, but it was expensive by our standards and there were no guarantees.

As we packed Landie, the rain started again from swirling dark grey masses which brushed the tops of the tall exotic pines standing around the Lodge. There would be no trips into the crater that day, or the next.

The road was muddy on the way down to Lake Manyara, the first time that Landie had slithered about on a slippery clay and mud surface. I was tempted to get out and switch over the front wheel hubs so we could use four-wheel drive for a legitimate reason. However, the rain was coming down hard and icy, so I continued in conventional fashion, driving carefully. Indeed, apart from getting out of scrapes where I had rashly gone off the road for fun, we never needed four-wheel drive anywhere on our journey. A tough pick-up with strengthened springs would have done just as well, but I would never have said that within Landie's hearing.

CHAPTER EIGHTEEN : *THE GREAT NORTH ROAD*

Cecil Rhodes and many others had a dream of driving a railway, and a road, from the Cape to Cairo through British territory. Rhodes could never see his dream come true because in his day there were the barriers of the Belgian Congo and German East Africa, which later became Tanganyika.

But after World War I it became possible when that magical pink-coloured, broad corridor did stretch from one end of the map of the continent to the other. With a wet-season break in the Sudan, because of the great Sudd swamps where steamers carried traffic on the Nile, the Great North Road did come into being although a railway was impossible because of economics. In the A.A. guide-book, *Trans-African Highways*, the route of the Great North Road was described and I had planned to travel along most of that legendary highway until the Russian constructors of the Aswan High Dam frustrated me. If it were not for that prohibition in Lower Egypt, we could have followed it in 1965.

The main towns southwards along the Great North Road are a romantic roll call and I enjoy listing them: Alexandria - Cairo - Asyut - Aswan - Abu Hamed - Khartoum - Malakal - Juba - Gulu - Tororo - Nakuru - Nairobi - Arusha - Iringa - Tunduma - Mbeya - Mpika - Kapiri Mposhi - Lusaka - Kafue - Livingstone - Victoria Falls - Bulawayo - Beit Bridge - Pretoria - Bloemfontein - Beaufort West - Cape Town.

During our local safari to Lake Victoria, we travelled a short distance on the Great North Road between Tororo and Nairobi and we joined it again at Arusha, from where we followed it well into South Africa, to beyond the Limpopo River. There were still people about in 1965 who talked about the Great North Road. Since then, fashionable contempt for the British Empire washed away the noble concept of a trans-continental highway linking nations with a common administrative system. Most nations along its route have been at odds with each other, civil unrest created insecurity and wars of various kinds have raged off and on. From Egypt to South Africa there was no clear peaceful or tranquil route at any time after 1965.

At the turn-off to Ngorongoro in the hamlet of Makuyuni we topped up with petrol and had Cokes. From there we were on gravel and laterite dirt roads all the way to Kapiri Mposhi in Zambia, a distance of 1,250 miles [2,000 kms].

The road crossed the wide expanse of the Masai Plain for maybe the first thirty or forty miles and we saw some of their famed cattle being herded in the distance by boys and men carrying spears. We stopped beside a party of Masai and Barbie negotiated with them to take a photograph. They wanted to bargain for what seemed quite a large fee and I guessed that they had become used to tourists going on safari to the Serengeti and Ngorongoro. Quite abruptly after that, we left the grassy plains and entered broken country covered by the endless acacia thornbush of Africa.

Thereafter it was a long, hard slog. The days merged into an endless rattling and hammering along many hundreds of miles of poorly maintained roads traversing a vast ocean of acacia thornbush merging later into mopane forest. Dust covering ourselves and everything within Landie became normal once again and our bodies and hair had to become used to it. I did not mind the dust; I welcomed it in a way because I much preferred that to damp and cold. I felt more at ease in the warmth and dryness and after the first few hours of getting thoroughly infused with dust, you can't really get any dirtier. Dry dust is 'clean' dirt anyway and I had been used to it from boyhood. Barbie, being a good Aussie girl, put up with it too after a few token complaints about her hair. The endless shaking and rattling along monotonous empty roads in the heart of Africa was a discomfort that had to be endured and there was no point in complaining about it.

In any case, there was an uplifting feeling about what we were doing which was always there at the back of our minds to buttress our stamina. On this stretch we were driving immense distances through lands which were as they were when the first Europeans explored them such a short time before. It was only ninety years since Stanley sought Livingstone, traversing exactly the same country that we were doing.

For many miles there was no sign of people apart from the road on which we bucketed along. The sight of another vehicle was

247

extraordinary and I do not remember passing any except within reasonable distance of one of the few towns. If we had broken down we would have had a long time to wait for assistance. We never saw a policeman or encountered any checkpoint except at the friendly border post between Tanzania and Zambia. The vast emptiness of the central African bushveld impressed itself so vividly on me.

It changed at the village of Babatiwe where we left the plains and descended a steep hill into a series of wide valleys interrupted by ranges of stony hills and rocky escarpments. Baobabs with pale skins and naked branches appeared in groups to provide some relief from the monotony of the thornscrub. The road snaked up and down the hillsides and the sky was clear with a silver sun bearing down on us. At that time of year, the beginning of the southern summer, the sun was about overhead at noon at that latitude and it was following us as we proceeded southwards. We never stopped that day except to have a pee and stretch. Our lunch was from boxes of sandwiches, biscuits and fruit which the Ngorongoro Lodge had given us.

We crawled over a pass which reached an altitude of 5,750 feet and then abruptly descended a dramatic section to the district centre of Kondoa Irangi which we never saw because it was some distance off the road. Between Kondoa and Dodoma there was a wide valley with escarpments along its edge and there were dried river beds filled by clear golden sand. In the brief rainy season when sudden storms passed over, that river must have come down in flash floods, but there was no water in it when we passed by.

Dodoma was one of the two towns between Arusha and the southern Tanzanian Highlands and I hardly remember it. There is a memory of a tarred street and a few dukas, a country hotel and a petrol station. There is a railway station there on the line from Dar-es-Salaam to Kigoma on Lake Tanganyika and we must have noticed it. Indeed I have scratchy memories about a railway station, but I could easily confuse it with another similar one somewhere else in Africa. Small colonial towns like Dodoma with remote railway stations were so much the same in those days.

What was interesting about that railway was that where it reaches Kigoma on Lake Tanganyika, it is not far from Ujiji which was the Arab-Swahili 19th century slave trading depot where David Lvingstone was stuck for several months and where Stanley met him with the famous greeting. From Dodoma, the railway passes through Tabora on its way to the lake and Tabora was another famous Arab slave-depot and resting place, ruled by a sheik appointed by the

Sultan of Zanzibar. Richard Burton and John Hanning Speke were laid up there for months during their pioneering exploration. Although we did not get excited about these events on that day when we traversed the region, I was aware of its importance and told Barbie stories about my heroes. I read the classic *The White Nile* by Alan Moorehead shortly before leaving home that year.

We went on some distance beyond Dodoma and pulled off the road into the scrub when I felt I could not drive any further. It was dry but chilly after the sun set. To warm ourselves we had a glass of 'Duval's Blood' brandy from the last of a bottle bought many days before in Mombasa. We were low on fresh provisions and ate a frugal dinner.

In the morning when I awoke, an elderly man was sitting beside Landie. He was worn and emaciated and probably no more than forty years of age but looked much older through living in a harsh environment. He waited at a respectful distance, watching our getting-up activity with interest and waved wistfully with a tentative smile when we departed. We had no bread for ourselves and breakfasted on water, so could give him nothing. I wonder what he was thinking as he watched us and how far away his home was, and how he had discovered us. Maybe he had heard our engine and rattling passage on the road the evening before and had got up early to see who had stopped close by. It is strange how an apparently insignificant human contact like that can often acquire far greater importance than grand events. I have a feeling of sadness and wonder about that man as I write.

We laboured up another escarpment after leaving that sleeping place and stopped on the crest for a break. Then it was onwards again. Along that stretch, Barbie noticed dark artificial shapes hanging in the trees in the bush near to a rough little settlement. We had read somewhere that people in those parts did not bury their dead, preferring to stick them in trees for predators to feed on. We assumed that what we were seeing were dead bodies and for some years afterwards I told that story. In 1985 when travelling further north in Tanzania beside Lake Victoria I saw the same thing and then again in the Rift Valley near Lake Baringo in 1991. It was then that I discovered that what we had thought were bodies all those years before had been beehives! There is an ancient tradition amongst some East African tribes of making coffin-like wooden hives for wild bees and hanging them in appropriate trees whose flowers the bees find attractive.

Descending a long hill, there were many baobabs and I stopped to take a photograph which became an epitome of that part of our journey. Landie is standing in the middle of the narrow dirt road with dry thornbushes on either side and a baobab looming. Beyond, a valley disappears into the hazy distance with hills far away. We were crossing the valley of the Great Ruaha River which later joins the Rufiji, one of East Africa's more important rivers. Some miles further on, we crawled up a winding track out of the Great Rift Valley, negotiating the Nyangolo Escarpment. From the bed of the Ruaha to Iringa we rose from 2,500 to 5,200 feet. It was very hot in the valley.

I remember Iringa more clearly than Dodoma, because we stopped there for petrol and to pick up whatever provisions were available in the dukas. There was long, low hotel with a gabled, Cape-colonial entrance and verandahs which looked as if they had been walled up rather tastelessly at some time. It was a substantial town and a provincial capital with public buildings and a cinema. The streets were tarred and there were bustling people and some pick-ups and farm trucks about. Directly to the south there were what were called the Southern Highlands where Germans settlers opened up coffee plantations before World War I and I believe there were still a number of white farmers and European-owned estates there when we were travelling through. Later, all foreign-owned land was appropriated by the state in Tanzania.

At Iringa, we joined the main road to Dar-es-Salaam and there was evidence of important road works in the vicinity with a workers' encampment and equipment. The road to the coast through the Ruaha gorges was being rebuilt and tarred. However, our road south west to Mbeya was still bad and had minimal maintenance since the last rainy season and we rattled and clattered ever onwards.

But we began to notice a change in the vegetation. There was a scattering of bigger trees and they were clothed in green leaves. There were ravines breaking the profile of the hillsides which had greater variety of shape than the broad curve of the escarpments further north. It looked like country that had regular rainfall in a more prolonged rainy season. We were entering a different geographical region. The road had many gullies in it and we began crossing rough little bridges and culverts.

About 3.30 in the afternoon there was a sign indicating a place to park off the road and on a whim I swerved onto the side-track. It was a picnic spot and there was a marvel at the end of a glade: a waterfall with real water splashing down. It was not difficult to decide to stop the night there. There was another party of travellers there too, which was a phenomenon. It was two car-loads of Indians who were having a civilised picnic with spread cloths and wicker baskets on their way from Dar-es-Salaam to Mbeya. One of the men said they were on business and were taking their families along because they were to stay with relatives. They were packing up when we arrived and soon departed leaving us with peace. Barbie washed some clothes and her hair in the clear stream while I leisurely arranged camp and prepared dinner with fresh food bought in Iringa. It clouded over and began to drizzle which confirmed the change in general geography we had noticed, but the drizzle was shortlived and we had a pleasant evening and rest in that place. It was cold later.

Next morning we emerged onto a plateau. There was grassland with a good scattering of acacias across it but these were a different variety, taller and spreading their branches. The dry thornscrub was gone. There were a few peasant farmers along the road and we saw cultivation for the first time since Arusha. The native huts were square and were decorated with designs and figures in different natural mineral washes. Children came out to wave and scream at us. Apart from the scattered acacia trees, most of the homesteads we saw had pawpaws or bananas growing around them. We stopped to photograph some women hoeing a field ready for planting and children lined up to be in the picture. We exchanged waves, smiles and friendly remarks with the women although we had no mutual language. It was pleasing to meet amiable, easy-going people with evidence of prosperity. Further on, there was a simple village school.

Having regard to the socialist rhetoric and propaganda I had read in the papers and heard on Radio Tanzania while at Bamburi, I could not imagine how collectivisation in a Soviet or Maoist model was going to help those few peasant farmers we saw there. Twenty years later I observed what the policy had done to degrade people in those isolated highlands, but that is another story.

Mbeya was a prosperous town built over attractive rocky hills with plenty of trees. We stopped for a while to change some money at a bank and fill up with petrol. The air was fresh and clear and the streets were neat and clean. We strolled for a while and went into an Indian café and bakery with an impressive Sikh gentleman behind the counter wearing an elaborate turban and an imperial moustache.

We bought huge samosas from him, still warm from the oven. They were delicious, full of spicy vegetables and finely ground meat. I have thought of those samosas at Mbeya a hundred times over the years. No matter how often I have eaten samosas in many different places, those at Mbeya became a yardstick.

It was not far to Tunduma and the border between Tanzania and Zambia where the immigration and customs officers of both countries shared a pleasant border post, all neat and freshly painted. The officers were still wearing typical British-style uniforms of white shorts and shirts with black epaulets and insignia. They were smartly turned out and it was difficult to decide which belonged to which country.

An extraordinary scene was being played out when we arrived and continued whilst we had our passports, customs forms and Landie's Carnet processed. A short, dumpy Englishwoman was passing through northwards and she had come up against the newly-imposed bureaucracy of the post-colonial era. The problem seemed to be that she had a collection of sporting rifles and shotguns and no international permit.

She stood in the centre of the circular hall, hands on hips, dressed in an old-fashioned khaki safari outfit with big bulging pockets and loops for ammunition. On her head was a large pith helmet. She was haranguing the officials of both countries who were at their counters on opposite sides of the room. Her driver or servant was standing mutely at one side with eyes cast down guarding a pile of long canvas gun-bags and rugged safari holdalls. His expression was unreadable, but I sensed a secret grin of either embarrassment or pride at her performance.

"I have never come across such a ridiculous situation," she was saying in a loud and penetrating voice with an upper-class accent. "I've been travelling in Africa for twenty five years and never encountered such stupid obstruction."

She moved nearer to an older man on the Tanzanian side. "You know me. I know you," she said, poking her finger at him. "I knew you when you put on your uniform for the first time. You didn't know your job then and we had to show you where to put your rubber stamps." The man grinned at her but said nothing. "And now you say I have to have a special permit which has to be issued in Lusaka. I never heard such nonsense! You hardly know where Lusaka is."

Her blue eyes blazed up at me. "You'll never believe what they get up to as soon as they get their so-called 'freedom'. *Uhuru*, they call it. Dear God! They don't know the meaning of freedom."

She turned around to aim a broadside at the Zambian side. "We are in Tunduma, not Lusaka. None of you have ever been to Lusaka. It's a thousand miles from here along your godforsaken roads through the blasted wilderness of Africa. I'm supposed to go back and get a permit?" Her voice reverberated with scorn. She swivelled back to the Tanzanians and she became almost gentle. "Come on, chaps, this is not reasonable. Just stamp my bloody forms and we can go and have a beer together. Like the old days. What do you say?"

"I'm sorry memsahib," the senior officer said, spreading his hands. "We are Tanzania now and I have to see the permits. If not, I shall be in trouble and lose my job."

"Job, fiddlesticks! I'll talk to the minister when I get to Dar. I knew him when he was a *toto* in short trousers..."

I took our completed forms over to one of the junior officers while the tirade continued. He was grinning as he listened to the grand lady and stamped my documents and our passports with hardly a look at them. I grinned back at him and there was a strange feeling of genuine bonhomie all around at the post. The men were not insulted or angered by this lady from another time. She was being abusive and shouting at them and they took it all with good nature. It was evident that they all knew her well.

The row was still going on when we went back to Landie. "I am not driving all the way back to Lusaka for those bloody forms. And that's my last word!" I heard her declaim as we drove off.

"What a to-do that was," I said, laughing with delight at the scene. "I'll always remember it."

"What do you think she will do?" Barbie asked.

"I expect she'll get away with it somehow. She'll get through on the phone to somebody in authority somehow even if it takes a day or two. It would be easier than trailing back and forth to Lusaka and I don't think she's the type to give up easily."

"I didn't think there were that sort of upper-class Pommy-type around any more."

"Nor did I," I said. "Somehow I'm glad there are. She was from the real colonial era."

"She was being pretty awful, though. She wouldn't talk like that back in London."

"Oh, I'm not so sure. Anyway, she was a bit of history and not really doing any harm to anybody. The officers seemed to be secretly enjoying her."

*　　*

From Tunduma the road descended from the Highlands through what I was to call the Tanganyika-Malawi Gap in a book years later and which had been important to ancient human history. The road continued to be bad; rutted and potholed where the laterite was hard, heavily corrugated where there was a soft or sandy surface. As we descended, the thick thornscrub closed in again and the heat built up to a fine intensity. The journey was increasingly one of maintaining our momentum for endless hours of monotonous jolting and crashing. I tried to keep up a steady speed of about forty-five miles an hour whilst steering on the best path to miss the worst holes and ruts. From time to time, I had to slow which meant changing down to third or second gear and grinding along for a while, then gradually speeding up. It was a tortuous passage and the country was pretty flat with occasional hills in the far distance, so there was no scenery to admire or break the monotony. The few villages were poor and primitive.

At Isoka there was a trading store where we bought warm Fantas. There was another great geographical divide there although I could not detect any reason for it. It must have been something to do with the timing of the rainy seasons because we were moving into the southern African region and were getting quite far from the ocean. Maybe we were now out of reach of the monsoon systems.

For whatever reason, the vegetation suddenly changed. The acacia scrub which spreads southward from northern Kenya, wherever it was not too high or too wet, abruptly disappeared. It was replaced by mopane forest which was quite different. Instead of the bush being filled by a variety of acacia species with different characteristics, the mopane was a single species and its only variation was in height or the closeness in which the trees crowded together, which in turn depended on the relative rainfall of the region.

Mopane stand straight and can be quite tall so that driving through them you cannot see beyond a few yards into their mass, even when it is the dry season and they have lost most of their leaves. They are deciduous and have large green leaves which become golden then russet and red before falling as the annual drought progresses. The wood is hard and makes very fine camp fires.

That first evening in Zambia we followed the advice of the trusty guide, *Trans-African Highways*, and sought out a government resthouse at Chinsali, eight miles from the main road on a track with a rather better surface than the highway. I was a bit dubious about what we would find and was prepared for it to be shut because we read that Zambia had begun closing the old colonial *bomas* or district headquarters. But, it was still functioning and was a delightful surprise.

It was on the slope of a gentle hillside and surrounded by some taller trees with dark green leaves and spreading branches. A small, middle-aged man with a wizened face came out to see who had arrived and greeted us with a grin and much friendliness. He was genuinely pleased to see somebody come to use his resthouse. He rushed away to put on a jacket and returned with a young assistant to help with our bags. He told us that he had few guests these days and everything was in order for us to stay over. He would cook our dinner and a fire would be lit immediately so that we could have a bath later. We produced our box of everyday food accessories such as tea, coffee, milk powder, sugar, cooking oil, salt etc and some food for dinner and these were whipped away to the kitchen somewhere at the back.

There was a verandah, a large living room with heavy, handmade furniture and a couple of bedrooms with mosquito nets. I was reminded of similar places in West Africa and was pleased to be there. The concept of government resthouses for travelling officials and approved civilians was new to Barbie and she was much taken by the kindness of the caretaker and his 'boy'.

Tea on an old painted metal tray was brought to us almost instantly, in the best British tradition of being the first essential for tired and needy travellers, and as it was getting dark this was followed by a hissing pressure lamp casting a bright white light.

There were old magazines, *Picture Post*, *The Illustrated London News*, *Sphere* and *Tatler*, which we feasted on with comment and laughter until our food was brought in, perfectly cooked and served on thick white china plates. When we had eaten, there was coffee and before we were left for the night we were told that the bath water was now hot. In the morning, coffee was brought at daybreak and we packed up when we were dressed. We had no suitable food with which they could make breakfast so I made the excuse that we wished to be away early. I tipped the caretaker and we had a pleasant little ceremony of farewell with much smiling back and forth.

There was an additional payment to be made in kind, however, because as we were about to leave, a young man was introduced and I was told he wished to go to Mpika urgently. He was smartly dressed and carried a battered little suitcase. There was no alternative to taking him on, and Barbie had to squeeze over and sit astride the gear lever for the next long stretch. I did not mind giving the caretaker's protégé a lift, how could I, but we were unused to having a stranger in the cab on long trips and felt inhibited.

After an hour or so, we wound down into the valley of the Luangwa River and up again with tall figs and other riverine trees beside the road which was a change from the endless mopane and straight road. A Zambian army convoy passed us in the valley with a Landrover in front flying a regimental pennant followed by six Bedford five-ton trucks grinding along with whining gears.

The closing of the *bomas* presented me with a problem which increased in urgency through that morning. I had used up the spare petrol in our cans during the traverse of Tanzania, my reasoning being that petrol was cheaper in southern Africa and therefore there was no point in continuing to fill up the tank with more expensive East African petrol while carrying a tankful in reserve. That was fine, except that I had reckoned without an inability to change money.

We had filled up the ordinary tank with petrol at Mbeya, and at the border post, Tunduma, I had changed the balance of our East African shillings into a few Zambian pounds and that had sufficed to take care of the resthouse. But I had been unable to change a traveller's cheque because there was no bank on the Zambian side of the border. The Zambian customs officer told me that I might find a *boma* to make change for me, but that there was no bank until Kapiri Mposhi, over six hundred miles away. The resthouse caretaker confirmed that the *boma* facility was no longer available to unofficial travellers, but there was a hotel with a white 'madam' at Mpika who he was sure would help me.

Whether the 'madam' would be helpful or not, Landie was running out of fuel. I increasingly drove with a light foot as the needle sank in the gauge. At Shiwa Ngandu, after the Luangwa River, there had been a *boma* and petrol seven miles from the highway, and that would have suited us very well had we been able to use it. There were still sixty miles to go after that. I thought of the opportunity we had to flag down the army convoy from whom I suppose we could have begged a couple of gallons, but the chance was gone.

Thirty miles from Mpika, the needle was firmly fixed on the empty position and I was driving at about 30 m.p.h. and dreading meeting some high escarpment up which we would have to crawl in low gear. But the road continued on long straight stretches, heavily corrugated but level. We met no other vehicles that day apart from the army convoy and I could not remember meeting one the previous day. Northern Zambia was empty of movement.

Luck was with us, of course, as it so often seemed to be, and we crawled into Mpika with maybe a pint or two left in the tank. There was a fork in the sandy track at the entrance to the village and our passenger directed us to the hotel before asking to be put down. I had explained our problem on the way and he had been getting nervous in sympathy, explaining that because of the *boma* problem many people were suffering with a lack of any cash with which to trade or buy essentials. What were the authorities thinking, I kept wondering to myself? The whole of that part of the country was at a standstill.

Gratefully, we parked on mown grass under a flame tree beside the Crested Crane Hotel and got out to stretch. A sprinkler was flashing silver sprays of water over the lawn and brilliant canna lilies were growing in a bed along the edge of the verandah. A flowering creeper hung over the entrance where the cement floor was shining with red polish. It was an oasis of old-fashioned colonial normality and I went into the reception office in fine spirits. The 'madam' turned out to be a Scotswoman, one of those amazing leftovers of the Empire, full of common-sense and energy, who made the wheels turn in the most unlikely places. She reminded me of the helpful manageress in the concrete-box hotel in faraway Tobruk. This 'madam' at the Crested Crane in Mpika was not pleased to see us, however.

"Oh, yes! I know all about you before you open your mouth," she said, looking me up and down. "You've come from the north no doubt?"

"Yes," I said. "And we have a bit of a problem. ..."

"Aye. I know you have," she interrupted me, her Glasgow accent strongly emphasised. "You've no money and no petrol. That's right isn't it? These bloody politicians are ruining the country. Nothing works any more." She threw up her hands. "And they have only been in power a bit more than a year. I'm not staying here longer than I have to, that I can tell you."

"Can you help?" I asked.

"Do you know that it takes two or three days for me to send cheques and so on to the nearest bank and get cash back? It costs a bloody fortune running my pick-up up and down to Kapiri Mposhi and everyone in town thinks that I am now the *boma* itself."

"I'll be spending most of what I change in buying petrol at your pump," I said. "And we'll have a bite to eat."

She gave me a brief smile. "Oh, yes, I know all that. And it's not your fault. ..."

She changed five pounds, my smallest denomination cheque, and sent someone to work the pump beside the hotel. After filling up we went onto the verandah for thick cheese and tomato sandwiches made with fresh bread, and very good coffee. There was a tame vervet monkey on a long leash who gambolled about and accepted bits of bread and small birds sang in cages hanging from the rafters. Guinea fowls strutted in a run at the back and Cape turtle doves called from the tall spathodeas and the flame trees shading the grounds. I would have been happy to spend a day or two at Mpika.

*   *

A hundred miles on from Mpika there was the turnoff to Livingstone's Memorial where he died and his heart and liver were buried under a tree. To pass the time, I told Barbie what I could remember of the great explorer's exploits.

The road ran on and on through that endless mopane forest which was getting drier and more stick-like as we progressed. Later, we were told that southern Africa was suffering one of its cyclical periods of exceptional drought which come about every seven years. It was hot and dusty as always and the elation at solving the immediate emergency at Mpika wore off as the hours passed. At the remote settlement of Mkushi River we were a few miles from the Congo border but did not realise it. We stopped for warm fizzy drinks at a duka and then went on for a few more miles before turning off into the bush to camp for the night.

I did not appreciate it at the time, but that was the last bush camp in true wilderness of the whole safari.

We had seen no traffic that afternoon and we were undisturbed fifty yards from the road. There were no native settlements within miles and nobody came to see who we were. In the distance we had seen the smoke of bush-fires and we were careful with cigarettes in that tinder dry place. Flies came out of nowhere to bother us but they went to bed when the sun set and we had a relaxed evening there.

The next day after breakfast of coffee it was stifling hot and the dust seemed to make it worse. We reached the small junction town of Kapiri Mposhi quite suddenly and there was a tarred road running north and south with normal traffic: saloon cars, pick-ups and trucks loaded with goods. There were buses crowded with people. I changed money in the bank and we topped up with petrol, drank iced Cokes and bought biscuits. Lack of everyday staples such as bread meant that we had been eating only one frugal meal a day. We had slimmed down considerably since leaving Bamburi where we had been living 'the good life' as far as food and drink was concerned. We were very fit. When I ran my hand over my stomach and pinched the skin there was no fat, only hard muscle.

Broken Hill was a substantial town and there were local white people about in numbers for the first time since Mombasa. Beefy, sunburnt farmers were in town wearing brief khaki shorts and long stockings. The womenfolk were shopping, dressed in flowery cotton dresses and carrying baskets. The main street was flanked by a line of stores with signs advertising South African brands of groceries which were familiar to me. I felt an immediate pang of excitement, we had passed some critical socio-economic barrier and entered a different world.

We had a toasted sandwich and fresh milk in a café in the main street and the act of doing so felt strange. White people were talking in a southern African accent around us. It was another milestone on our long journey and I felt that the adventure was now surely nearing the end even though we still had nearly two thousand miles to go.

There was a motel about ten miles south of Broken Hill and I slowed when I saw the sign and thought of stopping there, but Barbie wrinkled her nose. "It looks a bit crappy to me," she said and was quite right. It was run down and there were what looked like drunken blacks hanging around, so we headed onwards, spinning along the tar road.

Another two hours and we were in Lusaka, the capital of Zambia. From the north we entered the compact city centre quite suddenly through an avenue of flame trees and I drove slowly along the wide main boulevard, divided down the middle by islands alive with beds of well-tended, brightly-flowering plants. The modest two and three storied buildings looked newly decorated and smart and the people moving about were cheerful and well-dressed. There were men in business suits striding along carrying briefcases.

I stopped to take a photograph of this prosperous little metropolis before we drove on. Neither of us had any desire to stay in a city. On the southern side, there were a few small factories and warehouses. I noticed the names of well-known wholesale distributors and the brand names of South African food manufacturers. There were service garages and new vehicle showrooms and stockists of agricultural machinery. We stopped for petrol (we were eating up the miles on tarmac) and cold drinks and then, abruptly, we were back in the bush.

"It's a pity about that motel," I said. "I think we should try to stay at a cheap hotel tonight. We need to get cleaned up and sorted out."

"Too right, Den. My hair is disgusting!"

At the small town of Kafue there was what looked like a sugar mill and we crossed the river on a long steel girder bridge. I looked out for a congenial hotel, but there was nothing that suited us. I was wishing for something like the Crested Crane at Mpika. And then a few miles outside of town where the road divided, branching off to Salisbury, there was a sign announcing the Don Robbin Motel.

"This has to be it," I said confidently and pulled over.

*   *

They had a room available and we hauled our suitcases out from beneath the shambles in the back. The days of rattling and crashing about had created a jumble, all of which was covered in drifts of dust.

I stood in the hot little room with its simple beds, utilitarian furniture and mosquito mesh on the windows and looked about, lost in rumination about the ending of rough camping on our long journey down Africa. Because it *was* over, I realised, there in that simple roadside motel in Zambia.

The driving off into the desert or the bush to make our little camp, the stopping to have a pee beside Landie without thought, the freedom of empty Africa, these things were past now. There were fences along the road and traffic was frequently met. Africa was still relatively empty, but the commercial and industrial machine of South

260

Africa and Rhodesia was making itself felt and the arms of that 'civilised' octopus had reached out and touched us.

Barbie was in the bathroom and there was the hiss of a shower. "The water's hot!" she called.

Later we had iced Castle lager in the bar, crowded with local whites, talking in their distinctive southern African accents. They looked like farmers. Barbie thought that it was a bit like an outback saloon in Aussie even though the voices were different. Somebody asked us where we had come from when they noticed Barbie's accent and when we said we had come down overland there was a smile and a nod but no special interest. These were people used to the rough outdoors life. I had to admit that I felt a bit let down though. I wanted somebody to tell us we had done something out of the ordinary and give us congratulations. But I had to wait until I got to the big South African cities before I had that kind of recognition.

"Get on all right with the 'Affies' up north, did you?" one of the drinkers at the bar asked.

"Yes, fine. They were pretty friendly," I replied.

"Poor as dirt and bloody miserable round here," another observed. "Especially in this drought."

"Well, when you get down south you'll see different blacks there. Fat and prosperous, laughing and joking," the first one said, then sipped at his iced beer. "Cheeky, too," he added.

Coffee was brought to us at about 6.30 next morning by a maid and we had a cooked breakfast. In the grounds of the motel there was a peacock which made its siren call and two pathetic little antelopes, grey duikers, in a cage. Barbie loved their big soulful eyes. There was a VW combi full of American missionaries staying there too and we were amused by them and their careful preparation and elaborate packing arrangements. They seemed to be engaged in endless discussion about a journey of a hundred miles or so to their mission station.

The heat was increasing as we travelled southwards away from the equator, which did not seem to make sense, but it was the season of the year. It is always hotter in Central Africa in October and November just before the rains are due to start. The evidence of a particularly hard dry season was everywhere, thick dust and the bush devoid of any leaves with the bare branches a pale grey colour.

After Kafue and the junction of the main highway to Rhodesia, we still struck zones of mopane here and there but as we drove on to the border town of Livingstone we entered land which was primarily acacia bush again. It became almost empty again, too. Except that the road was tar and we were meeting the occasional truck or pick-up, even saloon cars, the countryside was similar to that far back up the Great North Road.

But there were now a series of small villages with petrol station and stores in the centre and we stopped twice for cold Cokes. We seemed to be especially thirsty, or was it that the easy availability of cold drinks made us feel more thirsty. After Choma and through Kalomo the road suddenly reverted to rough dirt and for thirty of forty miles we really did feel we were back in Tanzania, except for the stops for Coca Cola.

Livingstone was surprisingly big, a spread out township of leafy avenues of flame and jacaranda trees. We stopped to post cards at an efficient post office and have more Cokes. I had Zambian money to use up so we bought some dry provisions including vodka and bottles of Coke to celebrate our traverse of the Great North Road.

Out of town there was a sign to an 'African Culture Village' and we visited it. Examples of huts of the various local tribes had been built with care and authenticity within a large fenced compound with various traditional crafts on display. I was impressed and took several photographs. When a few other visitors appeared, a group of musicians gathered and began playing a battery of percussion instruments, marimbas and drums principally. The marimba players were good and the longer they played the better their hypnotic rhythm. I knew they could keep it up for hours in their real world and if there was sufficient reason would play the night through. Dancing to subtly varying but endless marimba and drum beat induces trance-states and is an important ingredient in the social and religious tribal life.

Those musicians were Chopi who have a particular reputation for their fine percussion music. Two dancers came out for a while, dressed in elaborate masking outfits made of a wooden frame with goatskins stretched on them, painted with designs and fringed and tasselled with fur and strips of skin: one simulated a hyena and the other a tortoise. They symbolised tribal totems and should only have been used in sacred ceremonies, which is probably why they did not seem to be dancing with great enthusiasm for the white tourists.

There was a curio and craft shop and on a whim I bought us each a large decorated spoon as souvenirs of our passing out of 'Black Africa'.

262

*   *

We were aware of a change in the atmosphere. There was a subtle dampness and the sky seemed to be a deeper colour of blue. Without warning we were driving alongside water and I pulled over to the side. There were palm trees on the bank.

"My God!" I called out. "Look at that. The Zambezi! It must be a mile wide."

"We must be close to the Victoria Falls," Barbie said. "What's that cloud of mist over there?"

"It must be spray from them." I could not keep the excitement out of my voice too. Muted thunder of tumbling water vibrated in the air.

There was a boy standing on a rock projecting into the clear rushing water of the mighty river. His fishing rod was held steadily as he waited for a bite. I took his photograph.

Another half a mile further and there was a parking place. We got out and crept to the edge of the Eastern Cataract. We could not hear each other speak, our nostrils were filled with damp air perfumed by the sweet aroma of fresh water. Within a few yards of where we were standing, white water was spewing past and disappearing into a gulf whose bottom was unfathomed in the swirling mists and spray. I was panting at the physical immensity of it all, my mind temporarily numbed with awe at the gigantic hugeness. On either side were hundreds of miles of dry, brittle scrub under a baking sky, here was more fresh water than one could have imagined; thousands of tons foaming and thundering past every minute.

I was so awestruck I did not even reflect on the impression it may have had on David Livingstone who had walked there from the far south. He had arrived on 16th November 1855, almost precisely 110 years before.

263

CHAPTER NINETEEN : *RHODESIA*

After passing out of Zambia we were met by young white immigration and customs officials on the Rhodesian side and the style of our processing was subtly different; more formal and correct with greater attention to Landie's Carnet and sharp questions about where we were going and where I was domiciled.

It was all rather 'British' and properly colonial and I did not like it. I was already feeling nostalgia for the easier yet less predictable manners of officials to the north. But it was efficient and we were through quickly enough.

Barbie grinned at me. "We are now in the 'White Supremacist Lands' of southern Africa I see. We'll have to be careful in case we contaminate their racial purity after coming through all those black countries..."

I grinned at her teasing. "At least we won't run out of money and petrol and stuff," I retorted.

But I was conscious of the sharp nostalgia I kept feeling as we passed each psychic milestone. I was pleased at successful progress and proud of our trouble-free passage down Africa, and excited at each new place or experience, but I was also shaken by bouts of deep sadness when a significant goal was reached. It was unnerving and was stronger as the journey's end was coming closer. I was aware that the final arriving was going to be very bad in its torment of conflicting emotions. I began to think of excuses to delay without making it ridiculous and counterproductive.

I had not visited Rhodesia until then but my mother had been to Victoria Falls in the 1930s and there were old snapshots in the family album. Of course, I had seen numerous other photographs and bits of movie film in travelogues over the years. But no illustrations were true to the reality. Some places are a disappointment when one reaches them, but the Victoria Falls were not. The bridge over the deep gorge with the foaming face of water within what seemed touching distance was one extraordinary experience.

Victoria Falls township was almost exclusively for tourists and had been long-established. There was a railway station still served by snorting steam locomotives, a grand hotel in 1920s style, a few shops and a petrol station. Hidden away amongst trees was a small residential area for the people who lived there and survived on tourism.

After quickly changing some money, we easily found the official camping park. There was a line of tiny little huts for hire, not much larger than a big tent and at a reasonable price, so I did not hesitate in taking one. We could unpack and relax properly for a real break after moving on daily all the way from Mombasa. They were furnished with nothing more than beds, so we had to use our own folding chairs and cooking equipment. There were communal showers and all about were mature old flowering trees and beds of cannas, crotons and hibiscus along the row of huts.

In the late afternoon we settled on our trusty camp chairs. A marvellous feeling of complete relaxation and happiness stole over me. Sitting outside our secure little hut, under a brilliant golden-flowered cassia in the balmy air as the sun set, sipping vodka and Coke and laughing and joking quietly, was supremely satisfying. In the air when we were silent there was the cheeping of little seed-eaters finding their nests, the trumpeting call of a hadeda ibis winging its way home, the clicking of insects and the murmur of voices from the line of huts. But behind all those friendly sounds, there was the subtle hint of rumbling noise from the mile-wide Zambezi plunging 350 feet into its gorge.

When it was dark we went to the Sprayview Restaurant, in the village centre, and had excellent grilled steaks, chips and salad. Accompanying it we drank a bottle of South African cabernet, our first bottle of decent wine at a reasonable price since leaving Egypt. We both felt particularly at ease and had a happy and carefree evening.

We breakfasted at the Sprayview the next morning and were joined by a neat little man who was touring alone. He was quiet and contained and though he must have been lonely he was quite at ease with himself. We exchanged the conventional information and to my surprise he was a colonial servant on leave from Nigeria, from one of the northern provinces. I told him that I had been working for The United Africa Company in the Niger Delta until three years previously and we had a bit of a chat. Barbie thought him strange, but once I knew his background, I was in sympathy with him. We gave him a lift down to the entrance to the Falls Nature Reserve. You never know how small the world is until you move in it.

We went on to the Falls Hotel, a fine old 'grand hotel' of the imperial period. Barbie cashed a cheque there and we looked into their curio boutique and bought postcards. From the verandah we looked across at the great steel truss bridge joining the two banks of the Zambezi over the narrow gorge below the falls, over which we had crossed the previous day, and behind it was the white water of the falls themselves. A cloud hovered over the horizon and the muted thunder was in the air. I imagined my mother there forty years before with her parents when there was a tramway from the hotel to lookout points and native 'boys' pushed the tourists there in little trolley cars with pretty candy-striped awnings to shade the ladies from the tropic sun. There were few tourists there with us because it was off-season and I could not imagine trolley cars in 1965.

Back in the village we did some shopping for food, we could not keep up the expense of restaurant eating, and there was a curio shop with a live crocodile in a miserable pen with a cement trough of smelly water. I supposed keeping a reptile like that is not as bad as a mammal, but we recalled the two little duikers at Robbins Motel and felt sad for the way humans thoughtlessly treat animals. There was a sour note at one of the shops where a white woman was abusing the rather slow black counter attendant.

"White racist supremacists!" Barbie angrily said to me outside. "That was a bad scene."

"I couldn't agree more," I said. "It's no more acceptable in South Africa than England or Australia. But, did you notice her accent? It was a London accent; she wasn't a local settler. Pommy immigrants are often the worst behaved towards Africans when they come out here."

After the inevitable cold Cokes we took the 'Zambezi Drive' into the wilderness reserve running along the south bank of the river. Away from lush riverine trees and their greenness, the bush reverted to the sunburned grey scrub we had been driving through for the previous week. From a hill, there were good views of the great river surging through the plain with its palms, figs and fever trees along the banks. We saw some wild animals: baboons gambolling about and chasing each other, warthogs, waterbuck, reedbuck, bushbuck, kudu and flocks of guinea fowl. Beside the river we heard hippos snorting and to our great delight there was a small herd of elephants coming to drink in the distance. On a hillside we suddenly saw a pair of sable antelope quite close which particularly delighted me. I have seen the rare sable only twice since that day.

It was very hot on the way back and we gulped at iced Cokes at the Sprayview before returning to our little hut for a brief snooze.

"This is a bloody hot place," Barbie said wearily, lying on her bed and fanning her sweaty face. Of course, we felt the heat more there because of the humidity from the falls.

When it was cooler we drove round the 'biggest baobab in the world' which was indeed a monster with a 67 feet diameter trunk, then parked near the Livingstone memorial. A bronze statue of the great explorer stood at the head of the Devil's Cataract, looking out across the river into the Africa which so fiercely held him in thrall. Standing beside him, looking along his line of sight, I could visualise places where we had crossed his path two or three times in the last couple of weeks which had taken him many years to reach. What contrasts there were between us and him, and yet the time of a hundred years was so short in the human history of Africa, just the twitch of an eyelid. I wondered what he would have thought of it all now.

Beside his statue, there was a path which almost touched the flying stream. If one wished, one could clamber down and trail fingers in it. And yet, twenty yards away there was the brink of the cataract and the bottom of it was invisible in the spray. The thundering roar filled your head and numbed your thoughts. I stood transfixed until Barbie tugged at my arm, wanting to get another view from further on. The path plunged into the thick rainforest which spread all along the cliff facing the mile-wide falls and within it the roar was reduced somewhat in volume. But the air trembled and on the whim of the breeze, showers of fine mist drifted through the trees so we were soon soaked.

At one point you could see along the whole length of the falls and could catch a glimpse of the bottom of the gorge far below and the surging waters there. Again, I was transfixed and Barbie sat entranced for a while on a log.

There could not be anything like it anywhere else in the whole world.

*   *

267

The charm of sitting outside our little hut while the sun set with a vodka and Coke in our hands was as strong as it had been the first evening. I cooked fat and tender steaks that we had bought in the little butcher shop in the village and we were jolly over our dinner. Later we had cold showers and still felt hot afterwards, lying naked on our beds.

The next day we gave Landie a rest and walked down to the falls and all along its length within the forest, stopping here and there to gaze at each new vista. There were benches in some places where we could rest but otherwise I was delighted by the way nothing had been done to spoil the natural beauty of the wilderness beside that amazing wonder. There was the well-worn path, of course, but there were no fences or guard rails and no signs or 'instructive' notices. Barbie commented on the lack of safety railing and we both praised the restraint of the authorities.

Despite drinking the Cokes which we bought wherever we could, we were both exhausted in the afternoon. I felt lousy and realised that the long walk in the high humidity had probably caused dehydration. We rested and then having rallied by late afternoon, went down for a final 'graak' of it all beside Livingstone's calm statue.

Baboons came by on the way to their roosts when we were cooking and we shooed them off. We were early to bed that night.

After a breakfast of scrambled egg and tomatoes and packing up Landie again, we were running with sweat and showered before setting off for Bulawayo. It was back to endless straight roads running through endless scrub bush. We stopped at Wankie where there was the headgear and tailings of a big coal mine for the inevitable cold drinks and again at Gwaai River where I filled up with petrol.

The road was quite good; it was two parallel strips of tar on which I could keep up a good fifty miles an hour. The problem was how to deal with an oncoming vehicle about which I was nervous at first. The locals seemed to have it exquisitely timed, waiting until the last minute before swerving off so that one wheel was on the outside strip and the other in the dirt beside. I thought they would never move the first few times so swerved right off almost into the ditch. But I became used to it and found that they would always give way.

Bulawayo was a quite large, very clean and tidy city with older, pre-war buildings in the centre which made it different to Lusaka. The main streets were vastly wide, designed to allow long spans of oxen to turn, which gave them a great air of spacious grace. There were many jacarandas and flame trees which were in bloom at that time of year making a fine show of mauve and scarlet. We checked into the Palace Hotel for the night because I wanted to get Landie serviced the next morning.

After a bath there was a bit of a panic because Barbie thought she had lost some cash. She worried about it and could not decide whether it was really lost, stolen at the camping park at Victoria Falls somehow or whether she had miscalculated. It was the only time on the whole journey we had that kind of worry, which was quite remarkable. I cannot remember if the problem was solved, I think she decided she had miscalculated when buying souvenirs at the Victoria Falls Hotel.

In the evening we sat in a beer garden at the back of the hotel in the company of some rowdy young white Rhodesians having a jolly time after a day in their offices. The dinner in the noisy dining room with clattering dishes was a very mediocre fixed-menu meal and we had hardly finished one dish before it was whipped away and the next plunked down before us. We were not used to that kind of service and were disconcerted by it.

I realised that it was in the style of cheap 'residential' or commercial hotels in South Africa and I looked with interest at the other diners. There were obviously a number of young residents there, some married, and the weary faces of travelling salesmen. They hung their suit jackets on the back of their chairs. Everybody was talking in hushed voices and the knives and forks were loud. Barbie and I were the only tourists.

I felt strange suddenly at the ordinariness of it all. We had never been in that kind of hotel, except probably the ones in Tobruk or Mombasa where the identity of the other guests had been blurred by the variety of nationalities or skin colours. It was the slightly seedy, properly respectable, British colonial feel to it all which struck me; the opposite side of the coin to the vision of wealthy settler life. The other guests were what an English snob might have described as working-class, or lower middle-class. I pointed this out to Barbie and I'm not sure whether she saw it with my eyes. She thought the scene was like an equivalent cheap small-town hotel in Aussie, which was exactly the same thing of course, but in a different context.

We had coffee and the local daily paper brought to us in bed the next morning. A notice said that there was room service for breakfast available, so I thought why not, and ordered it. The last

269

time we had breakfast in bed was in Cairo. It was a heavy English breakfast with eggs a bit congealed and toast rather limp by the time it reached us, but the idea of it was luxurious. The coffee was awful. The paper's front page was full of some 'crisis' and a speech by the Prime Minister, Ian Smith, with which I was not bothered.

The Landrover agents were easily found and told me that they would be done with a quick service by lunch time, so we strolled the streets casually window shopping, another strange activity. At the Post Office there was mail waiting and this had to be read back at the hotel. Afterwards there had to be post cards written in reply until it was time for cold drinks and a snack before picking up Landie who seemed to move more smoothly and have fewer rattles after the attention. We packed up, checked out of the hotel and drove out to the Matopos National Park twenty miles southwards.

It was a region of jumbled granite hills, most of them complete and unbroken domes of smooth grey rock: a most unusual landscape. Following directions we were able to find a rock shelter with extraordinarily fine Bushman paintings of a graceful hunting party racing after a herd of antelope. One of the figures which I photographed must be one of the most beautiful I have seen at any time.

From there we made our way to 'World's View' where Cecil John Rhodes was buried. A simple bronze plate was sunk into the smooth, hard granite dome overlooking that great jumble of rock ranging into the haze of distance.

"Did he die here?" asked Barbie.

"No, he died near Cape Town more-or-less in disgrace. A lonely and sad man whose dreams were lost. He engineered the Boer War in a way and he never recovered his political credibility after that terrible disaster."

"I don't know much about the Boer War," Barbie said. "At school we learned that some Aussie soldiers came over to fight the dreadful Boers under Kruger."

I laughed. "It was not a simple matter and it was a disaster for South Africa."

I thought for a moment about how I could explain the complexities. "Civil Wars are always the worst and the bitterness is still very strong today. The whole *apartheid* mess can be said to have been started by the Boer War. If the British hadn't started it all and treated the Afrikaners so badly, maybe they would not have been so insecure afterwards and be treating the blacks so terribly now."

I looked out at the endless wilderness of Africa before us, standing beside the lonely grave at our feet. "And this man who was so great in other ways is guilty of causing so much of all that..."

"In what way?" Barbie asked seriously.

I turned away, disconcerted at the impossibility of answering sensibly in a quick and easy fashion.

"He was greedy," I said eventually. "He wanted all the gold of the Witwatersrand and Rhodesia under his control. And when he got it, he was going to carve an empire with himself as the grand Viceroy which would cover the whole of south-central Africa. He did not care that the gold was not his to grab and in trying to do so he was going to cause misery to millions of people over the next sixty years. Bloody amazing isn't it?

"He got financial control of some of the Witwatersrand gold with commercial skills and shenanigans and then he seized Rhodesia by bamboozling the native kings and military conquest. When the Boer government of the Transvaal under Kruger resisted his attempts to further his ambitions by political means, because the foreign miners and other commercial immigrants were in the numerical majority of whites, he tried an armed coup. This failed dismally through incompetence but the British government were able to use that as an excuse to put pressure on the Boer government.

"The excuse was that Kruger was not allowing the immigrants to have a democratic vote and this would cause more violence. Britain wanted assurances about democracy which Kruger would not give, so the British had their war. It was supposed to last a few months because how could the Boers resist the might of Britain. But it went on for three years and a quarter of a million British and Imperial troops were needed, together with the destruction of the Boers' economy throughout South Africa. Thirty thousand Boers, mostly women and children and their coloured servants, died in British Concentration Camps.

"You see why the Afrikaners are still very bitter and resist alien control. To them the black majority is as alien and frighteningly dangerous as the British."

We were both quiet for a while, looking out on the silent majesty of that empty landscape.

*   *

271

Returning to Bulawayo, I sought out the municipal caravan and camping area in the central park. It was a large park and the camping section had tall old gum trees giving shade and protection from the weather and the grass was watered and neatly mown. I discovered an excellent ablution block while Barbie arranged our camp. There were a number of other parties there in caravans and tents, another 'first' in its way. These various events and situations which were part of a familiar world, and which we were steadily 'rediscovering', were gradually becoming commonplace. It was another slant to our southward progress that I was not happy about.

We seemed to be losing our special experience of the Africa outside of the westernised 'white south' all too quickly. I thought about that while sitting in the well-trimmed and well-arranged camping arena with other tourists about doing the same sort of things as we were, and I felt sour.

In the morning after packing up and when we were leaving, something seemed to crack. I was depressed and sensitive about our situation. We had been talking about our route over coffee as usual and I had been explaining that we should be through the border controls and well inside South Africa by evening. Unless we back-tracked, there was nothing else to do.

We had been silent when loading Landie and one or other of us made some thoughtless remark and we both lost our tempers. Afterwards, thinking about it, it was clear that we were both feeling the same kind of sadness, insecurity and worry about what was to happen when the journey ended. In the way these things happen, we exploded in anger at personal trivialities. The force of our mutual emotional explosion was stunning and we were both shaken badly. I was shocked at how close we came to a serious crisis, and it was a lesson for the future in similar situations of particular stress while travelling under pressure in the wilderness. I recognised events in the stories of Burton and Speke, and Livingstone.

By hook or by crook we had to see it all through to the last scene of parting and the finish of our adventure. Meantime, we would enjoy the rest of the time and get the most out of it. I don't believe there was another cross word from either of us after that. The value of our honourable friendship and what we had done together was too important to risk with unnecessary and groundless tantrums. Time was getting to be precious.

* *

272

By three in the afternoon we were at Beit Bridge, a small country town on the Limpopo River, the border with South Africa. We were both exhausted from the heat and the emotionally draining start to the day.

There was a motel on the Rhodesian side and we decided to stop there for the night rather than go thorough the border posts. There was a swimming pool and Barbie enjoyed that. We had vodka and Cokes beside it and the tensions left us. We were happy to be there together. It was a warm quiet evening and beyond the motel compound there were mopane trees.

Somebody we spoke to said that because of the exceptional drought, elephants had been coming down through farmlands to the few stagnant pools or to dig for water in the dry bed of the Limpopo.

Farmers were angry and complaining to the authorities. It was still Africa.

CHAPTER TWENTY: *THE LOWVELD*

We crossed the Limpopo River on the rattling old iron girder bridge from Rhodesia into South Africa on the 3rd November 1965.

I suppose we were aware that there was a serious political crisis brewing in Rhodesia. It had been rumbling for some years, ever since the break-up of the Central African Federation. The formation of a new constitution for 'independence' had been frustrated by conflict between the intransigence of the conservative government of the white settlers in Rhodesia and the intentions of the Labour Party in Whitehall where there was determination to create a Westminster-style parliament with equal voting rights for all.

Although we had seen newspapers in the hotel in Bulawayo, I had not taken much notice of the rhetoric and posturing of local politicians with whom I was not familiar. So although we were aware of the tensions that were building at the time, neither of us knew how close Central Africa was to years of conflict and war. The towns and the country roads were quiet and peaceful, people going about their business with complete normality. In fact, Ian Smith's government made its notorious unilateral declaration of independence (UDI) on 11th November, but when we left Rhodesia only a week or so earlier there was no sign on the surface of society that anything particularly momentous was about to occur.

What was of much greater concern for me that morning was getting Landie and our gear through the South African customs. Since leaving England, Landie had been covered by the international Carnet de Passage, but now we were entering my country of residence and Landie had to be imported and be issued with temporary registration and insurance documents. As we trundled across the iron bridge I was acutely aware of how ill-prepared I seemed to be. I did have the British road license, which luckily was still valid, and my original invoice from the Landrover agents in Durban, but otherwise had no documents. I had visions of needing a clearing agent and bills-of-lading and having to calculate c.i.f. values and worried about what I could do about such matters in a place where elephants were ravaging farmers' crops.

I need not have worried about documents. In the old-fashioned customs-hall of the South African border post, cavernous and echoing and almost empty of people that morning, I filled in the standard forms for any road traveller and in the inadequate space for showing goods to be imported I simply wrote "Landrover FXC248C", as if she was nothing more than a cheap camera or whatever, and handed it over to the uniformed official.

"Papers for your vehicle?" he asked without emotion. I handed over the Carnet, British license form and the original invoice which he studied for a while.

"O.K. You'll just have to hang on for a bit. I'll have to have the duty calculated and so on. Then you can pay and you'll be free to pass through."

"How much is the duty?" I asked anxiously. "We've driven all the way overland and I'm running short."

"Ja, well. You see, they'll have to make a calculation. It's a pity it is less than a year old, the duty would have been at a different rate if it was older."

"But it's not new," I protested anxiously. "We have travelled all the way. Algeria, Egypt, Kenya... Overland all the way. The Carnet de Passage proves it." My agitation was obvious.

He looked me over. "Well, I'll see what they can do." He smiled for the first time. "I suppose you can honestly guarantee that it is a used vehicle not to be re-sold as new, hey? Ag, no man, don't worry. I'll explain the problem."

I grinned nervously. "There's no doubt about it being used. The Carnet is there, and here is my passport if you like."

"O.K. Just hang on there."

We 'hung on' for quite a while. The customs officer came back and got on with other business, merely saying that his superior, the Collector, had to make a decision. Eventually, I was called over to be told that the duty had been estimated on a compromise between importing it as less than a year old and as a used, second-hand vehicle. The duty was 294 Rands (£147), but I would also have to purchase a temporary license and third-party insurance. If I did not like the scale of duty, I could appeal to the nearest customs and excise office to my place of residence, where I would have to get permanent registration anyway.

275

I did not have enough money left, so Barbie and I had a consultation. She would have to lend me a hundred pounds, which would allow us to have a reasonably free-and-easy trip down to Durban. I repaid her when we got there.

*   *

"Well, that's done with. Thanks Barbie," I said as we drove away.

"I suppose that means we can't stop over in Joburg or Pretoria?" she said. I knew she had wanted to see those cities, as a matter of principle, and no doubt also because she was itching for a bit of sophistication after the months of travelling rough. Her priorities and needs for adjustment at this end of the journey were increasingly different to mine. I was nearing my home base and my family, she was preparing to return to her 'normal' life which was that of a city girl however much she enjoyed the outdoors. I had not wanted to go through the centre of South Africa stopping off in Johannesburg, but super-conscious of the need to maintain accord during this increasingly sensitive period in our relationship, I had not made an issue of it. The matter of cash seemed to solve the problem, and I was selfish enough to be pleased.

"Stopping off in Joburg would be rather expensive," I said. "I suppose I could somehow get money from home, now that we are in the same country, but I feel awkward about that." That was truthful. It seemed to be wrong to phone my wife and ask for funds so that I could have a few days beating up the town a day's drive away at the end of our enormous journey. I was desperate to complete the grand safari with the most ease and harmony for all concerned.

"Yeah, you're right, Den," Barbie said. "That would not be a good idea really."

"Look. We'll go down to the Kruger Park and see the real Africa again, for the last time, then across to the Natal Drakensberg and camp there for a couple of days and sort everything out." I paused. "Then I suppose that takes us to Durban... We should have enough spare money with what I've borrowed from you to do it without counting every penny. In Durban you can get used to a big city again and live it up a bit."

She sighed and we drove in silence for a quite a while, overwhelmed by what was happening. What could we say to each other? We both knew exactly how we felt about it all.

                              *   *

We stopped at Messina, a small country town dominated by a big copper and zinc mine, for Cokes then once again at Louis Trichardt to fill up with petrol and get crisps and Cokes. We were really into having potato crisps and chips as snacks by then. At Louis Trichardt I sent a telegram to say that we had arrived in the homeland: another nail in the coffin of the long trans-Africa journey.

Twenty miles beyond Louis Trichardt, shortly after passing the village of Bandelierkop, we left the Great North Road and headed eastward to the Lowveld.

To pass the time and defeat the devilish monster of end-of-journey *cafard*, I told Barbie as much as I could remember about the history of the places we travelled through during the next few days. In the early nineteenth century no white people had explored the region and it had been sparsely populated by Bantu-speaking tribes who lived mainly in the hills and valleys where there was sufficient rainfall to cultivate their grains. They loved cattle and during the summer months there was some migration about on the grasslands but there were also huge herds of antelope, especially springbok, on the plains and they were followed by many predators. So the country was mostly empty of people.

The first Afrikaner migrant farmers, *trek-Boers*, thought these northern lands were paradise when they first arrived: no people, good grass, plenty of wild game and far away from the hated British. But for the same reasons that native Africans had not settled the country heavily, it was not suitable for the trek-Boers. Diseases to which the wild antelope were immune decimated their cattle and horses, in summer people succumbed to malaria, and they were tormented by lions and hyenas. When they attempted to move into the healthier and more congenial lands long-settled by the natives, there was territorial conflict and several skirmishes took place.

The trek-Boers returned southward for some decades and the area was in peace, until gold was discovered in the rivers and broken reefs of the eastern Drakensberg, the great escarpment that runs along the southeastern rim of the highland plains of South Africa. South Africa was never the same again and the fabulous gold-reef of the Witwatersrand was discovered soon afterwards.

We entered the mountainous country of the Drakensberg and the vegetation changed to low, tough bushes studded with patches of aloes and euphorbia on the sheltered side of mountains. In the valleys of rivers there were taller trees. Barbie commented on the improved greenness of the grasses and vegetation compared to the desert-like lands to the north, but it was still very dry. The rains had not started yet though it was well into the season. Soon, we descended a winding pass to the bottom of the mountains, into the lowveld, and entered pine and gum plantations that spread over the foothills.

Tzaneen was a sleepy old village with jacarandas in mauve bloom in the main street lined by shops and houses, many with corrugated iron roofs and verandahs supported by brick columns and decorated with iron or wood fretwork. This was the predominant architectural style of the region and reminded both of us of our colonial heritage.

"Something like the old places in the outback," Barbie said.

"Settled in the same time, the late nineteenth century," I explained.

From Tzaneen, the road became gravel, we left the plantations and the scene was sombre. The sky clouded over to a uniform dirty grey and the land we were traversing was scrappy scrub bush, devoid of leaves. The great escarpment of the Drakensberg marched some miles away on our right hand as we headed due south. I was disappointed in the scenery for some quirky reason although I kept up what I thought of as a cheerful commentary of the geography and history. The Drakensberg escarpment we were following was higher than any mountains we had seen since Kilimanjaro and should have been a great relief after the endless flat plains of Central Africa, but a decidedly different mood had overtaken me.

Somehow, after crossing the Limpopo I was no longer exploring: I was no longer on the grand safari, I was on some pointless local expedition or holiday trip. I had not been into that far north-east part of the Transvaal before so I was still 'exploring', but that did not change my depressed feeling. The *cafard* was at work.

Climbing back up the escarpment wall, passing through the finely-engineered Abel Erasmus tunnels, we wound through spectacular scenery. Barbie came to life, exclaiming at the colours of the strata of rock in the cliffs and the beauties of the scene. This revived my flagging spirits and when we stopped at Ohrigstad over the crest and back on the highveld I was more cheerful. We had strong coffees and the inevitable snack of chips and chattered with more liveliness. I explained more history, how the pioneering trek-Boers had struggled over these mountain passes, trying to find practical routes for their ox-waggons down to the lowveld and onwards to the sea at Delagoa Bay where the Portuguese had a port and trading centre.

Always they were trying to get away from reliance on the British who controlled the only ports from Cape Town to Natal.

In mid-afternoon we reached Pilgrim's Rest, an old mining town towards which I had been heading. I had visited it briefly on a family holiday two years previously and knew some detail of its romantic history. It was the site of a substantial gold rush. In 1873, a character known as 'Wheelbarrow' Alec Patterson (because he pushed all his belongings along in a wheelbarrow) found an exciting alluvial field in the valley below where the town was to grow. He was joined by a partner, William Trafford, who believed that their long search for wealth was over, hence the name of the new settlement. Large nuggets were found in the stream and by the end of 1875 the town had 21 stores, 18 pubs and many other establishments. After the First Anglo-Boer War, the Transvaal Gold Exploration Company took over and bought out the petty workings in the area and the Theta Reef was worked with great success.

Pilgrim's Rest was really nothing more than a ghost town in a conventional early colonial layout when we entered it that afternoon. A long main street, indifferently tarred and shaded by tall old gums, straggled up the side of a hill and it was flanked by rather dilapidated wood and iron cottages and shops, most of which needed a fresh coat of paint. I don't think Barbie was over-enthusiastic at the first impression.

"We're going to stop here?" she asked, trying not to sound disappointed.

"Yes, at the Royal Hotel. It's very historic and romantic; you'll see. Really it's very nice. Anyway, we've come far enough today."

We hauled out our suitcases and went up the shallow steps onto the verandah of the hotel and into its dim hallway. A cheerful woman checked us in and a silent porter took us through to a pleasant room with an old wooden floor and chintz curtains on the window. The beds had battered iron-frames and squeaked when Barbie sat on one. The window looked out onto a small grassy courtyard planted with roses and beds of bright Barbeton daisies. The room smelled of fresh polish and clean linen and it was quiet. I could hear the distant echoing voices of the African staff in the kitchen somewhere. Doves were calling in the trees.

*   *

We cleaned up and rested then walked in the garden of the courtyard at the back before a simple three-course meal. The diningroom was furnished with a mix of chairs set around small tables. Faded prints and old photographs were on the walls and a large sideboard stood against a wall. The horns of antelope hung over the fireplace. We were almost alone at dinner and were served by a silent and deft elderly waiter. We had a bottle of cabernet and chatted cheerfully.

Afterwards we went into the bar. In those days, women were not allowed in public bars in South Africa and native blacks were not permitted to buy white man's liquor at all. But there were no other guests about, the village was dead and the elderly white barman let Barbie stay when I started to ask him about the history of the hotel. I told him that Barbie was from Australia with mining antecedents.

"Well, you know, I'm not supposed to let ladies in here, but there's nobody around, so we'll take a chance!" His craggy face grinned. "Yes, this old bar has seen some interesting things in its time, I can assure you. Amazing characters and exciting times.

"You see, in the old days about eighty years ago when this town was just a mining camp, it was very rough and ready. Lots of little tin shacks and tents where the miners lived and some of the shacks were just a little bigger which were stores and bars. Some of the bars were very rough; you know, gambling and easy women and all that. It was not unknown for there to be a murder or two. To-morrow you can visit the graveyard if you have time and see some of the old inscriptions.

"Anyway, there were some respectable people who wanted to set up a church, so they got the money together to have a church sent out from England. Yes, all the materials designed and built in sections and shipped out to Delagoa Bay. Anyway, the church arrived and was brought up on transport waggons; across the lowveld and up these mountains. When it got here, I suppose people had changed and moved on and the town was getting bigger and more settled and there was no congregation to pay for the transport and erection and so on. So the church was auctioned off and was built as this hotel."

He grinned at Barbie's expression. "Yes, my girlie, this old hotel started as a church. You can see how it was if you go back into

280

the diningroom or have a look from the outside in the morning. You can see the shape of it."

He poured Barbie a beer and a brandy and ginger ale for me and went on telling us stories. The bar counter was the original and there were carved names with dates and dents in its surface from those days. "Can you just imagine the parties that took place here? In this very same old bar? Especially when someone had a good gold strike. Naked girls dancing on the counter, everybody with his own bottle of grog; the fights afterwards. And it started off as a church, built in England somewhere."

We had another round of drinks and he told us something of himself. He was a local man and loved this part of the country. He told us about the Rand Mine near the town which was closing down after sixty or seventy years. "Of course, our town is very quiet now. Houses are empty. But they are talking about opening up tourism. We don't get many people staying here now, but the owners are hoping that times will get better one day."

"I hope that they won't smarten it up too much and change its character," I said.

"Ag, no. Anybody who owns this place must make use of its history." He looked around his snug little bar with its glittering glass, the bottles stacked on shelves, the old advertising signs, some fading photographs and the bric-a-brac. "This is a good bar, though I says it myself. Come on, do you want another drink, then we can get off to bed?"

We declined and said good-night. When we were in the bedroom, Barbie yawned and said: "That was really interesting and what a nice old man. I found his accent difficult, though. He was a real Afrikaner wasn't he?"

"We're in a different part of Africa now, aren't we? Are you enjoying it?"

"Yeah, it is different. And this is a good place."

In the morning we had tea and coffee in bed and got up in a leisurely fashion. After breakfast we visited the old Rand Mine where there were many rusting corrugated iron sheds with piles of abandoned machinery, pipes, dismantled metal structures and strange pieces of domestic equipment. I photographed a lovely old wrought iron bath with brass taps standing forlornly. It had rusted through in a patch, so was useless, but it looked very sad amongst the rusting and battered equipment. An electric generator had been installed when the mine opened and there had been street lights in

281

town. We saw the tracks and the overhead pylons for an electric tramway that had been running in the 1890s and had carried on until quite recent years.

"Think of all the people who worked here and all the millions of pounds worth of gold that was dug up," Barbie said.

"It seems terribly sad that places where people have put so much effort into something and so many lives have been concentrated on something is just abandoned and lost," I said, looking at the dereliction.

We had picked up some tourist literature in the hotel and drove to Graskop, a bare little village standing on flat land on the crest of the great escarpment. From there we took a rough dirt track through pine plantations to a local beauty spot called God's Window where we stopped to get an awe-inspiring view into the dusty haze of the lowveld, stretching away to where it merged with the horizon.

The dull clouds of the previous day had moved away and the sun was shining brilliantly. At our look-out place the air was fresh and sweet but the sun was hot. Another car drove up and a middle-aged couple got out. They were Afrikaners and came over to talk when they saw Landie's number plates. They urged us to go and see the Blyde River Canyon and stay there where the local authority was starting a camping site, but it was on the way back to the north on another road, so we did not take their advice.

Nearby, returning to Graskop we came across genuine prospector's claims with registration numbers painted on them with recent dates. There was an old mine shaft penetrating the hillside with warning notices.

"It's all real enough, isn't it?" Barbie remarked. "And it's very lovely country." At Graskop we stopped for our usual Cokes and crisps.

She was entranced when we descended the escarpment again, going down to the lowveld through endless pine and tall bluegum plantations. There were saw mills and trucks carrying loads of cut logs on the road. The local forestry commission had erected large billboards warning against starting fires. The posters portrayed a sentimentalised antelope with a huge tear falling from its luminous eyes with burning trees in the background. Barbie loved those posters and I had to stop while she photographed one.

Down on the lowveld again, we left the plantations and drove through country reserved for local Africans and there were villages not unlike those we had seen in Rhodesia. And then there were

282

orange groves along the course of a river and I pulled over to visit the Sabie River Bungalows. It was another old hotel, but built for holiday-makers in a typically old-fashioned South African style: simple rondavels surrounding a central lounge and diningroom with a verandah and terrace, all encompassed by a mature garden with huge old indigenous trees and some exotic flowering bushes. Spathodeas and jacarandas mixed with giant figs and brilliant bougainvillaea which crawled over trees and parts of the building. We had iced beers on the terrace before moving on to the Kruger National Park.

Only the southern section of the Park was open during the summer season in those days. The roads in the northern part were not good enough to sustain tourist traffic when the big rains started and there was the risk of malaria. So, the only camps open at that time were Pretorius Kop and Skukuza. At the entrance gate, it was suggested that we go on to Skukuza because there was plenty of accommodation available there.

It was getting quite late and had clouded over again so I drove through quite fast, beating the restricting speed limit, but saw many wild animals. During our visit to Kruger Park we saw impala, baboons, vervet monkeys, kudu, wildebeest, zebras, giraffe, waterbuck, hippos, crocodiles and elephants.

At Skukuza we were allocated a rondavel and we settled in before having a look around. There was a small souvenir shop and notices advertising a film show that evening in the open-air assembly area under great old trees by the reception centre.

We had to cook our own dinners on a communal barbecue with a huge fire laid under a large circular grid, sheltering beneath a roof. There was also an old wood-fired stove and there was a bit of a scrum around it with pots and pans moved about by people from the neighbouring rondavels. But it was all very friendly and families were on holiday with children running about, all excited in the warm dusk. We enjoyed our simple meal and then went over to see the film show.

A jolly public relations-type showed us some scratchy old wild-life films on a noisy projector then gave us a colour slide show with witty and practised commentary. We laughed a lot. Back in the rondavel we were in bed when a furious thunderstorm exploded overhead with brilliant flashes of lightning instantly followed by detonations of thunder. It poured with rain for a while and the electric lights went out. I lit a lantern and we listened to the fury for a while before drifting off to sleep.

The next morning, Barbie said she had been woken in the night by shouts outside and running feet, so she had got up and seen torches bobbing about. I was sure that it had been a hyena and, although a game-ranger whom Barbie questioned denied knowledge of the incident, we learned later that a hyena had been in the camp and had tried to get into one of the rondavels where people had been sleeping with the top half of the stable-door open. It added a frisson of reality to camping in a game reserve.

"I said we would have a last taste of 'real' Africa," I told Barbie as we breakfasted off tinned fruit and chips. "We didn't have hyenas prowling around in Kenya or Tanzania."

"Who knows what was prowling around when we were sleeping inside Landie," she retorted.

*   *

At the reception we asked them to check if there was accommodation available at Pretorius Kop camp, which they were able to confirm, and we set off for a day of being 'on safari' in the bush.

It was a dull sort of day after the storm in the night, cool and humid. The rainy season had broken in the Lowveld and the land was damp and had a feeling of renewed growth. With the cool and damp, we did not see much wild life, but afterwards when writing her diary, Barbie reckoned that we had seen quite a lot during the day.

We drove along the Sabie River down to the Lower Sabie Camp, which was closed, and stopped off from time to time at convenient viewing places alongside the river. At one point, we saw crocodiles and a newly laid nest of their eggs in a scuffed up area on a sandbank beside the stream. Alongside the river there were fine riverine trees of various species that I could not identify, but they were dominated by glorious old figs. We saw several elephants, but lions or leopards eluded us. We had not seen any of the big cats on any of our excursions into game reserves and this was a great disappointment. I have often seen lions since then, and leopards, but had not seen lions in the wild myself at that time. So we were both equally frustrated. Inevitably, when we got to Pretorius Kop, there were people about who had seen lions in the last few days.

Barbie got talking to an American girl who was doing a similar trans-African journey, starting from the south. We wondered if she would finish it.

At Pretorius Kop there was a small grocery store and a simple restaurant, so we were able to buy some fresh provisions to cook in the communal 'kitchen', similar to Skukuza. Our rondavel was similar too, a small round room with thatched roof within which were two beds and a table and nothing more. It was all comfortable enough for us, and because of the rainstorms which struck again that night, we were glad of the shelter. It would not have been much fun had we been camping as we had done in Central Africa. But, as I had predicted to myself at Robbins Motel on the Kafue back in Zambia, our proper camping days were well behind us. My mood of false elation mixed with moments of sad depression continued. We finished our bottle of vodka that evening after eating, while the rain lashed down.

In the morning, we had a full breakfast in the restaurant before leaving. It was Saturday and people were arriving for the week-end and probably the camps would have been booked up. We had been lucky to have arrived during the week when there were plenty of vacancies.

From the Kruger Park, we headed for Natal, climbing up the Drakensberg escarpment once again onto the Transvaal highveld.

CHAPTER TWENTY ONE : *NATAL*

<u>Saturday, 6th November</u> :   .... *Attractive mountain scenery, then on highveld - farms, cattle, sheep on rolling plains through Carolina and Amersfoort. Stopped at Volksrust for a nice snack then through border into Natal: scene of much fighting during the Boer War. Through Newcastle-on-Buffalo* (Barbie lived in Newcastle-on-Hunter in N.S.W.) *with lots of coal mining. Raining now and then, nippy. Stopped at a motel not far out of Newcastle at Fort Mistake - quite nice - but pretty cold and windy. Den eventually got a fire going in our room. Voddies to cheer us up then had good dinner. 'Engie types' also there staying overnight.*

<u>Sunday, 7th November</u> : *Woke early, had coffee in bed - nice sunny day. Had breakfast in the restaurant and left soon after. On to Ladysmith, scene of great siege in Boer War, and had a look at the old church with names of many people who died in the fighting and admired the stained-glass windows. Branched off the main road shortly after. Lovely, hilly country. Very green. African villages. After Bergville, onto very rough dirt road for 27 miles to Royal Natal National Park. A little man put a sticker on Landie at the entrance gate. Suddenly we were close to fantastic mountains - the main Drakensberg range - much more jagged and higher than the scarp in the eastern Transvaal. There was an old hotel and a small river - Den said it is the source of the biggest river in that part - and then we were going up higher on a stony track to a camp with huts. They had one free and we unpacked Landie properly because we had to have a sort-out. 'Glooped' outside and 'graaked' the mountains for a while.*

Had tinned soup for lunch, we haven't much food, and found that African slaves do the cooking for you in this camp. Den had a large sleep then we took pics. It's very nice here and the mountains are so enormous and close to. When the sun faded it got nippy quickly. We started to separate all our goodies. Den organised dinner with the slaves, talking slave language: not

286

much, just baked beans and Irish stew from tins. Much coffee and chats after. Hot bath and early bed.

Monday, 8th November : Up pretty early, drizzling with rain, had coffee, washed, dressed then went to nearest village to get food in an African shop. On way back stopped at the hotel and booked horses for a ride later. Got some grog at their off-sales license shop. It was sunny in the valley, but dull still back at the hut though clearing slowly. Had coffee (with voddies) and biscuits. Still nippy. Den says its high here, maybe 7,000 feet at the camp.

Drove down to the hotel to pick up our nags, but they were very slow and lazy. We had to kick them along. Mine was traumatic and did not want to go past some places for some reason, while Den's would not do anything except follow behind, no matter how much it was urged on. The sun came out and it burned down, so it was lovely and warm. We ended up back at our huts so we stopped and let the nags have some lunch. They were more happy about going back and would trot for a bit. Both our bums were pretty sore when we got to the hotel; neither of us had ridden for a long while.

We had drinks on the hotel verandah. Den told me about when he was little, his family used to come there for Christmas hollies. King and Queen and the Princesses stayed there in 1947, that's why its 'Royal'. Drove back in our FAST Landie, compared to the nags.

Sat outside and had voddies while 'slaves' cooked the food we bought that morning. Got a bit 'slooshed'. Finished separating our goodies into separate suitcases - the first time since Spain.

Much sadness .... Later bath, then bed.

Tuesday, 9th November : Big storm during the night. Much lightning. Lovely sunny day. 'Glooped' it all. Had coffee and a cold sausage for breakfast. Then packed and left for Durban. ...

That, more-or-less, was that.

*   *   *

Barbie stayed at the Balmoral Hotel on the Durban beachfront for a while and came to terms somewhat with being on her own while I settled in with my family.

Of course, we were all happy to be together again and the children had noticeably grown and expanded their minds. They were all well and living normal lives with all the various trivia of everyday going on. I could not get used to sitting in soft chairs and sleeping in a comfortable bed. The huge space of the rather ordinary rooms of our home seemed built for giants. Food being cooked for me and brought to a table set properly for every meal was really very strange.

After a few days, when the excitement died down, I suggested that Barbie might stay at our home until she had to catch her ship for the return to England. Travelling by sea was cheaper than flying in those days. Sue was delighted to have the opportunity to get to know her and she settled in for the days before her ship was due. We had a celebrating dinner together at a smart restaurant in town and a day-trip down the coast to a seaside resort, which Barbie said was much like places in NSW.

Barbie sailed in the MV *Randfontein* of the Holland-Afrika Line from Durban to Southampton later that month.

We swore eternal comradeship and said we would always keep in touch, but there were uncertainties in both our lives. Barbie did not even have a fixed address. My career had been interrupted by the grand adventure and I was not sure what I was going to do now. I had to pick up the reins of normality again, but there was the Christmas holidays ahead of us and my soul had not caught up with me yet. It was still far north in the vacant wildernesses of Africa.

But, we did keep in touch, somehow. I met her briefly in London a year later. Two years later, in 1968, while in transit from Japan where I had been negotiating a contract, I met her again in London when she was married and her daughter, Sonya, had been born.

In 1978, I stayed with Barbie and her husband in their delightful home in a suburb of Newcastle, NSW. On the first morning of my visit with them, I went striding out on their back lawn in my bare feet, African-style, admiring the blue sky and listening to the weird calls of the galah parrots. Suddenly I leapt, cursing, into the air, my feet on fire with several thorns buried in them.

"You discovered our 'bindies'," Barbie called to me, laughing. "On our trip, I always told you Aussie was tougher than Africa..."

In 2005, while Sue and I were touring Australia, looking for places where my father had lived a century before, I stayed for a few days with Barbie and John in their retirement home on a smallholding on the Hunter River. Sue had been staying with other friends in Sydney and we all joined up for a great reunion in Newcastle.

It took me a long time to settle after my trans-Africa journey and there can be no doubt that it changed the direction of my life; and inevitably the lives of my family too. I'm certain that my life became richer afterwards.

In the late 1960s at a party in somebody's home in Johannesburg, I found myself next to a quiet man, about my age, who was alone and somewhat ill-at-ease. We began a conversation and discovered that we had both recently crossed Africa from north to south. In a few sentences we understood which routes we had taken and how it had been.

He smiled and said: "If you've done it, you don't have to explain anything to somebody who has also done it. But, if you try to explain to somebody who hasn't done it, you can't tell it in hours of talking."

In those years trans-Africa travellers were exceedingly rare. It was a long time before bus-loads of young tourists were doing it with professional safari companies.

~~~~~~~~~~~~~~~~~~~~~~~~~~~~~~~~~~

For to admire an' for to see,
For to be'old this world so wide -
It never done no good to me,
But I can't drop it if I tried.

RUDYARD KIPLING, 1865-1936.

If it must be so, let's not weep or complain
If I have failed, or you, or life turned sullen.
We have had these things, they do not come again.
But the flag still flies, and the city has not fallen.

HUMBERT WOLFE, 1886-1940.

CHAPTER TWENTY TWO: *TO THE SOUTHERN END OF AFRICA*

I became re-oriented to my home in December with Christmas parties and reunions of family and friends.

In January I was feeling 'civilised' again and had got accustomed to those strange comforts of a home with soft beds, a proper kitchen, space, good music and a well-tended garden. The children were on their summer school holidays for most of January and I spent much of the time either on family excursions or re-writing the novel, *Bamboo Assegai*, which I had drafted while at Bamburi.

By the end of that month I had completed much of the re-writing and was feeling a compulsion to finish my trans-Africa expedition by travelling some significant parts of the rest of southern Africa. I felt the pull of getting to the Atlantic shores in South-West Africa and down to the southern end. I had to start the draft of the story of my travels and was itching to do this. But, somehow I felt this need to get to the end. No doubt, it was an excuse to have one more carefree safari in Landie before the necessary final settling down after the enormous challenge and disruption of the soul-stretching experience of crossing Africa.

Sue was working, the children were back at school, I was feeling at a loose end anyway and already looking back on the vagabond months with enormous and often painful nostalgia. I made a few tentative starts to the travel story, but they ended in the waste basket. I knew that willy-nilly I had to return to the conventional world of a 9 - 5 job soon, but not yet!

Eileen, a friend from my Unilever years, contacted me to find out how my travelling had fared. She had been keen to do the trans-Africa journey with me but I had put her off because she only had South African citizenship which was 'no go' in most of Africa in those years. So it seemed natural that she should accompany me on the last part of my grand safari; to reach the Atlantic and the southernmost end. She was free, she said, and pleased at the opportunity of enjoying a camping holiday in the style of my recent adventures.

We arranged to meet at Estcourt and she turned up there as arranged, having been given a lift from Johannesburg. I was easily back into the rough-travelling routines with Landie and my trans-Africa gear and Eileen was an experienced camper.

*   *

Crossing Africa in Landie I had become used to driving long distances for long hours. The mostly tarred roads of South Africa enabled much greater daily traverses than the rough tracks further north. Nevertheless, a fair average speed in Landie on good roads was 45-50 miles in an hour and looking at maps today in re-creating my route I am surprised at the distances travelled. Of course, when one is driving continuously for maybe eight or ten hours in a day, you can cover a lot of ground.

The first day we left in the cool of dawn and had a late breakfast of a memorable hamburger parked under a weeping willow tree at a service station in Bethlehem in the Free State. It was before the arrival of franchised 'take-aways' and that hamburger has often been a remembered benchmark in the many years since.

That night we paused in a camp-site near Kimberley and the next day we were moving steadily across the western Free State and the Northern Cape towards' the Orange River. There was a particularly bad cyclical drought at the time and there had been negligible rain for three years in many parts of the interior. From Zambia southwards local people I had met complained of farming disaster. West of Kimberley there was no natural grass and the Karoo scrub was grey and dry. Dust blew across the land and the sky was a dull grey haze with a silver sun blazing a hole in it. I took an evocative photograph of a line of power pylons disappearing into the dust-fogged distance.

By noon we were at Prieska on the Orange River. I felt exhausted by the heat and glare and we needed to stop. I saw a track running down through some gum trees to the banks of the Orange and took it. There were a couple of battered pick-ups parked beneath the trees and quite a crowd of local Coloured people gathered there. I saw families lying in the shallows of the river with their clothes on, chatting while the children played. Greeted by waves and calls, we joined them, lying full length and fully clothed while the tepid brown river gently caressed us with its current. I shall not forget the relief from lying in the Orange River, gradually cooling, watching the branches of trees waving against the furnace-hot sky. Our scanty clothes were dry within minutes of leaving the water.

Having fuelled in Upington, had a snack lunch and cold Cokes in the park with its famous date palm avenue, and bought some groceries, I headed for the Augrabies Falls nature reserve where there were the most basic of camping facilities.

The reserve with its camping area beside the falls was deserted. There was no official caretaker and no other visitors. The holiday season was over. We set up camp beside some bushes not far from the brink of the great canyon into which the Orange River tumbled with constant roaring. In those days the hydro-electric dams further up the river had not been built and the take-off from irrigation was not much, so the river was full of water, thundering into its narrow cleft in the smooth pink rock walls, several hundred feet high. It was the strangest place: utterly deserted by people, the sun blazing on bare rock, the river plunging past into foaming destruction.

Away from the brink, the roar was muted and there was the perfect humming silence of desert wilderness. We wandered, exploring, when the sun lowered and cooked a simple dinner on my battered Primus stoves. We slept on my trusty camp-beds under the myriad stars with no artificial light in sight.

Inevitably, as I lay watching the brilliant stars in the black sky, Eileen breathing quietly a few feet away, I thought of all those other days and nights. I was twisted with nostalgia. I wondered how Barbie was getting on, back in London in the middle of winter. I reckoned I was enormously better off than she at that moment, and that added more sadness. Eventually I slept and woke to a dawn with the air already balmy.

The next day there was more exploring on foot and we roamed the cliff edges and stared for long minutes into the canyon, watching the turgid swirls far down below, or sitting close to the rush over the lip of the fall, feeling the spray wrap around us as the wind took it.

Not long before I had been at the Victoria Falls and had been equally mesmerised for long periods, but the two great African falls were distinct. The surroundings of Victoria were lush greenery and the Zambezi plunges over a mile wide ledge; the Orange at Augrabies is surrounded by desert and the river drops into the amazing narrow cleft. By noon we were suffering from the heat and I drove into the rough little town of Kakamas to buy fresh food for dinner that evening. But by four that afternoon I had no interest in food.

The temperature in the cab of Landie reached 118ºF (48ºC) and I was feeling physically ill. I forced Eileen and myself to drink water, but it produced a feeling of nausea. I knew we had to go south, there was no point in going on through the Kalahari and Namib Deserts to the Atlantic shores in those conditions. I had no imperative to follow that route.

"We'll head to the southernmost point of Africa and then across to the Atlantic on the west coast at Saldanha Bay," I told Eileen.

*   *

Before dawn at 0500 the temperature in Landie when we set off was 95ºF (35ºC). Doggedly, I drove south all that day, and when we had crossed the Great Karoo and reached Oudtshoorn it was noticeably cooler, though still at the normal hot summer temperature for that region. We stopped at the Kango Caves for refreshments and visited the famous spectacularly-lit caverns filled with giant organ-pipes of strange stalagmites and stalactites. It was the only time that I have gone underground there.

Spirits having been bucked by the normality of being tourists, we went on in high spirits over the Outeniquas and down to the Indian Ocean. I bought fine rump steaks in a local butchery and pan-fried them on a barbecue in the camping park at Heidelberg. Years later, Eileen could still remember the fracas which occurred when, having drunk a couple of glasses of Tassenberg wine, I knocked the steaks onto the ground and there was much scrambling about and cursing. They were cleaned up and eaten with great pleasure, our first good meal for some days.

The weather changed the next day. A cold front moved along the coast, constricted by the high coastal mountain range. It was chilly and drizzling from time to time. What a contrast to Augrabies.

From the main coast highway, I took the tarred road from Swellendam to Bredasdorp and on towards Agulhas, feeling gradually increasing excitement. I had not been that far south on land before.

After Bredasdorp the countryside became empty until we turned a corner and were faced by a small cottage: a low, whitewashed and thatched fishermen's cottage on a slight rise. There was a wind-tormented tree sheltering one side and at the half-open stable door a Coloured girl in a blue shirt was leaning out, contemplating the view. It was an extraordinarily evocative scene and I took a photograph which became a favourite for many years.

A short distance further on, I turned down a track to the fisherman's haven at Struisbaai where dories were sheltering behind a small natural promontory, lying at moorings out of the westerly wind. Another important photograph was taken there.

There were holiday beach cottages lightly scattered along the coast as we neared the cape and maybe a rough little country store. I do not remember detail. And then there was the lighthouse: a rectangular building supported at each end by stone castle towers and the red and white striped column of the lighthouse rising from the centre. I stopped on the level ground below the lighthouse and we walked to the shore where rollers tumbled and thundered on the rocks. We had reached the end of Africa.

Steady drizzling rain set in as the sun lowered and I looked for some sheltered place to spend the night. Further back from the cape a party had camped by the sea, somewhat sheltered by the headland, and were having a jolly time around a barbecue with demijohns of wine and much laughing and joking. I felt envious of them. Running up the cliff behind them was a rough track and I drove Landie up it until we were out of sight of the party and had some shelter from the weather. We had a poor meal there and were asleep soon, bundled in blankets in the back of Landie.

*   *

The next day, I headed for Saldanha and we camped for some days at the municipal site on the shore of the great bay.

On the way we called in at Langebaan, still a small simple fishing village then, and had cool drinks at a rough little café by the waterfront. There, I took other photographs which became icons in later years.

We explored places I had known as a seaman in the Navy and we sat, watching the ocean, on the rocks at the end of Hoedjies Point. Following a rough track we visited Danger Bay where I had swum naked in the icy ocean with a group of companions all those years before. There was much nostalgia for me. The weather was perfect and it was the best time of the whole of this last brief safari. I had spent most of 1951 in the Navy at Saldanha Bay and ever after have had a special feeling for that place.

There was that special ambience which old villages acquire when established beside cold sea and rocky shores, where men have gone out in small vessels to harvest the ocean. Away from the village and the harbour with its fish-processing factory and the small Naval Base, the lands beside the ocean were empty. It was bleak country, white sandy soil was covered by tough scrubby bushes and there were no trees except where people had planted them. The cold salt air off the sea, and the scream of gulls enveloped it all. Offshore there were guano islands where thousands of cormorants roosted and you could watch gannets diving vertically into shoals of fish. There were seals and whales.

Later, I dropped Eileen off with her friends at Seapoint in Cape Town and spent a couple of days with old Navy pals near Simonstown before driving home.

We had not travelled in South-West Africa, but we had touched the edge of the Kalahari Desert, reached the end of Africa and crossed to the wild Atlantic.

APPENDIX: 'LANDIE' AND SOME STATISTICS

Sundry notes from documents kept from 1965.

The passenger fare from Durban to Barcelona by the itinerant cargo vessel MV *Klostertor* registered in Hamburg, departing on 24th March 1965 was R160.00 (£80). The voyage lasted nearly four weeks. The agent was Cory Mann George (SA) (Pty) Ltd in Durban.

The passenger fare from Port Said to Mombasa by the cargo-passenger liner SS *La Bourdonnaise* of the Messagerie Maritime was about £70 and the freight for 'Landie' was about £110. The voyage lasted ten days. The agent was Thomas Cook in Port Said.

'Landie' was a long-wheelbase 4-cylinder petrol-engined Landrover in the most basic format with simple pick-up truck body and metal canopy without a separate cab. The colour was pale grey with cream canopy. She was fitted with a roof-rack and had two spare wheels, various extra spares, fuel and water cans, etc. She was purchased from the Landrover agents in Durban, South Africa, for delivery at the factory in Solihull, England. Her British registration number was FXC248C.

DISTANCES, FUEL PURCHASES & COSTS, 8 May - 10 November 1965

UK	653 miles	45.1 gallons	£41 7 5d
France	659	13.2	4 5 2
Spain	1315	64.0	16 3 5 (inc Ceuta)
Morocco	163	-	-
Algeria	977	45.6	14 2 -
Tunisia	762	62.2	21 5 7
Libya	1297	62.5	11 2 7
Egypt	702	13.9	4 16 8
Ship's passage	3450	-	110 - - (freight cost)
East/Central Africa	5540	277.9	60 3 4
South Africa	1164	54.0	9 - 5

Totals	18,682 miles	738.9 galls	£292 6 7d (inc. ocean freight)

Land Miles = 15,232   (24,513 kms)

Average petrol consumption = 20.62 miles per imperial gallon. (7.3 kms per litre.) Quantities by country are purchases, not consumption.

Average cost of petrol = £0.246 per imp. gallon. (nearly 25p), or 5.41p per litre. Petrol cost per mile = £0.012 (1.2p), or 0.75p per kilometre.

The cost of six full vehicle services in UK, France, Tunis, Mombasa (twice) and Bulawayo (including oils and spares) was £34 16s. 4d. Remarkably, during the whole of the journey, apart from work done during these services, 'Landie' never required oil or radiator water to be topped up, nor did she need tyre pressures to be increased. There were no punctures!

The invoiced Purchase Price, paid in advance in South Africa, of the long wheel-base Landrover, FXC248C, with extras collected at Solihull, was R1470 (£735). Duty paid to import it as a used vehicle into South Africa at Beit Bridge was R294 (£147). The South African registration number was NPN6057.

Total cost of the Landrover and all its running expenses UK to South Africa was £1209.

My budget for the whole of the round-trip journey from Durban to England and back to Durban was £1,000 and I met all of our travelling expenses en route through Africa. I spent less than that and would have had a handsome surplus except for the cost of freight for Landie from Port Said and the import duty into South Africa.

There were local registration and third party insurance fees paid at the borders of a few countries, but there was no general vehicle insurance cover available. We had no personal insurance and nothing was stolen from the vehicle or our campsites. Apart from an infection picked up in Algeria and a couple of 'tummy-bugs' we had no illness, not even a common cold. In East Africa, we took one Paludrine tablet a day and although we were swarmed by mosquitos on occasion, especially while camping, there was no hint of malaria.

'Landie' carried me and my family or friends something like another 75,000 kilometres in South Africa, Lesotho, Swaziland, and Mozambique, carrying camping gear and penetrating many other exciting places before being sold in 1970.

*

After 'Landie' was sold, I owned four more safari vehicles which carried me about southern Africa, camping roughly on occasion and exploring historical sites. All of these vehicles never let me down when travelling in remote places. It may be considered affected or even childish to name inanimate objects like vehicles, and use those names everyday. But, had I not succumbed to that whim and personified them, maybe I would have had disasters that luckily passed me by in many thousands of kilometres of wilderness travel? One can prepare well and be careful, but there is always bad luck ready to intervene around the next corner. Who knows?

~~~~~~~~~~~~~~~~~~~~~~

SOME STATISTICS OF THE RELEVANT COUNTRIES IN 1965.

	Independent Year	Estimated Population (millions)	
		1965	2005
Morocco	1956	13.25	33.00
Algeria	1962	12.00	32.50
Libya	1951	1.60	5.50
Tunisia	1956	4.60	10.00
Egypt	1922	29.60	78.00
Sudan	1956	13.50	41.00
Kenya	1963	9.10	34.00
Uganda	1962	7.70	28.00
Tanzania	1964	10.00	37.00
Zambia	1964	3.90	11.00
Zimbabwe	1965/80	4.30	12.00
South Africa	1910	15.90	45.00

Although population growth in all African countries has been prodigious, in sub-Sahara Africa it has been exceptionally high, generally outstripping infrastructures and food production. This growth together with the paucity of much of the land for easy peasant agriculture resulted in massive urban expansion which could not be sustained by formal development. The result has been huge informal settlements and massive unemployment leading to unrest, wars and repression, violent crime and poor or complete lack of services.

GENERAL GEOGRAPHICAL INDEX

301

302

Denis Montgomery
Chedburgh, Suffolk
21 December, 2006

African Insight